IRIS MURDOCH

a reference guide

A
Reference
Guide
to
Literature

Michael Begnal,
Editor

IRIS MURDOCH

a reference guide

KATE BEGNAL

G.K.HALL&CO.

70 LINCOLN STREET, BOSTON, MASS.

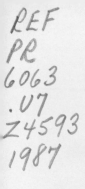

Library of Congress Cataloging-in-Publication Data

Begnal, Kate.
  Iris Murdoch : a reference guide.

  (Reference guide to literature)
  "Writings by Iris Murdoch": p.
  Includes index.
  1. Murdoch, Iris—Bibliography.   I. Title.   II. Series.
Z8606.3.B43   1987   [PR6063.U7]   016.823'914   87-25042
ISBN 0-8161-8646-4

This publication is printed on permanent/durable acid-free paper
MANUFACTURED IN THE UNITED STATES OF AMERICA

Contents

The Author

Kate Begnal, a graduate of the College of St. Elizabeth, received her Ph.D. from Pennsylvania State University with a dissertation on the fiction of John Barth. She has written on American and Dutch detective fiction. She has also written articles on such women novelists as Toni Morrison, Christine Stead, and Ivy Compton-Burnett. She is an associate professor in the English Department at Utah State University, where she teaches courses in women in literature and twentieth-century British and American literature. This project on the fiction of Iris Murdoch unites her research interests in the novel, in contemporary fiction, and in fiction by women.

Preface

Iris Murdoch: A Reference Guide contains a list of
major works by and about an important modern British novelist with a large body of work who has gained substantial
critical recognition. Other check lists of criticism of
her work exist. The principal bibliography is still Iris
Murdoch and Muriel Spark: A Bibliography by Thomas T.
Tominaga and Wilma Schneidermeyer, published by the Scarecrow Press in Metuchen, New Jersey, in 1976. That bibliography is not annotated. No primary bibliography that
is complete has yet been published. This reference guide
is the first annotated comprehensive bibliography of sec-
ondary sources. It covers Murdoch scholarship from 1953
to 1983.

This volume contains an introduction to Murdoch's
works, a chronological list of major primary works including novels, volumes of philosophical writing, published
plays, and verse. It includes annotations for the secon-
dary sources and an index that encompasses author, title,
and subject entries. The select list of primary works
notes the dates of the first British and American publications of Murdoch's writings. The annotated bibliography
is arranged chronologically, and it describes all major
books, monographs, critical articles, and dissertations
about the author. It includes some reviews to show the
critical reception of Murdoch's books and to illustrate
Murdoch's popular as well as academic reputation. Brief
reviews, uninformative plot summaries, encyclopedias,
literary histories, and foreign commentary difficult to
obtain have been omitted. Articles and reviews of Murdoch's philosophical writing have been noted and annotated
because critics of her fiction make substantial use of the
concepts in their interpretations of the novels.

Every attempt has been made to examine and annotate
available material. Important and readily accessible
studies are described. Items that could not be obtained
through interlibrary loan departments are followed by
their bibliographical sources. For the most part, anno-

tations of Ph.D. dissertations are based on summaries in
Dissertation Abstracts International.

I am indebted to the interlibrary loan staff of Mer-
rill Library at Utah State University, especially to the
persistence and ingenuity of Darlene Spence and Constance
Hatch. I would like to thank Pat Gordon formerly and
Shelley Hall presently of the Utah State English Department for their secretarial support. Translators I would
like to thank include Lonnie Kay, Gregory Hayward, Marie-
Paul Cellier, Marie Elena Andino, and Daniel Jones. I
wish also to thank my editor, Michael Begnal, for his
helpful suggestions.

Introduction

What has colored criticism of Iris Murdoch's fiction to a great extent is her beginning her career as a professional philosopher. Major full-length studies of her fiction in English began with A.S. Byatt's Degrees of Freedom (1965.5), which pointed out the importance of freedom as a theme in Murdoch's work. Byatt discussed the relation of the novels to existential and ethical questions, as well as Murdoch's inclusion of the strange and uncanny.

Peter Wolfe in The Disciplined Heart: Iris Murdoch and Her Novels (1966.39) investigated philosophical themes of choice and value. He related her ideas to those of Locke, Hare, Ayre, Hegel, Sartre, Dewey, Marcel, and Kant. Later Sally Cuneen explored Murdoch's relation to Sartre and to Plato (1978.18). W.K. Rose (1968.31) and Michele Morin (1978.36) also considered Murdoch as a Platonist, while Barbara Heusel examined Murdoch's fiction for ideas of Wittgenstein. Some critics in journal articles have isolated particularly influences of Sartre's La nausée on Under the Net (Vickery 1971.26, and Kellman 1976.14; 1980.17). Some discussed Murdoch's criticism of existentialism, especially of the early writings of Sartre (MacNiven 1970.11; Coventry 1971.3). Although many have dealt with Murdoch's criticism of Sartre's philosophy and fiction in her Sartre: Romantic Rationalist and her early essays, Obumsulu (1975.20) discussed Murdoch's debt to Sartre and named her existentialist despite herself. Of course, critics like A.S. Byatt have explained Murdoch's use of ideas from Simone Weil, especially her term "attention," a just and loving gaze at the world. In his monograph Iris Murdoch, Rubin Rabinovitz carefully and thoroughly connected ideas of Weil with Murdoch's early novels.

In Iris Murdoch (1974.5), Frank Baldanza discussed the alien-god figure and the artist-saint dichotomy of Murdoch's characters. Michael Bellamy in his dissertation (1975.5) also examined the artist-saint opposition. An early insight into that dichotomy can be found in

Ruth Heyd's interview with Murdoch (1965.15). Among
others who analyzed the alien-god figure were Arlene
Kuhner in her dissertation (1978.29) and a range of critics who analyzed what they called the enchanter figure,
especially with reference to The Flight from the Enchanter,
A Severed Head, and A Fairly Honourable Defeat. James
Grindin also discussed what he called "false gods" in the
novels (1971.8).

Donna Gerstenberger wrote a monograph, Iris Murdoch
(1975.13), which explored Murdoch's Irishness and its
effect on her writing, although Gerstenberger did not want
to distort Murdoch's fiction by confining her to a re-
strictive category. After anlyzing The Red and the Green
and Murdoch's use of Irish characters (usually as lower-
class aliens), Gerstenberger recognized Murdoch's Eng-
lishness as well. Colette Charpentier surveyed criticism
of Murdoch's "Irish" novels--The Unicorn and The Red and
the Green (1980.6; 1981.3)--after having previously studied the theme of enclosure in The Unicorn (1976.7).

In Iris Murdoch: The Shakespearian Interest
(1979.28), Richard Todd investigated the influence of
Shakespeare on Murdoch's work, not just in terms of finding sources and parallels in Shakespeare's plays for
techniques and plot situations in the novels but also in
terms of Murdoch's veneration for Shakespeare as the
ideal artist in his relationship to his characters and to
his artistic creation. Other critics have traced Shakespearian allusions and parallels. Robert Hoskins has analyzed the influence of A Midsummer Night's Dream on
A Fairly Honourable Defeat (1972.21) and parallels between Hamlet and A Severed Head (1981.15). Ronald Hayman
(1976.11) discerned four general Shakespearian elements
in the novel. Of course, most reviews and articles on
The Black Prince explicate the Hamlet connection.

Elizabeth Dipple's Iris Murdoch: Work for the Spirit
(1982.1) explored the strong impulse in Murdoch toward
moral philosophy, including the influence of Plato on her
moral thinking. An earlier study of Murdoch's spirituality is Wilma Schneidermeyer's dissertation (1974.32).
Other dissertations have also dealt with Murdoch's moral
philosophy: Kathleen Martindale's (1981.22), which concerned Murdoch's later novels, Samuel Ford's (1981.10),
which discussed the moralist as critic and storyteller,
and Sally Simpson Cunneen's (1978.18), which examined
the idea of the self and the sovereign good. Murdoch
herself discussed with Bryan Magee (1979.16) the extent
to which she considers her novels to be philosophical and
the extent to which she considers literature and philosophy to be separate, dissimilar disciplines.

Bernard Bergonzi (1970.3), Malcolm Bradbury (1977.5),
Patrick Swindin (1973.29), and David Lodge (1971.17) discussed the prospects of realism in the novel. They
applied Murdoch's ideas in "Against Dryness" to the question, as well as her idea of free characters. Murdoch's
ideal is to create characters who do not narrowly reflect
the prejudices of their authors and who do not simply
become mouthpieces of them in an ideological battle.
Mary McCarthy has discussed the disappearance of such
independent characters from the contemporary novel
(1961.19). Gerstenberger (1975.13) explored Murdoch's
practice compared to her theory. Kathryn Lenowitz related Murdoch's view of her characters to those of Nathalie
Sarraute, finding them less opposed than might be expect-
ed (1980.19). Critics like John Fletcher (1983.21) investigated the influence of her husband, critic and writer
John Bayley, on Murdoch's theory of character.

In interviews Murdoch has talked about her love for
the free characters of the English and Russian nineteenth-
century novels, citing as good examples characters of
Dickens and Dostoevski. Of course, her ultimate ideal in
creating free characters and in creating literary works
that encompass contingency is Shakespeare. Bad examples
Murdoch has mentioned have included some characters in
D.H. Lawrence novels (Interview, 1982.2) and characters
in her own novels like Nan Mor in The Sandcastle. Murdoch said that she should have let Nan develop more,
instead of confining her to the role of blocking wife.

Although negative critics like Christopher Ricks have
castigated Murdoch's characters as puppets because of
what seems to be arbitrary changes they make in their
affections and in their lives, more sympathetic critics
have seen evidence of Murdoch's fighting against her
natural tendency to write novels tightly controlled by
myth. Jean Kennard (1975.16) explained that Murdoch cannot follow the ordered nineteenth-century pattern of depicting characters' actions resulting in unambiguous con-
sequences without betraying her belief in surprise and
mystery, in contingency. Other critics like Robert
Scholes found it to be no problem that Murdoch is a fab-
ulist or allegorist whose genius is for plot and design
(1967.18). Several critics like Alice Kenny (1969.27),
C. Guido Mutis (1970.12), and Bernadette Bertrandias
(1975.6) have explicated Murdoch's use of myth in her
novels. Dissertations analyzing her use of myth have included those by Lois Keates (1972.24), Ellen Ashdown
(1974.4), and Rose Mohan (1977.19).

Genre studies of Murdoch's novels have not been lacking. Critics like Jack Dueck (1973.9), Ulrich Broich
(1967.4), and Bruno Schleussner (1969.38) have related
Under the Net to the picaresque tradition. Nina

Diakonova (1968.11) and Raymond Porter (1969.36) have considered Murdoch's novels as bildungsroman, with Diakonova finally distinguishing Murdoch's from the central bildungsroman pattern. Steven Kellman has characterized Under the Net as a self-begetting novel, a separate genre (1976.14, 1980.17). Linda Kuehl (1969.29), Morton Kaplan (1969.24), Dorothy Winsor (1979.33), and especially Zorah T. Sullivan (1970.19; 1975.31; 1977.35-36) have studied intensively Murdoch's use of the Gothic form. Charpentier (1980.6) found ten studies that dealt with The Unicorn as a Gothic novel. The Time of the Angels and The Italian Girl have also been examined as Gothic fictions.

Several critics have investigated Murdoch's use of comedy as a genre and a technique. Pamela Faust has examined how Murdoch uses the comic to comment on love (1965.9). Larry Jean Rockefeller has focused on comedy in the early novels of Murdoch (1968.21). In making connections between A Fairly Honourable Defeat and A Midsummer's Night Dream, Robert Hoskins discussed Murdoch's parody inversion and her ironic comparison (1972.21). In her dissertation, Nancy Wolf has analyzed the dark comedy of Murdoch, her comedies of moral education, her comic initiations, and her severely ironic tales (1972.39). Angela Hague, in her dissertation, stressed the importance of the comic dimensions and ironic tone of Murdoch's work, and she examined comic structure and tone in three of the novels (1979.12).

Many critics have traced literary influence in Murdoch's novels. I have already mentioned studies of Shakespeare's and Sartre's influence. Critics of Under the Net have discerned the influence of Samuel Beckett and Raymond Queneau on it. Steven Kellman (1976.14; 1980.7) and John Fletcher (1981.9) have made such studies, and Howard German (1969.16) has traced the influence of Ludwig Wittgenstein. There have been analyses of Murdoch's early novels for mid-East, Slavic, Scandinavian, Celtic, and Oriental Mythology (German 1969.16). Alice Kenny (1969.27) has charted the use of mythology and history in A Severed Head. William Hall has made a case for extensive references to Eastern mythology in Bruno's Dream (1969.17). Daniel Majdiak (1972.29) has studied the influence of Romanticism on Murdoch, despite her explicit criticism of Romanticism. Louis Martz (1971.18) has associated Murdoch with Dickens in the loving descriptions of London scenes, and John Mellors (1974.22) has seen resemblances between Murdoch's and Dickens's methods of characterization.

Critics like Dorthy Winsor have explored the influence of Freud on Murdoch's works (1981.37). Scott Dunbar has seen Freud's influence on Murdoch's idea that people have little freedom and the psyche is an obscure machine run on the principle of self-preservation (1978.21). In this scheme sexual love moves the person toward the world of others for gratification. But this dark eros is ambiguous and hard to control (Majdiak 1972.29). This impulse does not necessarily involve anything "uplifting." Characters in love can be deluded and can make fools of themselves, something clearly seen in A Severed Head, The Sea, The Sea, and The Black Prince.

An interesting critical dialogue has concerned Murdoch's depiction of male-female relationships. Gary Goshgarian (1974.15) has discerned in five of her novels a clear critique of male fantasies and romantic projections about women. Steven Cohan has found in her first-person male narrators an expression of a tension between male form and female contingency and a criticism of men's unconscious brutality in the name of love, culminating in The Sea, The Sea, its most skillful depiction (1981.4). In an interview with Murdoch, Michael Bellamy (1977.4) asked why Murdoch used first-person male but not first-person female narrators. Murdoch said that she identifies more with the male voice as generically human and sees the female voice as a special case, although she has portrayed many female characters.

Studies of the process of reading and interpretation have been applied to Murdoch's novels. Wolfram Volker in his Rhetoric of Love has investigated how Murdoch's novels themselves create the necessary reader for them (1978.51). Robert Scholes has asserted that The Unicorn itself teaches the method of reading a contemporary allegory (1979.27). Pat O'Donell (1979.19) and David Arnold (1983.3) have also explored the process of reading and the dialectic of reader and character in Murdoch's fiction.

Another important topic in Murdoch criticism has been the broad topic of art, referring sometimes to Murdoch's aesthetics, sometimes to her depiction of artist figures as characters, and sometimes to her use of visual works of art, influencing her characters. Michael Birdsall has explored how Murdoch uses art-related images and metaphors and how she presents the artist as an analogue to the good man (1980.12). Betty Foley has considered Murdoch's use of art as imagery and as giving an allegorical dimension to her plots (1979.10). In her dissertation, Gail Aiken related art as discussed in The Sovereignty of Good to The Black Prince, concluding that Murdoch's novels contradict the ideas in her philosophical essays (1979.2). Geneviene Lloyd considered in an essay Murdoch's defense of the ethical significance of truth in

the light of her refusal to separate art from truth
(1982.5). Criticism concerning the artist figure in Murdoch's novels often examines Under the Net and The Black
Prince. One interesting example is an essay by Elizabeth
Dipple, comparing the relation of art, immortality, and
mortality in Lolita and The Black Prince (1978.27).
Another is an article by Steven Kellman about the problematic status of art and the process of Jake's becoming
an artist in Under the Net (1976.14).

From a writer whose very productivity has been suspect
and one who has been accused of rewriting the same novel
each year, Murdoch has emerged as a writer of considerable stature, winning the most prestigious literary
prizes in England and becoming almost fashionable with
academic critics. As yet there is no Murdoch newsletter
or Murdoch literary society, but the day may not be long
in coming. The judgment that Murdoch is of the honorable
second rank of artists may be revised.

Writings by Iris Murdoch

This section lists chronologically the volumes of philosophy, fiction, drama, and verse discussed in the criticism. Primary bibliographic information is still scattered. Dates of the first English and American editions are noted. Writings other than novels are labeled as to their genre.

1953 Sartre: Romantic Rationalist (criticism). Cambridge: Bowes & Bowes; New Haven, Conn.: Yale University Press.

1954 Under the Net. London: Chatto & Windus; New York: Viking Press.

1956 The Flight from the Enchanter. London: Chatto & Windus; New York: Viking Press.

1957 The Sandcastle. London: Chatto & Windus; New York: Viking Press.

1958 The Bell. London: Chatto & Windus; New York: Viking Press.

1961 A Severed Head. London: Chatto & Windus; New York: Viking Press.

1962 An Unofficial Rose. London: Chatto & Windus; New York: Viking Press.

1963 The Unicorn. London: Chatto & Windus; New York: Viking Press.

1964 The Italian Girl. London: Chatto & Windus; New York: Viking Press.

1964 A Severed Head (play), with J.B. Priestley. London: Chatto & Windus.

1965 The Red and the Green. London: Chatto & Windus; New York: Viking Press.

1966 The Time of the Angels. London: Chatto & Windus;
      New York: Viking Press.

1967 The Sovereignty of Good over Other Concepts (lec-
      ture). Cambridge: Cambridge University Press.

1968 The Nice and the Good. London: Chatto & Windus;
      New York: Viking Press.

1969 Bruno's Dream. London: Chato & Windus; New York:
      Viking Press.

1969 The Italian Girl (play), with James Saunders. Lon-
      don: French.

1970 A Fairly Honourable Defeat. London: Chatto & Win-
      dus; New York: Viking Press.

1971 The Sovereignty of Good (essay). London: Rout-
      ledge; New York: Schocken.

1972 An Accidental Man. London: Chatto & Windus; New
      York: Viking Press.

1973 The Black Prince. London: Chatto & Windus; New
      York: Viking Press.

1973 "The Three Arrows," and "The Servant and the Snow":
      Two Plays (plays). London: Chatto & Windus;
      New York: Viking Press, 1974

1974 The Sacred and Profane Love Machine. London:
      Chatto & Windus; New York: Viking Press.

1975 A Word Child. London: Chatto & Windus; New York:
      Viking Press.

1977 Henry and Cato. London: Chatto & Windus; New
      York: Viking Press.

1977 The Fire and the Sun: Why Plato Banished the
      Artist (philosophy). London and New York:
      Oxford University Press.

1978 The Sea, The Sea. London: Chatto & Windus; New
      York: Viking Press.

1978 A Year of Birds (verse). Tisbury, Wiltshire:
      Compton Press.

1980 The Servants (libretto), for the opera composed by
      William Mathias.

1980 <u>Art and Eros</u> (play). London, Oliver Theatre,
2 April.

1981 <u>Nuns and Soldiers</u>. London: Chatto & Windus; New
York: Viking Press.

1983 <u>The Philosopher's Pupil</u>. London: Chatto & Windus;
New York: Viking Press.

1985 <u>The Good Apprentice</u>. London: Chatto & Windus; New
York: Viking Press.

1986 <u>Acastos</u> (philosophic dialogue). London: Chatto &
Windus.

Writings about Iris Murdoch, 1953–1983

1953

1 FOWLIE, WALLACE. "Figures from Two Tortured Gener-
   ations." Commonweal 59 (13 November):145.
        Review of Sartre: Romantic Rationalist. Notes
   Murdoch's comparison of the existentialist and the
   Marxist. Mentions the examination of surrealism and
   symbolist poetry. Praises the study as useful and
   objective.

1954

1 AMIS, KINGSLEY. "New Novels." Spectator, 11 June,
   p. 722.
        Calls Under the Net a "thoroughly accomplished
   first novel" and praises Murdoch's control and her
   use of a first-person male narrator.

2 "Briefly Noted: Fiction." New Yorker 30 (12 June):
   118.
        Reviews Under the Net, criticizing the characters
   as odd and wooden, deploring the "haphazard violence"
   and the talkiness of the novel.

3 CLARK, A.F.B. Review of Sartre: Romantic Rationalist. Canadian Forum 34 (April):19.
        Finds the book a profound study of Sartre but
   says he is already overpraised.

4 FOX, JOAN. Review of Under the Net. Canadian Forum
   34 (October):164.
        Calls it an able first novel but asks if it is
   meant to be intellectual or funny.

5 FULLER, EDMUND. "Talented But Lazy." New York
   Times Book Review, 20 June, p. 15.
        Praises the "high sense of comedy" and intricate
   plot of Under the Net and finds it "casually existen-
   ialist."

6   HAMPSHIRE, STUART. "The Latest Hegelian." New
    Statesman and Nation 47 (2 January): 19.
        Reviews Sartre: Romantic Rationalist as wide-
    ranging, constructive criticism to explain the nature
    of Sartre's existentialism.

7   HODGART, PARTICIA. "American Social Groups." Man-
    chester Guardian, 10 June, p. 11.
        Criticizes Under the Net as a "sentimental fan-
    tasy," objecting to its whimsey.

8   HOLZHAUER, JEAN. "A Palpable Romantic." Commonweal
    60 (4 June):228-29.
        Finds Under the Net odd and "strongly flavored"
    with existentialism, noting the discontinuity between
    the characters' thoughts and actions.

9   "Humor and Verse." Nation 178 (26 June):548.
        Praises Murdoch's wit and urbanity in Under the
    Net and notes the "sure touch" and delightful manner.

10 LANE, MARGARET. "Under the Net by Iris Murdoch."
    London Magazine 1 (September):104-6.
        A review of Under the Net that describes it as
    highly intelligent and extremely funny. Calls Jake's
    interlude in Paris moving and poetic.

11 PAULDING, GOUVERNEUR. "Are Women Necessary: A
    Witty and Intelligent Novel." New York Herald
    Tribune Book Review, 6 June, p. 4.
        Says that Murdoch has an "almost doctrinal dis-
    taste" for women but finds Under the Net a "successful
    mixture of high comedy and deep purpose."

12 RAYMOND, JOHN. "New Novels." New Statesman,
    5 June, pp. 737-38.
        A review of Under the Net that compares it
    unfavorably with Hurry on Down and Lucky Jim, calling
    it a bluestocking fantasy and long-winded cafe writ-
    ing.

13 Review of Under the Net. Booklist 50 (15 May):359.
        Calls the number of characters "bewildering" but
    recommends the "humorous episodes."

14 ROLAND, ALBERT. Review of Sartre: Romantic
    Rationalist. Books Abroad 28 (Autumn):481.
        Brief review that states that the book attempts
    an objective evaluation of Sartre's contribution to
    our culture. Sartre's writing provides a sensitive
    portrayal of contemporary man who has lost the com-
    forting certainties of religion and progress and who
    stands alone. Murdoch's book is interesting, but it
    should analyze Sartre's texts in more detail.

15 ROLO, CHARLES T. "Potpourri." Atlantic Monthly 194
    (July):85.
        Mentions the "raffish characters" in the "pic-
    aresque tale" and praises the original style of Under
    the Net.

16 "Romantic Rationalist." Times Literary Supplement,
    15 January, p. 45.
        Review of Sartre: Romantic Rationalist. Judges
    Murdoch's commentary to be penetrating and extremely
    intelligent.

17 "Town and Country." Times Literary Supplement, 9
    July, p. 437.
        Review of Under the Net. Praises Murdoch's
    sense of comic timing and her creation of characters.
    Calls it a minor weakness that some characters are not
    integrated into the plot.

18 WALBRIDGE, EARLE F. Review of Under the Net.
    Library Journal 79 (15 April):771.
        Recommends the novel as very amusing.

19 WEBSTER, HARVEY CURTIS. "Grasp of Absurdity."
    Saturday Review 37 (3 July):15.
        Says Under the Net satirizes Sartre's fiction
    and appreciates the "too intelligent" characters.

20 WILSON, ANGUS. "New Novels." Observer, 6 June,
    p. 17.
        A review of Under the Net, finding it "seriously
    conceived" but not clever or funny enough to be suc-
    cessful. Notes a lyrical strain in the novel but com-
    plains that the poetic scenes are set pieces.

                           1955

1   FITZSIMMONS, THOMAS. "Four Novels." Sewanee
    Review 63 (Spring):328-30.
        A review of Under the Net that finds the satire
    subordinate to a larger purpose--Murdoch's concern
    with the "distortion of reality by personality." Says
    that Jake is forced to confront the world of everyday
    action.

2   KALB, BERNARD. "Three Comers." Saturday Review 38
    (7 May):22
        Mentions Amis, Wain, and Murdoch as a group of
    contemporary British writers, referring to the good
    reviews of Under the Net.

1956

1 AARON, DANIEL. "Seven Novels." Hudson Review 9
   (Winter):624-25.
        A review of The Flight from the Enchanter that
   compares it to Sartre's "No Exit," calling the novel
   brilliantly artificial and praising Murdoch's style.

2 "Bad Spell in London." Time 67 (14 May):133-34.
        Calls Murdoch "a great tragicomic talent" and
   describes The Flight from the Enchanter as "brilliant
   in detail."

3 BOSTOCK, ANNA. Review of The Flight from the
   Enchanter. Manchester Guardian, 27 March, p. 4.
        A review of The Flight from the Enchanter that
   notes two kinds of relationships between the characters: completely superficial and extremely intimate.
   Commends the comic scenes and disparages the serious.

4 BRETT, HARVEY. "Enchanter." New York Times Book
   Review, 22 April, p. 8.
        Some biographical information about Murdoch and
   mention of her as an important postwar British novelist.

5 "Briefly Noted: Fiction." New Yorker 32 (12 May):
   177.
        Describes The Flight from the Enchanter as "cur-
   iously diverting" but criticizes the characters as
   "inhabiting a private world."

6 ENGLE, PAUL. "Astonishing Novel of Odd Characters."
   Chicago Sunday Tribune, 17 June, p. 3.
        A review of The Flight from the Enchanter that
   praises the wit and the surprising insights, calling
   the society odd but convincing.

7 F., E.W. "New Form for the Novel." Christian
   Science Monitor, 19 April, p. 11.
        Calls The Flight from the Enchanter a "macabre,
   satirical, disjointed tale" but claims that Murdoch
   has taken the novel "out of its strait-jacket" of
   traditional form.

8 FIEDLER, LESLIE A. "The Novel in the Post-Political World." Partisan Review 23:358-65.
        Review of The Flight from the Enchanter, assert-
   ing that Murdoch's world, like those of many contemporary writers, is "post-political." Compares her to
   Dickens in her portrayal of British bureaucracy.

9 GEORGE, DANIEL. "New Novels." Spectator, 30 March,
   pp. 418-19.

Praises the beautiful writing and Murdoch's "in-
fallible comic sense" even if The Flight from the
Enchanter does not explore "the dilemma of our time."

10   HUGHES, RILEY. Review of The Flight from the
Enchanter. Catholic World 183 (July):313.
Complains of ambiguities and the mixture of surrealistic and comic scenes and the reader's inability
to tell if this is an existentialist novel or a satire
on existentialism.

11   PAULDING, GOUVERNEUR. "Laughter, Horror Together
in This Dream-Like Novel." New York Herald Tribune
Book Review, 29 April, p. 6.
Notes the wild humor in the nightmare world and
praises the real characters and the extraordinary
suicide scene in The Flight from the Enchanter.

12   "Perpetual Motion." Times Literary Supplement,
6 April, p. 205.
Review of The Flight from the Enchanter. Notes
a "mood of intense feeling" but finds it not related
to the characters or situation.

13   PIPPETT, AILEEN. "Moonshine and Asphodel." New
York Times Book Review, 15 April, p. 31.
Calls The Flight from the Enchanter "preposterous
and enchanting," an account of fantastic adventures
related matter-of-factly.

14   Review of The Flight from the Enchanter. Booklist
52 (1 May):363.
Considers the subplots confusing but admires the
"intellectual and sensitive work."

15   RHODES, ANTHONY. "New Novels." Listener, 19 April,
p. 475.
A review of The Flight from the Enchanter that
asserts it amuses by depicting petty minds disturbed
by the trivia of daily life and by showing the London
intellectual scene as a zoo.

16   RICHARDSON, MAURICE. "New Novels." New Statesman
and Nation 51 (31 March):315.
Judges Mischa Fox "a cardboard box" and accuses
Murdoch of "suffering from metaphysical affectations"
in The Flight from the Enchanter.

17   SISK, JOHN P. "Uncrystallized Matter." Commonweal
64 (11 May):158-59.
Sees The Flight from the Enchanter as a vision
of absurdity and futility and finds the half-concealed
meaning "to inhibit the laughter" and make it part of
the grotesque.

18 VAN GHENT, DOROTHY. "New Books in Review." Yale
    Review 46 (Autumn):153-54.
         Calls Murdoch's talent spell-binding and notes
    her working against pattern in a labrinthine tale in
    The Flight from the Enchanter.

19 WEBSTER, HARVEY CURTIS. "Four from Abroad." Satur-
    day Review 39 (21 April):14.
         Finds The Flight from the Enchanter an excellent
    novel, comic and philosophic at the same time, with
    many layers of meaning.

                            1957

1   ENGLE, PAUL. "Vigorous and Lively Tale." Chicago
    Sunday Tribune, 30 June, p. 4.
         A review of The Sandcastle, praising Murdoch's
    comic sense and her probing of the emotions. Calls
    the novel original and Murdoch vigorous, perceptive,
    and subtle.

2   GEORGE, DANIEL. Review of The Sandcastle. Specta-
    tor, 17 May, p. 657.
         Predicts a large public for this satisfying novel
    of "comic, poignant, and unnerving events."

3   HOPKINSON, TOM. "A Natural Novelist." Observer,
    5 May, p. 17.
         Finds Mor to be an individual, yet Everyman.
    Calls Murdoch a "natural" novelist with "great pen-
    etration into character." Says that the women charac-
    ters are portrayed with less sympathy than the men in
    The Sandcastle.

4   LEHMANN, JOHN. "Foreword." London Magazine, 4
    (August):7-9.
         A discussion of the contemporary English novel as
    characterized by social comedy as opposed to the
    French and American novels of existentialist despair.
    Groups Murdoch with Amis and Wain as vigorous, young
    English novelists.

5   LERMAN, LEO. "English Novelists." Mademoiselle 45
    (September):167-68.
         Names Murdoch a brilliant young British novelist
    whose forte is savage, intellectual comedy.

6   MADDOCKS, MELVIN. "Miss Murdoch's Sandcastle."
    Christian Science Monitor, 16 May, p. 13.
         Evaluates the novel as "more conventional and
    more profound" than Murdoch's earlier ones. Compares
    her to Henry Green in her style's being integral to
    character depiction.

7   MORTIMER, RAYMOND. "Notable Novelist: Miss Iris
    Murdoch's Three Books." Sunday Times (London), 5
    May, p. 6.
        A review of The Sandcastle that compares it to
    Murdoch's first two novels and finds it confronting
    actuality more directly. Interprets the theme as the
    duty of making choices and acting them out.

8   "New Novels." Listener, 16 May, p. 800.
        A review of The Sandcastle that compares Murd-
    och's techniques to those of the Post-Impressionist
    painters, with bold, simple characters arranged in
    geometrically complex relationships. Asserts that
    the design is secured by Murdoch's personal symbols--
    nets, rivers, fish, and jewels.

9   "Out of School." Times Literary Supplement, 10 May,
    p. 285.
        Review of The Sandcastle. States that Murdoch
    developed her idea more fully than usual and embodied
    it with simplicity and sensitivity.

10 PAULDING, GOUVERNEUR. "A Wealth of Life in Iris
    Murdoch's Latest Novel." New York Herald Tribune
    Book Review, 12 May, p. 5.
        A review of The Sandcastle that asserts Murdoch
    uses her imagination to deepen character and to form
    a moving, comic conclusion. Extols her independence
    and maturity.

11 "Philosophical Pixie." Time 69 (10 June):106.
        Sees an "extra dimension" to the story of a love
    affair but objects to Murdoch's use of witchcraft in
    The Sandcastle.

12 PIPPETT, AILEEN. "The Women in the Case." New
    York Times Book Review, 12 May, p. 4.
        Review of The Sandcastle that credits Murdoch
    with an "authentic narrative gift" and sees her
    moving to the front rank of novelists.

13 PRICE, MARTIN. "New Books in Review." Yale Review
    47 (Autumn):146-47.
        Sees the influence of T.S. Eliot in the depic-
    tion of Mor, while it considers Murdoch's theme to be
    freedom. Praises the tenderness and humor of the
    Sandcastle.

14 QUIGLY, ISABEL. "Miss Murdoch and Others." Tablet
    209 (May 18):472.
        Criticizes the awkward symbolism but commends
    Murdoch's new direction away from brilliance toward
    humanity and warmth in The Sandcastle.

15 RICHARDSON, MAURICE. "New Novels." New Statesman
    and Nation 53 (11 May):616.
        Compliments Murdoch's sense of detail and her
    convincing characters, while criticizing her use of
    epithets in The Sandcastle.

16 RIDLEY, M.R. "A Schoolmaster Falls in Love."
    Daily Telegraph and Morning Post, 10 May, p. 12.
        A review of The Sandcastle that notes the inten-
    sity of the story, the convincingly real characters,
    and the significance of the theme.

17 SHRAPNEL, NORMAN. "New Fiction." Manchester
    Guardian, 28 May, p. 4.
        A review of The Sandcastle that disparages the
    dusty plot and the unconvincing climax but names Mur-
    doch a true novelist, in tune with the times.

18 SISK, JOHN P. "A Sea Change." Commonweal 66
    (31 May):236-37.
        Finds "less surface sparkle" but good and often
    brilliant writing in The Sandcastle. Declares the
    theme--"the isolation and mystery" of human existence
    and the need for love--to be common to The Flight
    from the Enchanter.

19 TRACY, HONOR. "Passion in the Groves of Academe."
    New Republic 136 (10 June):17.
        Calls Murdoch the only interesting postwar
    British novelist, praising her "truly original mind."

20 VOILES, JANE. "A Third Murdoch Novel Comes as a
    Surprise." San Francisco Chronicle, 10 May, p. 10.
        A review of The Sandcastle that calls it more
    explicit and more appealing to American readers,
    commending the clean, tight writing.

21 WYNDHAM, FRANCIS. Review of The Sandcastle.
    London Magazine 4 (August):64-65.
        Judges The Sandcastle a consolidation of Mur-
    doch's impressive reputation and finds the familiar
    theme treated with patient intelligence. Calls the
    subtle characterization of Nan a triumph and the
    depiction of the married relationship in chapters one
    and twelve unsurpassed.

                              1958

1   ALLSOP, KENNETH. The Angry Decade: A Survey of
    the Cultural Revolt of the Nineteen-Fifties.
    London: P. Owen, pp. 88-95.

An assessment of Murdoch's ability, judging it
to be solid and professional. Predicts that of all
the postwar novelists, Murdoch may have the most
potential.

2   BETJEMAN, JOHN. "Mis Murdoch's Lay Community."
    Daily Telegraph (London), 7 November.
        Review of The Bell, praising Murdoch as someone
who really knows how to write, who can tell a story
and delineate character, who can capture an atmosphere, who can enter the private thoughts of a man
and make it believable. Complains that she does not
understand the purpose of the religious life and that
her plot deviates into a mere adventure story. Calls
it a splendid novel anyway.

3   BLAIR, HOWARD. "The Legend of a Bell--and Three
    Frantic People." San Francisco Chronicle, 2 Novem-
    ber, p. 20.
        Categorizes The Bell as a novel of ideas con-
cerning Christian ideas of innocence and the spiritual life . Criticizes the bell as symbol.

4   BOWEN, ELIZABETH. "Sensuality in a Secluded World."
    Saturday Review 41 (25 October):28.
        Praises the remarkable authority of Murdoch's
writing and the "sensuous exactitude" of The Bell.

5   "Briefly Noted: Fiction." New Yorker 34 (22
    November):233.
        Finds The Bell to be very dull, criticizing the
"vaporous symbolism."

6   Current Biography, 1958. Edited by Marjorie Dent
    Candee. New York: H.W. Wilson Co., pp. 293-94.
        Information about Murdoch's life and work to
date, calling her a major young British novelist.

7   GANNETT, LEWIS. "At the Bottom of a Lake Was a
    Bell." New York Herald Tribune Book Review, 16
    November, p. 8.
        Objects to the "Delphic pronouncements" but
describes the story of The Bell as entertaining.

8   GINDIN, JAMES. "The Reassertion of the Personal."
    Texas Quarterly 1 (Winter):126-34.
        Groups Kingsley Amis, John Wain, and Angus
Wilson with Murdoch as writers of comic novels that
affirm the value of the individual. Contrasts Murdoch as setting her characters in a religious framework.

9   GRAHAM, A.F. "All Our Failures Are Failures of
    Love." New York Times Book Review, 26 October,
    pp. 4-5.
        Praises the wisdom and wit of The Bell and
    states that Murdoch has achieved her "true voice" in
    it.

10 HARVEY, W.J. "The Reviewing of Contemporary Fic-
    tion." Essays in Criticism 8 (April):182-87.
        Claims to be not a review but a sermon against
    critics' refusal to recognize good in contemporary
    literature. Calls The Sandcastle a disappointment
    because of the gap between fantasy and contemporary
    reality, but calls Murdoch the most promising novel-
    ist since the war.

11 "In the Heart or in the Head." Times Literary
    Supplement, 7 November, p. 640.
        A review of The Bell, discussing Murdoch's pre-
    vious novels and dissociating her from the Angry
    Young Men. Also lauds her "literary transvestism."

12 "It Tolls, but for Whom?" Time 72 (27 October):94.
        Calls the bell a symbol of innocence and finds
    distinction in the various sermons, praising the
    novel's "ethical insight."

13 KERMODE, FRANK. "Novels of Iris Murdoch."
    Spectator 201 (7 November):618.
        Discusses the "double life" of Murdoch's stories,
    saying that her precise descriptions validate the
    improbable situations she creates.

14 "New Fiction." Times, 6 November.
        A review of The Bell, declaring it a strong,
    positive novel, "a joy to read." Estimates that it
    may be a little long with a little too much symbolism
    but praises the purpose, intelligence, and delightful
    prose.

15 "New Novels." Listener, 18 December.
        A review of The Bell that remarks on the elab-
    orate construction and ambitious scope, perceiving a
    haunting quality in Murdoch's description but seeing
    the symbolism as externally imposed. Calls her gifted
    and remarkable.

16 PERROTT, ROY. "Miss Murdoch Rings the Bell."
    Manchester Guardian, 13 November, p. 11.
        States that Murdoch catches the atmosphere of the
    community brilliantly and says that she may bring
    greatness back to the novel.

17 PRICE, MARTIN. "The Self-Deceivers: Some Recent
    Fiction." Yale Review 47 (December):272-75.
        Names The Bell a "comedy of the existential
    plight" and finds Murdoch's wit and intelligence
    impressive.

18 QUINTON, ANTHONY, et al. "The New Novelists: An
    Enquiry." London Magazine 5 (November):13-31.
        A symposium of critics, all of whom consider
    Murdoch an important contemporary writer, although
    Frank Kermode chides her for giving up "information"
    about the world.

19 RAYMOND, JOHN. "The Unclassifiable Image." New
    Statesman 56 (15 November):697-98.
        A review of The Bell that sees Murdoch as a
    satirist who is tender toward human frailty. Notes
    her interest in institutions and praises her honest
    and subtle treatment of the homosexual theme.

20 ROLO, CHARLES. Review of The Bell. Atlantic 202
    (November):173-74.
        Calls the novel entertaining but bewildering
    because sometimes Murdoch seems to be satiric and
    sometimes to be "playing it straight."

21 SISK, JOHN P. "Melodramatic Story and Novel of
    Ideas." Commonweal 69 (7 November):154-55.
        Review of The Bell. Sees Murdoch's melodrama as
    part of her vitality. Finds the ideas integrated
    completely into the story and states that Murdoch
    has "few equals" among contemporary novelists.

22 TAYLOR, GRIFFIN. "What Doth It Profit a Man. . .?"
    Sewanee Review 66 (January-March):137-41
        A review of The Sandcastle, critizing Mor, the
    protagonist, as a weak character and criticizing the
    shifting points of view of the novel.

                        1959

1 BALAKIAN, NONA. "Flight From Innocence." Books
   Abroad 33 (Summer):261, 268-70.
       Discusses a new generation of British writers,
   including John Osborne, Kingsley Amis, John Wain,
   John Braine, J.P. Donleavy, and Iris Murdoch. Says
   that they are all in flight from romantic belief in
   innocence. Praises Murdoch as the most distinguished
   one, for her experimentation and inventiveness.

2 BOWEN, JOHN. "One Man's Meat: The Idea of
   Individual Responsibility." Times Literary Supplement, 7 August, pp. xii-xiii.

                         11

A consideration of Wilson, Golding, Durrell, and
Murdoch as novelists refusing to accept "group values"
and asserting the worth of the individual.

3 FRASER, G.S. "Iris Murdoch." In International
   Literary Annual. No. 2. Edited by John Wain.
   London: John Calder, pp. 37-54.
       An interpretation of Murdoch's novels from Under
   the Net to The Bell, maintaining a continuing theme in
   them to be the relation of the private will to the
   social spirit. Praises Murdoch's depiction of the
   "solidity of the normal," subsequently a much discussed phrase.

4 GINDIN, JAMES. "Comedy in Contemporary British
   Fiction." Papers of the Michigan Academy of
   Science, Arts, and Letters 44:389-97.
       A discussion of Britain's "Angry Young Men,"
   including Kingsley Amis, Angus Wilson, John Wain, and
   Iris Murdoch. Sees them not as a new social movement
   but as a group of comic writers. Interprets Murdoch's
   first two novels.

5 HOWE, IRVING. "Realities and Fictions." Partisan
   Review 26 (Winter):132-33.
       Review of The Bell that calls it, and Murdoch
   also, formidable. Says that Murdoch's ideas "twist
   themselves through the action." Sees important symbolic implications but asks Murdoch to write a simple
   story of love.

6 KAUFMAN, R.J. "The Progress of Iris Murdoch."
   Nation 188 (21 March):255-56.
       Discusses Murdoch's first four novels, judging
   each one better than the last. Calls her a humanistic existentialist like Camus and says that The Bell
   qualifies her as the "most potent" British talent
   since the war.

7 LANOIRE, MAURICE. Les lorgnettes du roman anglais.
   Paris: Librairie Plon, pp. 234-39.
       A discussion of several young women characters
   in Flight from the Enchanter including Agnes Casement,
   Rosa, and Annette. Sees disorder in their relationships to society and holds that Annette's brother
   Nick is guilty of an evasion of his responsibility to
   his heritage.

8 SIMON, IRENE. "Some Recent English Novels."
   Revue des langues vivantes 25:229-30.
       Review of The Bell that praises the lively,
   exciting story and the warm, intense feeling. Sees
   the bell as a symbol of innocence and self-knowledge
   but finds some of the symbolism ambivalent.

1960

1 COLLINS, A.S. English Literature of the Twentieth
  Century. With a postscript on the 1950s by Frank
  Whitehead. London: University Tutorial Press,
  p. 383.
  An assessment of Murdoch's work through The Bell,
praising the first novel and her flair for invention,
characterizing the next two as disappointing, and The
Bell as impressive, compassionate, and penetrating.

2 FELHEIM, MARVIN. "Symbolic Characterization in the
  Novels of Iris Murdoch." Texas Studies in Language
  and Literature 2 (Summer):189-97.
  Asserts that in four novels Murdoch builds much
of the action on contrasting or complementary pairs
of women: In Under the Net, Anna and Sadie Quentin;
in The Flight from the Enchanter, Annette Cockeyne
and Rosa Keepe; in The Sandcastle, Rain Carter and Nan
Mor; and in The Bell, Dora Greenfield and Catherine
Fawley. The women characters are living symbols that
carry the burden of Murdoch's theses. They combine
strangeness and reality, and in the novels they function on two levels: the world of present-day England
and a more significant realm of art.

3 GINDIN, JAMES. "Images of Illusion in the Work of
  Iris Murdoch." Texas Studies in Language and
  Literature 2 (Summer):180-88.
  Declares that each of Murdoch's first four novels
refers in its title to an image of a type of illusion
that its characters face. Under the Net involves nets
from logical-positivist philosophy and left-wing
politics. The Flight from the Enchanter concerns
spells and emotional captivity. The title The Sandcastle refers to the love affair between Bill and
Rain Carter, as impermanent as a castle of sand. The
bell in The Bell stands for people's efforts to con-
struct their own means of salvation although their
efforts are undermined.
  Most of the images in Murdoch's titles are rela-
tive. Different characters interpret the symbol in
the title in their own ways. Only in The Sandcastle
does the title refer to a single illusion. While
each novel expresses symbolically the characters'
desire to create form out of their contingent experiences, each attempt is unsuccessful.

4 MICHA, RENE. "Les romans 'à machines' d'Iris
  Murdoch." Critique (Paris) 16 (April):291-301.
  A discussion of Murdoch's novels through The Bell
that begins by considering the covers of the books.
Also considers Murdoch's use of objects raised to the
status of people like the dog's cage in Under the Net,

the chandelier in <u>Flight from the Enchanter</u>, and the portrait in <u>The Sandcastle</u>. Analyzes the quests and peregrinations of the characters.

5 O'CONNOR, WILLIAM VAN. "Iris Murdoch: The Formal and the Contingent." <u>Critique</u> 3, no. 2:34-46.
    Discusses Murdoch's book on Sartre, her first four novels, and three of her early essays. Distinguishes Sartre's fiction from Murdoch's, praising her creation of character and her sense of humor.

6 RAYMOND, JOHN. <u>The Doge of Dover and Other Essays</u>. London: MacGibbon & Kee, pp. 179-83.
    Murdoch is the foremost contemporary British novelist. With <u>The Bell</u>, she has expanded her field of moral vision. She has the ability to enfold her characters in a density of scene, and she communicates a delight in description of engineering. Her comedy is dry and acute but tender toward human frailty. She presents the homosexual theme with honesty and intelligence. Murdoch sees the irreducible uniqueness of people, while believing in the essential human being behind the accidents.

7 SOUVAGE, JACQUES. "The Unresolved Tension: An Interpretation of Iris Murdoch's <u>Under the Net</u>." <u>Revue des langues vivantes</u> 26:420-30.
    Opposes Murdoch's interest in the surface of life and in the fantastic to her concern for the "deeper issues" of life. Sees <u>Under the Net</u> as an unsuccessful combination of elements of the picaresque novel and the Bildungsroman, creating an uneven tone.

8 STEVENSON, LIONEL. <u>The English Novel: A Panorama</u>. Cambridge, Mass.: Riverside Press, p. 493.
    A brief mention of Murdoch as a young novelist, saying that, in general, young British writers follow Huxley or Woolf.

9 WOOD, FREDERICK T. Review of <u>The Bell</u>. <u>English Studies</u> 41:50-51.
    A review of <u>The Bell</u>, applauding Murdoch's skill and insight into human motivation but deploring the obscurity of her central idea.

<u>1961</u>

1 ALLEN, WALTER. "The Surface Isn't All." <u>New York Times Book Review</u>, 16 April, p. 5.
    Review of <u>A Severed Head</u>. Compares it negatively to <u>The Bell</u>, calling the later novel artificial and the surface events "unacceptable."

2 BARROWS, JOHN. "Living Writers--7: Iris Murdoch." John O'London's 4 (4 May):498.
Interview with Murdoch about her method of writing. Reports that Murdoch has no general intention beyond creating a particular book and that she enjoys planning, more than actually writing, a novel.

3 BRADBURY, MALCOLM. "New Novels." Punch, 12 July, p. 67.
Names A Severed Head as the best thing Murdoch has written, admiring her intelligence and fine moral poise. The novel's superb and complex moral irony compares with that of Ivy Compton-Burnett and Jane Austen. The symbolism and fantasy are not allusions in a realistic story but agents in a highly stylized one. The novel assumes the tone of a civilized tale about civilized people, only in the end to turn against civilization.

4 BRYDEN, RONALD. "Phenomenon." Spectator 206 (16 June):885.
A review of A Severed Head that names it Murdoch's "most masterful" novel. Discusses the theme of human dependence and the force "that drives men and women" together. Says that Murdoch can be compared with E.M. Forster as a comic novelist.

5 COSMAN, MAX. "Priapean Japes." Commonweal 74 (9 June):286-87.
Finds A Severed Head more than "a phallic game" because of Murdoch's serious intention; praises her humor and her inquiry into freedom and loneliness.

6 DERRICK, CHRISTOPHER. "Truth on a Hill." Tablet 215 (24 June):609-10.
Calls A Severed Head a sermon on the besetting sin of the times, lies and deception, but says that the novel is not as "sorted out" as The Bell.

7 EVERETT, BARBARA. "Review and Comments." Critical Quarterly 3 (Autumn):270-71.
Finds the novel to be moral comedy in a New Wave film style. States that Murdoch has fully worked out her previous material in A Severed Head and looks forward to an unspecified new direction.

8 FALLE, GEORGE. Review of A Severed Head. Canadian Forum 41 (November):187.
Judges the novel a sentimental melodrama that is a disaster, comparing it unfavorably to all previous Murdoch novels except The Flight from the Enchanter.

9   FRASER, R.A. "A Complicated Minuet of Love--in the
      English Manner." San Francisco Chronicle, 30 April,
      p. 27.
          Calls A Severed Head a tour de force, an elabor-
    ate minuet by bloodless mannequins, but praises Mur-
    doch's depiction of personal relationships.

10 GEORGI, CHARLOTTE. Review of A Severed Head.
      Library Journal 86 (1 April):1479-80.
          Recommends the novel only for large collections,
    judging it a waste of Murdoch's talents.

11 GREEN, PETER. "Bond in a Bloomsbury Eden." Daily
      Telegraph and Morning Post (London), 16 June, p. 18.
          Finds A Severed Head to be a satire on rational-
    ist ethics and psychoanalysis, saying that it will
    consolidate Murdoch's already high reputation.

12 HICKS, GRANVILLE. "Acute Angles of a Triangle."
      Saturday Review 44 (22 April):19.
          Appreciates the compelling movement of the story
    from revelation to revelation, finding A Severed Head
    complex and well written.

13 HOBSON, HAROLD. "London Comment: Miss Murdoch's
      Latest." Christian Science Monitor, 22 June, p. 7.
          A review of A Severed Head that praises Murdoch's
    wit and mental toughness in depicting people's expos-
    ing their own worthlessness.

14 HOPE, FRANCIS. "The Novels of Iris Murdoch."
      London Magazine, n.s. 1 (August):84-87.
          An evaluation of Murdoch's first five novels
    that says she has come full circle in arguing against
    too much seeking for explanations and against the
    pretence of rationality.

15 JACOBSON, DAN. "Farce, Totem and Taboo." New
      Statesman, 16 June, pp. 956-57.
          A review of A Severed Head that credits Murdoch
    with consolidating the advances she made in The Bell,
    objecting only to the character of Honor Klein.

16 "Ladies Quintet." Books of the Month 76 (July):15.
          A brief review of A Severed Head that finds the
    characters hard to keep track of.

17 LEHMANN, JOHN. "English Letters in the Doldrums?"
      Texas Quarterly 4 (Autumn):56-63.
          A consideration of contemporary British litera-
    ture that calls Murdoch one of the two or three most
    important younger novelists, placing her in the trad-
    ition of Henry Green and Virginia Woolf.

18   "Leisured Philanderings." <u>Times Literary Supplement</u>,
     16 June, p. 369.
         Compares <u>A Severed Head</u> to a Restoration comedy,
     noting its brilliance, but finds the meaning elusive
     and the symbols probably intentionally obscure.

19   McCARTHY, MARY.   "Characters in Fiction." <u>Partisan</u>
     <u>Review</u> 28:171-91.
         Article often mentioned by critics of Murdoch
     because of its similar concern with character,
     although Murdoch herself is not mentioned.   Claims
     that there are no characters in modern fiction
     because writers have lost interst in the social.   The
     fictional experiments of the twentieth century pro-
     duced two kinds of novels, those of sensibility like
     Virginia Woolf's and those of sensation like those of
     Ernest Hemingway.   At the center of modern literature
     is the dissociated outsider.   Finds problematical
     books that are dramatic monologues like <u>Lolita</u> and
     <u>Henderson the Rain King</u>.

20   MALCOLM, DONALD.   "To Everyone with Love." <u>New</u>
     <u>Yorker</u> 37 (6 May):172-76.
         An ironic, even sarcastic review of <u>A Severed</u>
     <u>Head</u> that charges Murdoch with reusing old material
     and with creating a melodramatic atmosphere of por-
     tents and omens.

21   MEHTA, VED.   "Onward and Upward with the Arts: A
     Battle against the Bewitchment of Our Intelligence."
     <u>New Yorker</u> 37 (9 December):59-159.
         An interview with Murdoch and other contemporary
     British philosophers that sees her as an existential-
     ist.   Reports the connection between her philosophy
     and fiction to be only the general concern with making
     decisions.

22   MEIDNER. OLGA McDONALD.   "The Progress of Iris Mur-
     doch." <u>English Studies in Africa</u> 4 (March):17-38.
         A consideration of Murdoch's novels through <u>The</u>
     <u>Bell</u> that criticizes what is seen as her increase of
     intellect over intuition and her loss of artistry in
     handling words, a disregard of her verbal medium.

23   MEIDNER, OLGA.   "Reviewer's Bane: A Study of Iris
     Murdoch's <u>The Flight from the Enchanter</u>." <u>Essays</u>
     <u>in Criticism</u> 11 (October):43-47.
         An interpretation of Calvin Blick as a projec-
     tion of Rosa's and Hunter's minds, rather than Mur-
     doch's reported intention of Calvin and Mischa as two
     sides of one character, symbolizing the evil of great
     power.

24 "New Fiction." Times (London), 15 June, p. 17.
        A review of A Severed Head that apprehends it as
macabre and violent, not really light-hearted satire.
Murdoch embodies her philosophy and mysticism in comic scenes that are purely emotive and quite perfect.
Suggests that the Russians will see the novel as an
exposé of the decadent West.

25 PENDRY, E.D. "William Golding and 'Mankind's Essen-
        tial Illness.'" Moderna Sprak 55:1-7.
        A discussion of William Golding's fiction that
compares Golding to Murdoch in the seriousness of
their writing and in their semiallegorical fiction.

26 PRICE, MARTIN. "The Novel: Artifice and Exper-
        ience." Yale Review 51:152-58.
        A characterization of contemporary novels as
formula novels, journalistic novels, or great novels,
with a discussion of Murdoch's concept of the "neurotic" novel as an overly subjective, limited form.

27 QUENEAU, RAYMOND. "A World of Fantasy." Time and
        Tide 42 (6 July):1119.
        An examination of A Severed Head that discovers
no moral judgments but sees the novel as exploring
people falling in love arbitrarily.

28 Review of A Severed Head. Booklist 57 (1 May):546.
        Calls the novel a compelling story of a tangled
web of relationships, told with subtlety and irony.

29 ROLO, CHARLES. "Liaisons dangereuses." Atlantic
        207 (May):98-100.
        Review of A Severed Head, praising Murdoch's
imagination and "first-rate" intelligence, her command
of the language and comic sense. Finds in the novel
not the plausibility of daily life but the evocative
truth of a dream.

30 SAXTON, MARK. "Ingenious and Bizarre Novel of Emo-
        tional Ambushes in London." New York Herald Trib-
        une Book Review, 16 April, p. 27.
        Review of A Severed Head that finds the plotting
to be constructed in terms of "emotional ambushes,"
but sees the book redeemed from mere cleverness by
Murdoch's descriptive power, creating the reader's
sense of things seen.

31 SCOTT-KILVERT, IAN. "English Fiction 1958-60, II."
        British Books News, no. 248 (April), pp. 237-44.
        A discussion of young novelists that praises
Murdoch's deep and subtle characterization, along with
her compassion and assurance.

32 "Short Notices." Time 77 (19 May):109-10.
        A review of A Severed Head that calls it a
    "sophisticated shocker," exploring the complicated
    rules of adultery.

33 SINGER, BURNS. "New Fiction." Listener, 15 June.
        A review of A Severed Head, calling it a "glor-
    iously artificial world" with a complicated plot.
    Wonders how the novel will be interpreted in Russia
    where Murdoch's work is said to be popular.

34 THOMPSON, JOHN. "Plot, Character, Etc." Partisan
    Review 5-6:707-13.
        Compares Murdoch to Kingsley Amis, both reliable
    comic novelists who know how to control the machinery
    of fiction. Finds in A Severed Head some of the same
    power of strangeness as in The Flight from the Enchan-
    ter, but finds the meaning of the new novel too clear
    and systematic.

35 TOYNBEE, PHILIP. "Too Fruity To Be True."
    Observer, 18 June, p. 28.
        A review of A Severed Head that criticizes Mur-
    doch as a novelist of ideas with the wrong approach
    to fiction. Judges her situations to be preposterous
    and her characters impossible.

36 WARNLE, F.J. "New Books in Review." Yale Review
    50 (June):632-33.
        Calls A Severed Head most impressive, praising
    its symbolic richness and psychological insight.
    Finds the formal qualities delightful.

                            1962

1 BALLIET, WHITNEY. Review of An Unofficial Rose.
   New Yorker 38 (15 September):178-79.
        Criticizes the writing as female, academic, and
   self-conscious, and charges that the novel is a cha-
   rade and that it creaks,

2 BARRETT, WILLIAM. "Roses with Thorns." Atlantic
   Monthly 209 (June):108-9.
        A review of An Unofficial Rose that praises the
   graveside scene but finds the book as a whole ambiguous and diffuse.

3 BRADBURY, MALCOLM. "Iris Murdoch's Under the Net."
   Critical Quarterly 4 (Spring):47-54.
        Sees Murdoch's first as a "dialectical novel in
   comic form," with the protagonist moving from wrong
   thinking to reappraisal to true vision. Praises the
   flexibility of Murdoch's style.

4 _____. Review of An Unofficial Rose. Punch, 27
  June, p. 989.
       Deals with the violence and mysteriousness of
  love, using the Romance of the Rose as a structuring
  device. An Unofficial Rose is one of Murdoch's most
  mature and richest books with a subtlety and precision of observation of a complex web of persons. The
  opening falters, but the novel is rewarding.

5 BRADLEY, VAN ALLEN. "The Emotional Perils in Path-
  way of Love." San Francisco Chronicle, 29 August,
  p. 39.
       A review of An Unofficial Rose that calls it a
  compelling, involved tale of marriage, praising Murdoch's skill and understanding.

6 BRYDEN, RONALD. "Living Dolls." Spectator 208
  (June):755-56.
       Categorizes An Unofficial Rose as a study in
  "will," naming it a solid achievement and seeing a
  steady development of Murdoch's talents and accom-
  plishments.

7 BUCKLER, ERNST. "People Survive Somehow." New
  York Times Book Review, 20 May, p. 5.
       A review of An Unofficial Rose that compares
  Murdoch with Ivy Compton-Burnett and Mary McCarthy.
  Appreciates the articulation of the complex plot and
  the sure-footed writing but notes that the reader
  remains a spectator, not an imaginative participant.

8 DERRICK, CHRISTOPHER. "The Burden of the World."
  Tablet 216 (23 June):595-96.
       A review of An Unofficial Rose that compares it
  to a chess problem with survival an arbitrary but
  necessary value and causality unpredictable. Finds
  the novel electric and alive but the characters clich-
  éd.

9 ENGLE, PAUL. "Human Behavior in the Grip of Love."
  Chicago Sunday Tribune, 17 June, p. 3.
       Sees An Unofficial Rose to be about the fantasies,
  duplicities, and entanglements of the person in love
  and praises the luminous writing.

10 GINDIN, JAMES. "Images of Illusion in the Work of
   Iris Murdoch." In Postwar British Fiction: New
   Accents and Attitudes. Berkeley: University of
   California Press, pp. 178-95.
        Extension of his article (1960.3) exploring the
   images of illusion suggested by the titles of Murdoch's first four novels. Against the images of man-
   made structures, Murdoch poses images of the natural
   world. Through her first four novels, the creature

is opposed to the nets or traps. A Severed Head
mocks the spurious rationality man invents for himself, ignoring the unconscious creature. In it Honor
Klein represents the primitive, human force that the
other characters are dissociated from--the id. In
the earlier novels the God-figure was comically destroyed as a fabrication, while the creature remains
inviolate. In The Severed Head, Murdoch mocks the
faith in the creature by inflating the pretensions of
the id.

11 HICKS, GRANVILLE. "The Operations of Love." Sat-
    urday Review 45 (19 May):32.
        A review of An Unofficial Rose, praising Mur-
doch's sustained presentation of character and her
understanding of the complexity of human motivations.
Compliments her tenacity and lucidity.

12 HOBSON, HAROLD. "London Comment: Miss Murdoch's
    Unofficial Rose." Christian Science Monitor, 19
    July, p. 11.
        Characterizes the tone of the novel as "autumnal,
quiet sympathy," sometimes sentimental. Sees the
dazzling skill and depth of comprehension of the book
to be further evidence of Murdoch as one of England's
most important contemporary novelists.

13 JACKSON, ROBERT B. Review of An Unofficial Rose.
    Library Journal 87 (15 April):1630.
        Judges that the novel will not be popular but
that it should be included in collections of important fiction. Names Murdoch a major talent.

14 KARL, FREDERICK R. A Reader's Guide to the Contem-
    porary English Novel. New York: Noonday, pp. 260-
    65.
        Murdoch's novels are intelligent and well writ-
ten but lack clear definition. In Under the Net,
The Flight from the Enchanter, and The Bell, Murdoch
is unable to sustain the humor, and the novels
decline into triviality. The Bell resolves the serious conflict with an extended practical joke in
which the characters and the reader lose interest.
The lack of sharp focus in The Sandcastle, a romance,
keeps everything undramatic and tedious.

15 KERMODE, FRANK. "Myth, Reality, and Fiction."
    Listener 68 (30 August):311-13.
        A summary from a symposium from the Third Pro-
gramme with contributions from distinguished novelists, including Murdoch. Asked to explain "journalistic" versus "crystalline" novels, Murdoch con-
trasted the tendency to give importance to people in
a novel with the tendency to create a carefully con-

structed object, with the ideal being to combine the
virtues of both.

16 MILLER, VINCENT. "Unofficial Roses." National
    Review 13 (11 Septmeber):194-96.
        A review of An Unofficial Rose that sees Mur-
    doch's subject to be absurd man, viewed tolerantly and
    sometimes lovingly, but the reviewer objects to a
    glorification of muddle.

17 MINER, EARL. "Iris Murdoch: The Uses of Love."
    Nation 194 (2 June):498-99.
        A review of An Unofficial Rose that comments on
    all her previous novels, judging A Severed Head to be
    seriously flawed. Calls the new novel a triumph,
    clear and convincing, with its profound penetration
    of human behavior and its mature attitude.

18 "Observer Profile: Iris Murdoch." Observer, 17
    June, p. 23.
        A combination of biographical information and
    discussion of Murdoch's writing, based on an inter-
    view but filtered through the reporter's perceptions.

19 O'CONNOR, WILLIAM van. "Iris Murdoch: A Severed
    Head." Critique 5 (Spring-Summer):74-77.
        A discussion of Murdoch's novels up to and in-
    cluding A Severed Head, calling her a "twentieth-cen-
    tury Congreve" writing about amoral characters.
    Asserts that the real game is not between the charac-
    ters and the reader, but between Murdoch and the read-
    er, with the characters just puppets.

20 _____. "Two Types of Heroes in Post-War British
    Fiction." PMLA 77:168-74.
        Relates the sensitive, artistic, self-conscious
    modern hero to postmodern heroes. Contrasts the
    working-class heroes of Allan Sillitoe, David Storey,
    and John Braine to the Amis, Waterhouse, Murdoch type
    of protagonist who is comic, not heroic. Sees a
    change in focus from individual consciousness to the
    relation of man to man in society.

21 O'SULLIVAN, KEVIN. "Iris Murdoch and the Image of
    Liberal Man." Yale Literary Magazine 131 (Decem-
    ber):27-36.
        A discussion of Murdoch's first six novels that
    sees her exploring other people's reality. Praises
    the power of her mind and imagination, the range of
    her characters, and her supple, precise prose. Pre-
    dicts for her a career of increasing achievement.

22 PEARSON, GABRIEL. "Iris Murdoch and the Romantic
     Novel." New Left Review, nos. 13-14 (January-
     April), pp. 137-45.
        A consideration of A Severed Head in terms of
     Murdoch's critical ideas in the essay "Against Dry-
     ness." Criticizes the novel as a romantic or symbol-
     ist one that degenerates into private fantasy.
     Affirms Murdoch still as one of the best contemporary
     writers.

23 RYAN, MARJORIE. "Iris Murdoch: An Unofficial
     Rose." Critique 5 (Winter):117-21.
        Divides Murdoch's novels into either fantastic
     or realistic novels, finding An Unofficial Rose to be
     a fusion of the two categories. Relates the theme to
     a conflict between a desire for experience and a de-
     sire to give experience form and meaning.

24 "Soap Opera and Sensibility." Time 79 (25 May):
     100-1.
        Review of An Unofficial Rose that calls Murdoch
     a "literary magician" who operates here without many
     of her usual props. Notes the marvelous suspense of
     the novel and the richness of motive of the charac-
     ters.

25 SOUVAGE, JACQUES. "The Novels of Iris Murdoch."
     Studia Germanica Gandensia 4:225-52.
        A study of Murdoch's novels through A Severed
     Head that applies ideas from two Murdoch essays on
     art and morality. Distinguishes her novels from
     Sartre's in terms of their social sense and places
     her in the tradition of Jane Austen and E.M. Forster,
     praising her irony and wit.

26 _____. "Symbol as Narrative Device: An Interpre-
     tation of Iris Murdoch's The Bell." English Studies
     43 (April):81-96.
        An interpretation of the bell in The Bell that
     uses ideas from Murdoch's essay "The Sublime and the
     Beautiful Revisited" and sees characters moving from
     subjective illusion to objective reality. Considers
     Dora's "moral self-discovery" to be a central theme.

27 "Stretching the Net." Times Literary Supplement,
     8 June, p. 425.
        A review of An Unofficial Rose that claims Mur-
     doch is sacrificing her humanity and wit to a "fan-
     tasy of sexual violence" and a seemingly inevitable
     game of passion. Calls the novel cynical and clever.

28 TAUBMAN, ROBERT. "L'année derniere à Dungeness."
     New Statesman 63 (8 June):836.

Relates An Unofficial Rose to the tradition of
The Faerie Queene and Les liaisons dangereuses with
love as a fatal attachment. Calls it a stunning
novel, "in deep focus."

1963

1 BARRETT, WILLIAM. "English Opposites." Atlantic
   211 (June):131-32.
       Review of The Unicorn that criticizes it for
shifting between symbolism and realism but recommends
it for readers who enjoy Gothic romance.

2 BRADBURY, MALCOLM. "Under the Symbol." Spectator,
   6 September, p. 295.
       Calls Murdoch a surrealist and The Unicorn the
most mythic of her novels. States that the portrayal
of Hannah is "unsure," but the book is remarkable.

3 BUITENHUIS, PETER. "The Lady in the Castle." New
   York Times Book Review, 12 May, pp. 4, 24.
       A review of The Unicorn that credits it with the
magnetism of a detective story but finds the story
well rooted in the realism of the characters. Asserts
that it leads the reader into the terror and mystery
of existence.

4 COOK, ELEANOR. "Mythical Beasts." Canadian Forum
   43 (August):113-14.
       A review of The Unicorn, praising Murdoch's hol-
istic creation that does not fall apart into separate
strands of myth and present reality. Compares the
ironic presentation of Effingham Cooper with Austen's
less sophisticated Mr. Collins in Pride and Prejudice.

5 DAVENPORT, G. "Books in Brief." National Review
   14 (18 June):505.
       A review of The Unicorn that names it a convinc-
ing depiction of suffering with a "first rate" plot.

6 "Deep Mist and Shallow Water." Time 81 (10 May):104.
       Describes The Unicorn as a parody of a nineteenth-
century romance, witty and strange, a "parable of
guilt."

7 DENT, ALLEN. "At the Play." Punch 244 (22 May):75.
       A review of the play A Severed Head that calls
it fascinating but faulty and compares it to the
dramas of Wycherley and Etherege.

8 DERRICK, CHRISTOPHER. "The Moated Grange." Tablet
   217 (14 September):986-87.

A review of The Unicorn that judges it Murdoch's best so far, making the reader reappraise realism and the tension between the actual, what the artist portrays, and what the artist envisions.

9 "Fable Mates." Times Literary Supplement, 6 September, p. 669.
      Criticizes The Unicorn for having no sexual comedy, no satire, and none of Murdoch's usual bizarre social types. Rejects the possibility that the novel illuminates experience allegorically. Disparages the "unsatisfactory talk" about God.

10 GASCOIGNE, BAMBER. "Sex in the Head." Spectator 210 (17 May):638.
      A review of the play A Severed Head that finds funny the "farcial mathematics" of the plot and the characters' mimicry of passion.

11 GELLERT, ROGER. "Quaint Honor." New Statesman 65 (5 July):24.
      A review of the play A Severed Head, shaped by J.B. Priestly, that states it reveals itself as outrageous farce about the alienation of body and mind. Compares Martin to the hero of a Jacobean tragedy, judging the play witty and bizarre.

12 GRIGSON, GEOFFREY. "Entre les tombes." New Statesman 66 (13 September):321-33.
      A review of The Unicorn that sees in it too much symbolism and criticizes Murdoch's treatment of the symbolism as vulgar. Asserts that the characters are "lifted" from a woman's magazine serial.

13 HAGLER, MARGARET. Review of An Unofficial Rose. Books Abroad 37 (Winter):80.
      Brief review contending that the blend of real and fantastic elements makes it far more than a conventional, realistic work. Each chapter is written from the viewpoint of the character who plays the most important role in it.

14 HEBBLETHWAITE, PETER. "Out Hunting Unicorns." Month 30 (October):224-73.
      A review of The Unicorn that praises the mythic quality and discusses the identity of the unicorn in the novel. Discerns in it the existentialist question of the relation of guilt to action and inaction, with guilt an inescapable part of being human.

15 HICKS, GRANVILLE. "Entrance to Enchantment." Saturday Review 46(11 May):27-28.

Calls The Unicorn a thriller with exciting narrative movement and praises the characters who refuse
to fit a preconceived pattern.

16 HILL, W.B. "Fiction." America 109 (23 November):
    682.
       A review of The Unicorn that relates it to the
    Brontes' novels and finds it "fundamentally sound."

17 HOBSON, HAROLD. "New Novels by Iris Murdoch and
    Hortense Calisher." Christian Science Monitor,
    9 May, p. 8B.
       Judges The Unicorn a recovery from An Unofficial
    Rose, and exploration of the conflict between freedom
    and order. Calls it a strange romantic story with an
    extraordinary use of landscape, distinctive characters,
    and fascinating adventures.

18 JACKSON, ROBERT B. Review of The Unicorn. Library
    Journal 88 (15 April):1688.
       Recommends the novel for all "serious" collec-
    tions of fiction and predicts it may attract readers
    who are not usually Murdoch fans.

19 KERMODE, FRANK. "House of Fiction: Interviews
    with Seven English Novelists." Partisan Review
    30 (Spring):62-82.
       An interview with seven novelists including Mur-
    doch, Greene, Wilson, Compton-Burnett, Snow, Wain,
    and Spark, Discusses with Murdoch her distinction
    between the "crystalline" novel and the "journalistic
    novel." Murdoch says that her works alternate be-
    tween novels of character and intense novels with
    powerful stories.

20 KIELY, ROBERT. "On the Subject of Love." Nation
    196 (25 May):447-48.
       A review of The Unicorn that relates it to the
    Gothic tradition of Ann Radcliffe and Mary Wollstone-
    craft Shelley. Discovers behind the Gothic trappings
    the mystery of love and the ambiguities of knowledge.

21 McDOWELL, FREDERICK P.W. "The Devious Involutions
    of Human Character and Emotions: Reflections on
    Some Recent British Novels." Wisconsin Studies in
    Contemporary Literature 4 (Autumn):352.
       A consideration of some novels from late 1961 to
    early 1963, including An Unofficial Rose and The
    Unicorn. Praises Murdoch's inventiveness and energy
    but declares neither book completely satisfactory.

22 MAES-JELINEK, HENA. "A House for Free Characters:
    The Novels of Iris Murdoch." Revue des langues
    vivantes 29:45-69.

A discussion of Murdoch's novels through An
Unofficial Rose that sees self-knowledge as a condition of freedom, and conventions, morality, and personal chaos as enemies of freedom. Also explores the
characters' need to recognize the reality of other
persons.

23 MOODY, PHILIPPA. "In the Lavatory of the Athen-
    aeum--Post War English Novels." Melbourne Critical
    Review 6:83-92.
        An attack on the mistrust of language found in
    critical essays by Murdoch, Wain, and Snow and in the
    novels of Murdoch and Snow. Charges that after the
    first two novels Murdoch substitutes philosphy and
    psychology for a central concern for language.

24 MURRAY, J.G. Review of The Unicorn. Critic 21
    (June):77.
        Classifies The Unicorn as a writer's, not a
    reader's, novel, concerned with technical display and
    parodying the modern Gothic romance, the Sleeping
    Beauty motif, classic mystery stories, the "belle
    dame san merci" legend, and Poe's tales of ratiocina-
    tion.

25 O'CONNOR, WILLIAM van. "Iris Murdoch: The Formal
    and the Contingent." In The New University Wits
    and the End of Modernism. Carbondale. Southern
    Illinois University Press, pp. 54-75.
        Interprets Murdoch's first five novels, saying
    that she is playing an intellectual game with the
    reader, a technical feature that is her strength and
    her limitation. She is a contemporary Congreve whose
    characters are interesting puppets and symbols. The
    world of Under the Net is close to the world of
    Queneau's Pierrot. Her second novel has an allegory-
    in-wonderland quality. The theme of the more realis-
    tic The Sandcastle is that freedom must come to terms
    with necessity. The Bell shows Murdoch to be probably
    the best young novelist. Her talent is for evoking
    the concrete and a sense of mystery. The characters
    in A Severed Head are amoral with no true identities,
    and Honor signifies that no goddess and no principle
    is completely reliable.

26 PAULDING, GOUVERNEUR. "Even the Landscape Has
    Homicidal Properties." New York Herald Tribune
    Book Review, 19 May, p. 3.
        A biographical sketch and review of The Unicorn
    that discusses Murdoch's use of landscape for Gothic
    effect and relates it to British landscape painting.

27 PICKREL, PAUL. "Mostly about Women." Harper's 226
    (June):107-8

A review of The Unicorn that sees it as an attack
on our tendency to categorize, neutralize, and deaden
experience. Notes Murdoch's seven brilliant novels
and praises her power of invention.

28 PONDROM, CYRENA NORMAN. "Iris Murdoch: The Unicorn."
    Critique 6 (Winter):177-80.
        The Unicorn tries to reveal contemporary meanings
    of basic moral concepts, especially refuting the idea
    that freedom is the key to the good. The ambiguity
    of Hannah can be understood through Kierkegaard's dis-
    cussion of the inwardness of religious experience.
    The characters crave love, but there is little evidence
    of grace that makes possible the leap of faith.

29 Review of The Unicorn. Booklist 59 (15 April):769.
        Characterizes the novel as a "semi-allegorical"
    tale and finds the atmospheric setting appropriate.

30 RYAN, MARJORIE. "Iris Murdoch: An Unofficial Rose."
    Critique 5 (Winter):117-21.
        Classifies the novel as a well-constructed com-
    edy of sexual manners in which one cannot separate
    "the plain from the symbolic." Considers the theme to
    be the tension between messy experience and the urge
    to give it form.

31 SIGGINS, CLARA M. "Fiction: The Unicorn." Best
    Sellers 23 (15 May):71.
        A review of the novel that sees it to be an ex-
    ploration of guilt in love, with the guilt and suffer-
    ing weaving people together in a demonstration of Ate.
    Notes seven sections of the book reflecting the
    seven-year spell.

32 TUCKER, MARTIN. "Love and Freedom: Golden and
    Hard Words." Commonweal 77 (21 June):357-58.
        A review of The Unicorn noting its extraordinary
    moments of revelation in Murdoch's moral comedy,
    praising her mastery of the incongruous and her com-
    edy, as well as her wit.

33 WALL, STEPHEN. "The Bell in The Bell." Essays in
    Criticism 13 (July):265-73.
        An interpretation that disputes that the bell has
    a single, allegorical meaning, instead seeing it as
    a fluid symbol that shifts with the development of
    the main characters.

34 WEST, PAUL. The Modern Novel. London: Hutchinson,
    pp. 126, 134, 145.
        Credits Murdoch with integrating realism, psych-
    ological probing, wit, and dream but criticizes the

overanalysis of her well-trained mind. Discusses her novels through An Unofficial Rose.

35 WHITEHORN, KATHERINE. "Three Women." Encounter 21 (December):78-82.
     A review of The Unicorn that censures it for lacking a historical sense, accusing Murdoch of refusing to provide realistic details. Alleges the novel would be refused publication as an unsolicited first manuscript.

1964

1 ALLEN, WALTER. The Modern Novel: In Britain and the United States. New York: Dutton, pp. 282-84.
     An assessment of Murdoch's work through A Severed Head that sees her as the leading contemporary symbolist. Asserts that she seems to have the ability to become a great novelist but that her development has been puzzling. Judges The Bell her best novel and says that she moves the reader the way that poetry does.

2 "An Arion Questionnaire: 'The Classics and the Man of Letters.'" Arion 3 (Winter):66-67.
     A questionnaire of British writers asking what influence the Greek and Latin classics had on their work. Murdoch named Homer as the classic author she turned to most.

3 BARRETT, WILLIAM. Review of The Italian Girl. Atlantic 214 (November):201-2.
     Feels disappointed by Murdoch's novels. Finds Edmund an unsympathetic and unsatisfactory narrator and complains that the Gothic tale seems serious but may be parodic.

4 BRUGIERE, BERNARD. "L'univers romanesque d'Iris Murdoch." Mercure de France 352 (December):699-711.
     Discusses The Flight from the Enchanter, The Sandcastle, A Severed Head, and The Bell. A constant theme in Murdoch is the discovery of oneself through freedom. Although Mischa is a tyrant of the spirit, he is the agent of the process of self-discovery. In the next novel, passion is the medium of freedom. A Severed Head presents a closed world of well-informed people who are unable to be themselves. The Bell illustrates the existential dialectic through the homosexual theme. Michael struggles to discover the truth of his life and of his failure in love. Murdoch has an ethical intention, using elements of existentialism including authenticity, choice, freedom, and subjectivity.

5   CASEY, FLORENCE. "Gothic Murk in Murdochland."
    Christian Science Monitor, 25 November, p. 17.
        A review of The Italian Girl that accuses Murdoch
    of reworking the same themes continually and of being
    preoccupied with guilt and suffering. Calls the
    latest novel disappointing.

6   CHAPMAN, JOHN. "A Severed Head Tricky Comedy."
    New York Theatre Critics' Reviews 25 (9 Novem-
    ber):178.
        A review of the play A Severed Head in New York
    that sees it as a tricky comedy about sex. Chides the
    actors for throwing away lines but declares the play
    amusing.

7   "Circles of Hell." Time 84 (11 September):110.
        A review of The Italian Girl, praising its wit
    and urbane prose and characterizing it as a formal
    dance of sexual mismatchings. Finds the theme to be
    that any life at all is better than no life.

8   DAVENPORT, GUY. "Turn the Other Face." National
    Review 16 (3 November):978-79.
        A review of The Italian Girl that compares
    Murdoch to a pre-Raphaelite painter whose precise
    images radiate meaning, judging her characters to be
    allegorical monsters of our vices.

9   "Enter Someone." Times Literary Supplement, 10
    September, pp. 8, 37.
        Critizes The Italian Girl as a novel with a good
    beginning that degenerates into farce and melodrama.
    Asserts that the implied significant revelation that
    the plot leads to never comes.

10 FRASER, GEORGE. The Modern Writer and His World.
    Rev. ed. London: Penguin; New York: Praeger,
    1965, pp. 29, 175, 184-87.
        Under the Net, despite its rogue hero like the
    one in Lucky Jim, is a roman philosophique, question-
    ing social life. Murdoch's imagination works with
    contradictory ideas--that everything must obey the
    laws of logic and that everything is free and con-
    tingent. The combination of those ideas produces the
    ambivalent effect of her novels. Her fictional world
    resembles the ordinary world, but with more insistent
    implications of significance. Her best novel, The
    Bell, reflects her chief theme, that people build
    fantasy worlds and evade self-knowledge. Of all the
    recent novelists, she possesses the greatest penetra-
    tion and the most striking individuality.

11 FURBANK, P.N. "Gowned Mortality." Encounter 23
    (November):88-90.

Connects The Italian Girl to earlier Murdoch novels in terms of their common Platonic themes, characterizing the theme of this novel to be that of heal-
ing. Claims, however, that the characters become
less substantial as the action continues and that they
act things out broadly as in farce.

12 GRIFFIN, LLOYD W. Review of The Italian Girl.
    Library Journal 89 (1 September):3186.
        Recommends the novel for broadminded readers,
    saying that in it the saint becomes the sinner and
    the sinning leads to suffering and finally under-
    standing. Criticizes the portrayal of the male char-
    acters.

13 HILL, W.B. Review of The Italian Girl. America
    111 (28 November):718.
        Finds the novel to be a neo-Gothic romance with
    a weird atmosphere.

14 HOFFMAN, FREDERICK J. "Iris Murdoch: The Reality
    of Persons." Critique 7 (Spring)48-57.
        Discusses Murdoch's critical commentary in
    "The Sublime and the Beautiful Revisited" and in
    Sartre: Romantic Rationalist and applies the com-
    mentary to her novels. Murdoch believes that fiction
    must restore the whole human being. Her novels pre-
    sent the conflicts between symbol and the contingent
    person and between the conscious person struggling
    for domination and the resisting other. Murdoch is
    also struggling to control her characters and yet to
    separate them from her.

        The Bell, her clearest success, maintains a bal-
    ance of people and symbol, with the symbol not threat-
    ening to take over the novel. Instead, characters
    with separate existences are set in a formal pattern.
    On the other hand, in A Severed Head, the characters
    in their shifting sexual relationships are all but
    blurred. An Unofficial Rose provides space for Mur-
    doch to develop the apparent absurdities of the char-
    acters into human weakness. Murdoch has not yet
    achieved the proper balance between fantasy and real-
    istic detail to change her good novels into great ones.

15 HOPE, FRANCIS. "Iris Murdoch." In On Contemporary
    Literature. Edited by Richard Kostelanetz. New
    York: Avon, pp. 468-72.
        In Murdoch's new novel, A Severed Head, she seems
    to be extending her range, paring away her well-known
    characteristics. She is known for the grace of her
    writing, the complexity and depth of her imagination,
    and her extraordinary mixture of the real and the
    fantastic. In her first two novels, Murdoch seems to

be using the novel to make the point that novels
should not make points. The Flight from the Enchanter
gives the impression of a world that defies explanation, full of loose ends and ambiguity.
     The Sandcastle, more conventional, and The Bell
share themes of freedom and deception. The structure
of The Bell is carefully worked out with pages of
analysis of aphoristic clarity. A Severed Head is
almost all form with characters performing an elaborate minuet in an intricate scheme of personal relations. Martin's love for Honor makes nonsense of the pretensions to rationality of Palmer and Antonia. Murdoch again argues
against too much seeking for explanations.

16   JANEWAY, ELIZABETH. "But Nobody Understands."
     New York Times Book Review, 13 September, p. 5.
          A review of The Italian Girl that asserts that
     Murdoch has set her story not within the human world,
     but within the human psyche with the characters arche-
     typal figures from myth and dream. Criticizes the
     dialogue in the novel.

17   KERR, WALTER. Review of A Severed Head. New York
     Theatre Critics Reviews 25 (29 October):178.
          Finds the play to be a trip into Wonderland in
     which nothing is what it seems and the characters need
     their images supported by onlookers. But gauges the
     irony and wit as quickly spent and the comedy as over-
     played by the actors.

18   KRIEGEL, LEONARD. "A Surrender of Symbols."
     Nation 199 (9 November):339.
          A review of The Italian Girl, accusing Murdoch
     of becoming cute and merely clever. Contends that the
     suffering of the characters is told but not felt and
     the figure of the Italian girl is lifeless and unsub-
     stantial.

19   LEECH, ANASTASIA. "Anyone's Devil." Tablet 218
     (10 October):1144.
          Finds the images of The Italian Girl full of life
     but expressing a central concern with the fact of
     death. States that the Italian girl both judges and
     frees the members of the family.

20   "Love in the Mind's Eye." Time 84 (6 November):52.
          A review of the play A Severed Head, judging it
     to be sophisticated and urbane. Names it an unset-
     tling philosophical comedy depicting the tyranny of
     mind over instinct.

21 McCLAIN, JOHN. "Sustained Punch Lacking." New York
    Theatre Critics' Reviews 25 (9 November):177-78.
        A review of the play A Severed Head that declares
    it a strange mixture of sex and psychopathy with some
    terribly witty moments but without the punch to sus-
    tain it.

22 NADEL, NORMAN. "Severed Head Is a Stunning New
    Commedy." New York Theatre Critics' Reviews 25
    (9 November):180.
        A review of the play A Severed Head that compares
    the play's motion to that of a pendulum, swinging from
    comedy to terror. Extols the play's sophistication
    in ridiculing the unrestrained sexuality of the upper
    classes in high style.

23 NEILL, S. DIANA. A Short History of the English
    Novel. London: Collier-Macmillan; New York:
    Collier Books, pp. 394, 401-3.
        An assessment of Murdoch's writing that first
    associates her with and then distinguishes her from
    the social realists like Amis and Wain. Credits
    Murdoch with seriousness, cultivation, and intellect
    but asserts that her novels lack a significant action
    for the plot.

24 PICKREL, PAUL. "Heading toward Postcivilization."
    Harper's 229 (October):128-32.
        A review of The Italian Girl that finds Murdoch
    concerned with "pre-scientific dimensions of exper-
    ience" and the everyday world in her novels providing
    only a surface tension. Judges The Italian Girl to
    be uneven and the ending to be impatient.

25 SALE, ROGER. "Provincial Champions and Grand-
    masters." Hudson Review 17 (Winter):608, 612-13.
        A review of The Italian Girl, calling it the
    least satisfactory Murdoch novel, a repeat performance,
    lacking inevitability. Murdoch's career is credited
    with making the English novel unprovincial.

26 SALVESEN, CHRISTOPHER. "A Hieroglyph." New States-
    man 68 (11 September):365.
        Criticizes the characters of The Italian Girl as
    impossible and their antics as ridiculous. Credits
    Murdoch's narrative talents but calls her material
    tiresome.

27 SHEED, WILFRED. "Making a Meal of Antipasto." Book
    Week 2 (13 September):5, 12.
        Asserts that The Italian Girl is inferior as a
    whole to its individual scenes and its English nature
    writing and that Murdoch is more a philosopher-com-
    edian than a novelist.

28 _____. "Nursery Politics." Commonweal 81 (4 December):354.
    A review of the play A Severed Head that sees
the characters behaving like children with crushes on
each other, arbitrary and evanescent. Calls Murdoch
a tease and her use of Freud a good joke.

29 "Speaking of Writing, XII: Iris Murdoch." Times
    (London), 13 February, p. 15.
    An interview with Murdoch in which she declares
Homer, Shakespeare, and Jane Austen to be inspirations
to her and Henry James to be her most conscious influence. Affirms that she writes to correct the mistakes
of her last novel.

30 TAUBMAN, HOWARD. "Theater: Minuet of Marital
    Affections." New York Theatre Critics' Reviews 25
    (9 November):179-80.
    A review of the play A Severed Head that finds
it thoroughly English, understated, but remote and
bloodless. Contends that the predictability of the
changes of partners robs the audience of the joy of
surprise.

31 TRACY, HONOR. "Misgivings about Miss Murdoch."
    New Republic 151 (10 October):21-22.
    A review of The Italian Girl, criticizing it as
not a combination of imagination and realism like The
Bell and The Sandcastle, but an embodiment of abstract
ideas. Praises the character of the Italian girl, but
little else.

32 TUCKER, MARTIN. "More Iris Murdoch." Commonweal
    81 (30 October):173-74.
    Finds glaring weaknesses in The Italian Girl,
including the character of Maggie, the symbolism, and
the disunified effects. Instead of intellectual
comedy, the reviewer sees melodrama and sentimentality.

33 WARD, A.C. Twentieth-Century English Literature,
    1901-1960. Methuen University Paperbacks. New York:
    Barnes & Noble, p. 80.
    An account of Murdoch's writing through the stage
adaptation of A Severed Head. Discerns compelling
power in Murdoch's fiction but deplores her heavy symbolism.

34 WATTS, RICHARD, Jr. "Witty British Rigadoon of
    Sex." New York Theatre Critics' Review 25 (9 Novem-
    ber):179.
    A review of the play A Severed Head that per-
ceives it to be witty, original, and fascinating--an
intellectual sex comedy excellently acted.

35   WHITESIDE, GEORGE.   "The Novels of Iris Murdoch."
      Critique 7 (Spring):27-47.
            Murdoch is a realist and a satirist. Five of her
      seven novels are about main characters who develop
      romantic preconceptions, act on them, lose them, and
      thus are back where they started, an ironic circular
      pattern. She writes about romantic love because as a
      moral philosopher she wants to know how people make
      or avoid making decisions, and it is romantic love
      that enables people to avoid making decisions. Roman-
      tically involved people feel that they have been
      driven to act by a force beyond their control.
            There are two kinds of romantic love: protec-
      tive love, in which you feel superior to your loved
      one, and abject love, which is the love of a child
      for a parent or courtly love. Only unromantic couples
      feel equal.
            In Under the Net it is Jake who is abjectly in
      love with Hugo Bellfounder. The novel is a satire
      becauses in satires the hero, though made wiser,
      always ends up back where he was before his adventures
      began.
            The Bell is a triumph of realism. It focuses
      attention on two romantic protective loves: Michael's
      failure to get over his love of Nick and Dora's
      success in escaping the similar love of her husband
      Paul. When Dora rings the bell, making it bespeak
      reality, she breaks the spell of her husband's love.
      When Nick destroys himself for love of Michael,
      Michael realizes his failure.

                              1965

1   BALDANZA, FRANK.   "Iris Murdoch and the Theory of
      Personality."   Criticism 7 (Spring):176-89.
            Endeavors to compare Murdoch's theory with her
      practice in depicting personality. Murdoch finds
      that the Liberal-Democratic theory of personality is
      vitiated by certain Romantic tendencies inherited
      from Hegel and Kant.
            Kant opposed the liberal tradition by envision-
      ing people as bearers of an essentially abstract
      universal reason. Sartrean existentialism and
      Stevenson's linguistic analysis both reduce man to
      solipsism. Through literature, however, the reader
      can discover a sense of the density of human lives if
      characters are represented as opaque and contingent.
      The novel should represent the degrees of freedom in
      which man exists and the struggle of the characters
      for meaningful relations like love.
            In A Severed Head, Murdoch shows full respect
      for the autonomy of her characters and provides
      devastating formal ironies. The novel concerns

                              35

Martin's coming to accept and love the otherness of
separate people. In the final pairings one forth-
right character is matched with a partner who has been
blind to the reality of others. In the general movement away from incestuous unions, there is a symbolic
advance in accepting the strangeness of other persons.
Martin and Honor understand the perils and rewards of
the relationship between them.

2 BOWEN, JOHN. "One Must Say Something." New York
   Times Book Review, 7 November, pp. 4-5.
        A review of The Red and the Green that calls it
   mechanical and contrived, comparing Murdoch to paint-
   ers who think the essence of art is the artificial.
   Charges her with writing too much.

3 BRADBURY, MALCOLM. "The Romantic Miss Murdoch."
   Spectator 214 (3 September):293.
        A discussion of Murdoch's career to date, inspir-
   ed probably by the publication of A.S. Byatt's
   Degrees of Freedom: The Novels of Iris Murdoch, which
   it reviews. Asks why there is disappointment with
   Murdoch's development and ascribes it to a misappre-
   hension of her aim, to work in the romance tradition,
   using allegory and symbolism for metaphysical spec-
   ulation.

4 BROOKE, JOCELYN. "New Fiction." Listener, 28
   October, p. 677.
        A review of The Red and the Green, alleging
   Murdoch's other novels to be like fairy tales but this
   new novel to be rooted in reality. Applauds the
   tight construction and unifying theme and estimates
   this novel to be one of Murdoch's best.

5 BYATT, A.S. Degrees of Freedom: The Novels of
   Iris Murdoch. London: Chatto & Windus, 224 pp.
        All Murdoch's novels can be seen as studies of
   degrees of freedom available to individuals. The
   first two novels focus on the possibility of man's
   freedom in society. The later novels are more concerned with freedom within personal relationships,
   studying one person's power over another. Murdoch
   respects the normal as an aspect of human life that
   contributes to the opacity of the person and to the
   mystery of freedom.
        Murdoch disclaims a didactic philosophical inten-
   tion, but the characters are approached from the
   theme and not the other way around. Her first two
   novels are fantasy-myths, in which the action is unreal, events happen with suddenness, and all the characters are related as concepts to a theme. Other
   novels are symbolic, and some are in between the two
   categories.

Murdoch is a prolific writer still in the middle
of her career. She deals honestly with real, important problems. But she has difficulty with the stuff
of life, a charge she leveled against Sartre. Some
philosophical idea provides much of the underlying
framework of each of her novels. She has a natural
ability to organize the form, but she seems to regret
her metaphysical talent.

Murdoch has a natural ear for the banal, ordinary
conversation. Her first two books possess a unity
of style and tone. Critics complain about aspects of
her style in later novels. Murdoch overuses certain
key words, evocative to her. Her last two novels contain long passages of unsuccessful rhetoric and philosophical shorthand. Out of a reaction to the high
praise for her early work, critics now tend to emphasize Murdoch's inadequacies. She is, however, an
inventive, structurally skillful, morally perceptive
writer.

6 CLARKE, JOHN. Review of The Red and the Green.
   Best Sellers 25 (15 November):324-25.
      Complains that the novel is sentimental and the
reader confused about the characters' relationships
to each other. Praises Murdoch's language and her
research but asserts that she halts the action too
much to examine her characters' thoughts.

7 COOK, RODERICK. "Books in Brief." Harper 231
   (November):129.
      A review of The Red and the Green that applauds
her change from "Freudian Gothic tales" to a highly
civilized novel, reflecting compassion for her
characters. Calls the novel her best since The Bell.

8 DeMOTT, BENJAMIN. "Dirty Words?" Hudson Review
   18 (Spring):31-44.
      A discussion of Under the Net and J.D. Salinger's
Seymour Glass stories as evidence of a new literary
theme of "holy silence." Ascribes the "attack on
public language" to a reaction against the lower-class
man's power of words. Identifies Belfounder as a
manager who stole words from the artist Jake.

9 FAUST, PAMELA. "Iris Murdoch: The Comic Commentary
   of Love." M.A. thesis, Sacramento State College,
   56 pp.
      Purpose of the study is to trace how Murdoch uses
the comic to comment on love and clarify its nature.
Innocent love implies an absence of the knowledge of
evil. Grotesque love is twisted and springs from
abnormality. Illusory love is uninformed of the
realities of the lovers and their situations. The
love that leads to understanding results in a clear

perception of the beloved's existence. Analyzes the
novels through An Unofficial Rose.

10   FYTTON, FRANCIS. "The Red and the Green by Iris
     Murdoch." London Magazine, n.s. 9 (November):
     99-100.
         A review that characterizes the novel as one of
     atmosphere, painstakingly analyzing the characters.
     Asserts that the Rising is portrayed as fratricide,
     caused by incest.

11   GALLOWAY, DAVID D. "The Iris Problem." Spectator
     215 (22 October):520.
         A review of The Red and the Green, calling it
     ambitious but decrying the melodramatic treatment of
     the revolutionaries. Charges that the episodes have
     no consistent point of view and that the novel is
     almost a self-parody.

12   GREGOR, IAN. "Toward a Christian Literary
     Criticism." Month 33 (April):239-49.
         A consideration of Lawrence's Women In Love and
     Murdoch's A Severed Head because both treat love as a
     key to man's destiny. A theme identified in the
     Murdoch novel is the debasement of understanding. In
     trying to reclaim love, the motive of both novels is
     religious, but Murdoch's wit and irony corrode the
     serious theme.

13   GRIFFIN, LLOYD W. Review of The Red and the Green.
     Library Journal 90 (1 November):4807.
         Calls the novel less shocking than usual, power-
     ful and sensitive, and names Murdoch one of the
     finest contemporary novelists. Commends the plenti-
     ful, good talk.

14   HALL, JAMES. "Blurring the Will: The Growth of
     Iris Murdoch." Journal of English Literary History
     32 (June):256-73.
         In recent fiction, characters have changed from
     senstive, reflective consciousnesses to representative
     forces colliding. Murdoch has responded to the aesthe-
     tic problem by trying to reconcile sensitivity and
     will. In her novels an original play of forces is
     blurred to present the uniqueness of people and their
     relationships to each other.
         Two metaphors control the action of Under the
     Net: property as a metaphor for daily experience and
     idyll as a dream of harmonious communications between
     two people. The novel enacts the rhythm of expecta-
     tion, reversal, disappointment, and the reassertion of
     the will.
         In The Sandcastle, the play of forces is original
     but narrow. The energy of the novel comes first from

from the awakening of love as an anxious idyll. Later
the family reactions provide the energy. Every
attempt at change produces a counteraction for norm-
alcy.
The Bell is a novel with a setting instead of a
hero. Dora is the angry skeptical mind in conflict
with a community based on high sentiment and the reg-
ulated life. Dora defines herself through destructive action against the community, but she gets
educated. The bell is a floating symbol, meaning
what each character thinks it means. The novel brings
Murdoch's best talents together and the highly structured actions mesh. Michael fights against the will
to directionlessness. Reality refuses to conform to
the will of Dora or to the will of Michael. Murdoch
communicates a sense of the complications of living.
The Bell is first-rate.

15 HEYD, RUTH. "An Interview with Iris Murdoch."
    University of Windsor Review (Spring):138-43.
        An interview with Murdoch that elicits specific
information about her intentions in her novels to date.
Says that many of the views of Max Lejour in The
Unicorn originated in Simone Weil's philosophy. Characterizes Belfounder's fireworks and watch repair and
the market gardening at Imber Court as marked by virtue because immersed in the outward and the simple.
Names as artists Donaghue and Randall Peronett and
saints Tayper Pace, Belfounder, and Ann Peronett.

16 HICKS, GRANVILLE. "Easter Monday Insights."
    Saturday Review 48 (30 October):41-42.
        A review of The Red and the Green that calls it
more a comedy of manners than a historical novel.
Describes it as Murdoch's most straightforward and
lucid novel, very readable.

17 HOFFMAN, FREDERICK. "The Miracle of Contingency:
    The Novels of Iris Murdoch." Shenandoah 17
    (Autumn):49-56.
        A discussion of Murdoch's essays "The Sublime and
Beautiful Revisited" and "The Idea of Perfection" and
an interpretation of The Italian Girl. Says that
Murdoch struggles for a balance of "intimate fact"
and symbol, that she opposes the existentialist
picture of man as lonely will, and that she portrays
a person's view of another changing slowly through
meditation and love.

18 "Irish Stew." Newsweek 66 (22 November):113-14.
        A review of The Red and the Green, considering
it to be a conventional novel that will not impress
Murdoch's admirers.

19 KITCHIN, LAURENCE. "The Zombie's Lair." Listener
    74 (4 November):701-2, 704.
        An article about the changing role of the country
    house in the twentieth century that discusses the work
    of D.H. Lawrence and E.M. Forster and mentions Mur-
    doch's The Bell in which the country house has been
    institutionalized.

20 KRIEGEL, LEONARD. "Iris Murdoch: Everybody
    through the Looking Glass." In Contemporary British
    Novelists. Edited by Charles Shapiro. Carbondale
    and Edwardsville: Southern Illinois University
    Press, pp. 62-80.
        Asserts that Murdoch is on the verge of achieving
    a major reputation in contempory English fiction
    based on the totality of her work. One continues to
    expect a major work from her but is continually dis-
    appointed. Her novels include a free play of intel-
    ligence, incisive prose, a sense of craft, humor, and
    broad human sympathies. But her world contains Vic-
    torian order at the expense of postmodern rage.
    Missing in her novels is the sense of the age.
        Her most contemporary novel is Under the Net,
    strong in its sense of lived vitality. Murdoch's
    finest novel, The Bell, successfully blends myth
    and reality. In it the reader experiences as real
    suffering the horror of Nick's suicide and Catherine's
    mental wreckage.
        Murdoch has still not written the novel that
    The Bell seemed to promise. She indulges her taste
    for myth and allegory at the expense of reality. Her
    novels lack vision. In most of them she fails to
    portray real sexuality or real violence. A failure
    of emotion, a failure of involvement with the real
    and the human keeps Murdoch from being a major novel-
    ist.

21 KUEHN, ROBERT E. "Fiction Chronicle." Wisconsin
    Studies in Contemporary Literature 6:135-37.
        An article that attributes Murdoch's current
    reputation as almost a "highbrow hack" to her produc-
    ing novels quickly and regularly. Calls The Italian
    Girl one of her best, along with The Sandcastle and
    The Bell. Claims that the theme is that characters
    must fall into humanity to be redeemed.

22 LERNER, ARTHUR. Review of The Italian Girl. Books
    Abroad 39 (Summer):351.
        Brief review, finding it a most dynamic, memor-
    able tale. Estimates it to be Murdoch at her best,
    writing lucidly with an appreciation of human
    strengths and weaknesses. Sees Edmund as highly
    believable, initially very egoistic but finally
    psychologically mature.

23 McCABE, BERNARD. "The Guises of Love." Commonweal
   83 (3 December):270-73.
   A review of The Red and the Green that attacks
   Murdoch's heavy symbols, her elaboration, and porten-
   tous tone. Criticizes her for being almost a "lady-
   novelist." Claims that Ireland and the Rising are
   in the novel only as painted background.

24 MARTIN, GRAHAM. "Iris Murdoch and the Symbolist
   Novel." British Journal of Aesthetics 5 (July):
   296-300.
   An article that seeks to establish Murdoch not
   as a social novelist but as a symbolist novelist
   whose most successful novels contain characters that
   remain opaque. Contends she avoids traditional allegory by making the visions of the characters private
   and individual.

25 "Notes on Current Books." Virginia Quarterly
   Review 41 (Winter):x.
   A review of The Red and the Green that calls
   Murdoch Britain's foremost novelist writing today and
   praises her glittering prose. Evaluates the narrative
   surface as brilliant and the novel as most impressive.

26 PELL, EDWARD. "Irish Adolescence." New Leader 48
   (20 December):19-20.
   A review of The Red and the Green that characterizes its mood as the suspended expectancy of adolescence, with the mood arising from the structure and
   character revelation. It sees the characters unable
   to touch each other, struggling with their fantasies,
   sexual and political.

27 POIRIER, RICHARD. "Biting the Hand That Reads
   You." Book Week 3 (14 November):5, 21-24.
   A review of The Red and the Green that sees the
   public and private sequences joined by the characters'
   desire for an act to free them from historical and
   personal "muddle." Interprets the story as a dream
   of escape from personal and sexual involvements.
   Attributes the drabness and heaviness to Murdoch's
   reminding the reader of the artificial form.

28 POORE, CHARLES. "The Lady Millicent and Her Quad-
   ringa." New York Times 4 November, p. 45.
   A review of The Red and the Green characterizing
   it as entertaining and brilliant with Lady Millicent
   an explosive force. Views the style as a blend of
   Sartre and Stendhal. Praises Murdoch for balancing
   all the personal and historic turbulences.

29 PRICE, R.G.G. "New Novels." Punch 249 (27 October):625.

Predicts that The Red and the Green will be Murdoch's most commercially sucessful novel because it has life all through it, rooted as it is in history. The milieu is brilliantly established. There is no feeling that a philosophical pattern determined the particulars. Her usual sexual dance is here funny and touching.

30 PRYCE-JONES, ALAN. "The 'Creative Waywardness' of Iris Murdoch." New York Herald Tribune, 4 November, p. 23.
A review of The Red and the Green that praises Murdoch's wit and courage and distinction of mind. Asserts that the novel is not a good one but is interesting with its ingenious story. Calls Murdoch arbitrary in her search for symmetry in intrigue.

31 "Republic and Private." Times Literary Supplement, 14 October, p. 912.
Reviews The Red and the Green as a serious novel about real people in a realistic context that is just about ruined by the ridiculously contrived ending. Commends the accurate details and the careful description of Dublin.

32 RICKS, CHRISTOPHER. "A Sort of Mystery Novel." New Statesman 70 (22 October):604-5.
A review of The Red and the Green that complains that the sexual permutations demean Irish history. Criticizes the authorial manipulation in Millie's incest, the coincidences, the formulaic repetitiveness and the use of adjectives to assert mystery.

33 RIPPER, JOSEPH S. Some Postwar English Novelists. Frankfurt am Main: Diesterweg, pp. 71-103.
Asserts that Murdoch's world has become more and more complex. She has moved from fantasy and light humor in her first two novels to tragicomedy in the third and fourth to comic human geometry in the fifth. Few of the newer English writers have such a wide range, such maturity and breadth of experience, such pertinence to the contemporary scene.
In Under the Net and The Flight from the Enchanter, the characters are larger than life, and they reject the rules of normal social behavior for unconventional high jinks. The first novel depicts a world of nonengagement, of farce and irony with lightly constructed episodes and the debunking of conventional standards. The second is a comedy of incongruity with humor the most satisfying aspect of the novel.
The ambiguity of situation in The Bell and The Sandcastle is one illusion and a conflict of obligations. Murdoch's characters in these two novels are

anything but flat. In The Bell, Nick is a truly evil
person, betraying Michael, and yet a pitiable creature.
A Severed Head is a mocking portrayal of a society
whose rationality is close to sterility. Free from
preconceived ideas and taboos, Honor is the only
really vital character in the novel.
 Murdoch has explored the spheres of fantasy, the
unconscious, the tragicomic, gentle satire, and irony.
Her novels are becoming more complex in plot and char-
actization. She is advancing toward a deep comic
classic.

34 SULLIVAN, RICHARD. "Millicent the Magnificent."
    Critic 24 (December-January):63.
     A review of The Red and the Green, applauding
its craftsmanship, structure, and style but denying
being moved by the novel. Names Millicent the most
fascinating character and Barney the most touching.

35 "Unbelievable Don." Time 86 (19 November):139.
     Reviews The Red and the Green, finding Murdoch
knowledgeable about history and the Irish character.
Sees her using poetic gifts in describing Dublin and
the Irish rain but considers her characters unbelievable.

36 WALKER, PEREGRINE. "Unlikely Quintet." Tablet 219
    (30 October):1213-14.
     A review of The Red and the Green that acknowl-
edges her virtuosity and subtlety of mind but complains that the novel is slow and heavy.

37 WARDLE, IRVING. "A Dublin Romance." Observer, 17
    October, p. 28.
     A review of The Red and the Green that complains
of the claustrophobia of the closed emotional situations and judges the novel mediocre, lauding only
the descriptions of the Dublin rain.

38 WEEKS, EDWARD. "Easter 1916." Atlantic 216
    (December):138.
     A review of The Red and the Green that calls it
an anticlimax to Murdoch's earlier good writing.
Asserts that the confrontation at Millie's house is
not plausible drama or comedy.

39 WOLFE, PETER. "Philosophical Themes in the Novels
    of Iris Murdoch." Ph.D. dissertation, University
    of Wisconsin, 379 pp.
     An account of Murdoch's speculative writings with
a novel-by-novel interpretation to date of the moral
problems she deals with and the artistic worth of her
fiction. An examination of her reinterpreting existentialism and logical analysis.

1966

1 ALLEN WALTER. "Anything Goes." New York Times
   Book Review, 25 September, p. 5.
        A review of The Time of the Angels that calls
   Murdoch's starting point of a group of isolated
   characters driven to frenzy predictable. Judges all
   but two main characters, Carel and Elizabeth, to be
   well drawn and praises Murdoch's creation of minor
   symbols like the fog, the snow, and Eugene's icon.
   Complains of the obscurity.

2 "Altar to Evil." Newsweek 68 (26 September):118.
        Describes The Time of the Angels as a combina-
   tion of black theology and gothic action, saying that
   Murdoch turns comic situations into sheer horror,
   praising her intriguing technique and sharp dialogue.

3 BANNON, BARBARA A. "Forecast of Paperbacks."
   Publishers' Weekly 189 (13 June):129.
        An announcement of the publication in paperback
   of The Bell, noting that Murdoch probes her characters with skill and wit.

4 "Briefly Noted." New Yorker 41 (8 January):111.
        A review of The Red and the Green that finds the
   action awkward and giddy and the Irish rebellion used
   as "comic-melodramatic" relief. Asks why Murdoch
   bothered to write the novel.

5 COLEMAN, JOHN. "Sexual Permutations." Observer,
   11 September, p. 27.
        A review of The Time of the Angels, classifying
   Murdoch as a high-brow Gothic novelist who provides
   for the common reader a variety of "naughtiness."
   Complains of her adjectives that propose reactions,
   instead of create reactions.

6 COOK, RODERICK. "Books in Brief." Harper 233
   (November):141-42.
        A review of The Time of the Angels that calls
   Murdoch highly original but repetitious. Notes the
   Sleeping Beauty figure and the Gothic trappings but
   says that the reader will be fascinated.

7 DAVENPORT, GUY. "History with Its Eyes Wide Open."
   National Review 18 (29 November):1227.
        Calls The Time of the Angels a timely novel with
   wisdom in it, an expression of Murdoch's conviction
   that the inward look is poisonous and that the self
   must be dissolved in the world.

8   ____ . "Messages from the Lost." <u>National Review</u>
     18 (8 February):119-20.
          A review of <u>The Red and the Green</u>, judging it
     the work of a novice writer, a story told more bright-
     ly before by Sean O'Casey.

9   DICK, BERNARD F. "The Novels of Iris Murdoch: A
     Formula for Enchantment." <u>Bucknell Review</u> 14
     (May):66-81.
          An article interpreting Murdoch's novels from
     <u>Under the Net</u> to <u>The Italian Girl</u>, calling them all
     variations on a theme that theorizing without partic-
     ulars is self-delusion, a kind of enchantment. What
     breaks the enchantment is love, the awareness that
     something else, apart from the self, is real.
     Describes Murdoch as the leading contemporary symbol-
     ist novelist.

10   DONOGHUE, DENIS. "Magic Defeated." <u>New York Review</u>
     of Books 7 (17 November):22-23.
          A review of <u>The Time of the Angels</u> that maintains
     that Murdoch's imagination has no interest in ordin-
     ary life and that it is not suited to the genre of
     the novel. Contends that her imagination is more
     like Poe's than Tolstoy's or Henry James's. Calls
     this novel an elegy, with Murdoch's will trying to
     substitute for imagination.

11   EIMERL, SAREL. "Choreography of Despair."
     <u>Reporter</u> 35 (3 November):45-46.
          A review of <u>The Time of the Angels</u>, judging it
     hollow and too intellectual. Asserts that it exag-
     gerates the modern problem, a condition of moral dis-
     integration and despair. Decries Murdoch's excess of
     technique.

12   GRIFFIN, LLOYD W. Review of <u>The Time of the Angels</u>.
     <u>Library Journal</u> 91 (1 September):3973.
          Calls the novel Gothic, grotesque, and sexually
     unusual, classifying the characters as most uncommon,
     but recommends it highly.

13   HALIO, JAY . "A Sense of the Present." <u>Southern</u>
     Review 2 (Autumn):952-66.
          A review of <u>The Red and the Green</u> that surveys
     Murdoch's earlier novels and sees the new novel
     extending her usual concerns into the sphere of
     politics, told in the more realistic style of <u>The Bell</u>.

14   HALL, WILLIAM F. "'The Third Way': The Novels of
     Iris Murdoch." <u>Dalhousie Review</u> 46 (Autumn):306-18.
          An article interpreting Murdoch's novels in
     terms of her philosophical ideas expressed in <u>Sartre</u>
     and "The Sublime and the Beautiful." Contends that

her ideal for her characters is unchanged since
Under the Net -- recognition of the other.

15 HICKS, GRANVILLE. "Rector for a Dead God."
    Saturday Review 49 (29 October):25-26.
        A review of The Time of the Angels, praising it
    as her best novel since A Severed Head. Finds
    elements of melodrama and slapstick, saying that Mur-
    doch combines fantasy and the ordinary, showing a
    respect for reality.

16 HILL, W.B. "Fiction." America 115 (26 November):
    707.
        Reviews The Time of the Angels as profound and
    most readable.

17 JONES, DOROTHY. "Love and Morality in Iris
    Murdoch's The Bell. Meanjin Quarterly 26:85-90.
        An analysis of The Bell that begins with ideas
    from Murdoch's critical essays and identifies the
    theme of The Bell to be the relationship of love, art,
    and morality to the discovery of reality. Discusses
    the conflict between the pattern-making impulse and
    contingency, including the opaqueness of persons.

18 KIELY, BENEDICT. "England and Ireland." New York
    Times Book Review, 5 June, p. 5.
        A review of The Red and the Green, describing it
    as an impressionistic version of the intertwined
    fates of England and Ireland, commending Murdoch's
    ability to distinguish precisely Irish rain.

19 LEECH, ANASTASIA. "Fiction and Fact." Tablet 220
    (24 September):1074.
        Reviews The Time of the Angels, asserting Mur-
    doch's seriousness, examing the problem of evil. Com-
    pares the novel to The Unicorn in its prisoner, its
    guilty rather than guiltless scapegoat, and its dark
    tower.

20 LEONE, ARTHUR T. Review of The Red and the Green.
    Catholic World 203 (June):188-89.
        A review that sees The Red and the Green as
    engaging and Murdoch's eye for detail as superb but
    judges Millicent's taking of lovers to be the novel's
    undoing, plunging it into preposterous melodrama.

21 NETTELL, STEPHANIE. "An Exclusive Interview."
    Books and Bookmen 11 (September):14-15, 66.
        An interview of Murdoch that provides substantial
    information about her writing habits, including her
    conviction that novels should aim at being beautiful
    and at mirroring nature. Expresses the importance of
    scenery and weather to her and notes that she begins

on a novel with a germ of a situation or a provocative image.

22 "Notes on Current Books." Virginia Quarterly Review
    42 (Spring):xlvii-xlix.
        A review of The Red and the Green that interprets
    its theme to be freedom in relation to memory or his-
    tory. Finds the novel to be more conventional and to
    have a sparser texture than Murdoch's mythic novels.

23 OSTERMANN, ROBERT. "Miss Murdoch's Morality Play
    Ignites a Roaring Dramatic Blaze." National Observer,
    17 October, p. 23
        Reviews The Time of the Angels, saying that Mur-
    doch makes one care about the ultimate questions she
    poses and that the drama emerges from the interaction
    between human actions and ideas taken seriously.

24 PHILLIPSON, JOHN S. Review of The Time of the
    Angels. Best Sellers 26 (1 October):236.
        Names The Time of the Angels an existentialist
    novel, built on a series of contrasts: warm-cold,
    light-dark, open-hidden, love-hate. Judges Murdoch
    to be a major contemporary English novelist.

25 "Picking Up the Pieces." Times Literary Supplement,
    8 September, p. 798.
        A review of The Time of the Angels that finds
    it to be readable, technically skilled, and intel-
    ligent but not finally satisfying. Asks what has gone
    wrong since Murdoch's early novels and sees this novel
    as a Gothic extravaganza.

26 POORE, CHARLES. "The Walls Came Tumbling Down."
    New York Times, 29 September, p. 49.
        Reviews The Time of the Angels as an excellent
    melodrama, asserting that Murdoch retailors Sartre
    but is a born storyteller.

27 PRICE, R.G.G. "Fitful Backward Glance." Punch 251
    (28 December):970.
        A retrospective review of The Time of the Angels
    that faults it for having its roots in philosophy, not
    in character, asserting that the world of experience
    should be the starting point of a novel.

28 _____. "The Personal Art." Punch 251 (14 Septem-
    ber):415.
        A review of The Time of the Angels, finding it
    unconvincing and factitious, with the characters like
    pieces in a jigsaw puzzle and the only interest in-
    spired by the argument. Calls it a bore.

29 Review of The Red and the Green. British Book News,
    no. 305 (January), pp. 79-80.
        Finds The Red and the Green to be dramatic and
    highly readable but not part of Murdoch's serious fic-
    tion. Sees that the family conflicts reflect the
    absurdity and tragedy of the large-scale political
    troubles.

30 Review of The Red and the Green. Choice 3 (June):
    310.
        Recommends the novel for large libraries, prais-
    the artistic daring of the conception but saying that
    Murdoch does not bring it off, judging much of the
    novel to be ordinary.

31 SALE, ROGER. "High Mass and Low Requiem." Hudson
    Review 19 (Spring):124, 128-29.
        A review of The Red and the Green that credits
    Murdoch with many strengths, especially the inability
    to see anything as truly ordinary. But it implies
    that her best work has already been done and that she
    is no longer interested in her characters.

32 SHESTAKOV, DMITRI. "An Iris Murdoch Novel in
    Russian." Soviet Literature 7:169-75.
        Extracts from the afterword to the Russian
    edition of Under the Net by a young Russian critic.
    Distinguishes Murdoch from the Angry Young Men in
    that Jake can feel amazement or wonder. Sees Jake's
    freedom as a grotesque parody of the freedom modern
    man seeks.

33 SIDNELL, M.F. Review of The Red and the Green.
    Canadian Forum 46 (October):166.
        Describes history as manipulating the characters
    in The Red and the Green, calling them stereotyped
    figures. Finds a certain palatability to the story
    but not the vigor and warmth of some other treatments
    of the uprising.

34 TAUBMAN, ROBERT. "Uncles' War." New Statesman 72
    (16 September):401-2.
        A review of The Time of the Angels, charging it
    with willful obscurity and with characters borrowed
    from fiction, not life. Concedes Murdoch's skill at
    "knockabout Freudian comedy," but asks what it all
    means.

35 TOYNBEE, PHILIP. "Miss Murdoch's Monster Rally."
    New Republic 155 (22 October):24.
        A review of The Time of the Angels that judges
    it a victim of its own machinery of Gothic horror and
    melodrama, praising only Murdoch's writing.

36 TRACHTENBERG, STANLEY. "New Books in Review."
    Yale Review 55 (March):448-49.
        Reviews The Red and the Green as Murdoch's
    attempt to reconcile a symbolist concern for form with
    an existential concern for contingency. Sees the
    characters as independent of the plot and so illus-
    trating only the lack of causality. Says Murdoch
    uses farce to resist the reader's attempts to make
    sense of things.

37 TUCKER, MARTIN. "The Old Fish in Iris Murdoch's
    Kettle." New Republic 154 (5 February):26-28.
        A review of The Red and the Green, criticizing
    Murdoch's tendency to explore the grotesque and amoral,
    finding this novel to be better than other of her
    recent novels because of its deeper feeling and simp-
    ler style and fewer tricks of intellectual comedy.

38 WEEKS, EDWARD. "Satan in a Fog." Atlantic 218
    (October):138, 140.
        A review of The Time of the Angels that sees its
    atmospheric pressure skillfully done and its charac-
    terization fascinating but criticizes some passages
    as labored.

39 WOLFE, PETER. The Disciplined Heart: Iris Murdoch
    and Her Novels. Columbia, Mo.: University of
    Missouri Press.
        Discusses Murdoch's novels from Under the Net to
    The Italian Girl. The first chapter studies the
    static elements of Murdoch's thought, including her
    basic assumptions and influences on her. The study
    then analyzes her work novel by novel. Interested in
    social morality, Murdoch does not openly discuss
    philosophical ideas in her fiction. She emphasizes
    the free discovery of the self and other selves in
    the world. Her novels are exciting literature and
    penetrating moral philosophy. Compares Murdoch's
    philosophy with that of Locke, Hare, Ayer, Hegel,
    Sartre, Dewey, Marcel, and Kant.
        Because the final test of morality is actual
    social experience, Murdoch's novels depict closely
    observed character interaction. Instead of writing
    novels of ideas, she writes novels of social educa-
    tion. Murdoch agrees with W. H. Auden on the impor-
    tance of disciplined love.
        Under the Net is one of the most ambitious first
    novels of our time. It employs the English comic
    novel as a vehicle for weighty philosophical ideas.
    The novel projects its theme against the interplay
    of contingent human life.
        Many of the ideas from her first novel appear in
    the next three novels but with more lucid psycholog-
    ical interpenetration. The Sandcastle is better than

The Flight from the Enchanter in its unity and psychological depth. It is the first major statement of
Murdoch's moral vision, her first sustained depiction
of the uncertainty of human values.

Murdoch's eight novels establish a moral focus:
the importance of free choice. She depicts concrete
individuals, but her novels contain events that defy
rational explanation and that are not controlled by
human volition. She portrays man in an intractable,
discontinuous world, with the potential for value and
meaning within himself. Her basic attitudes remain
the same while she experiments with setting, character,
point of view, and narrative pace.

1967

1 BALDANZA, FRANK. "Iris Murdoch." Wisconsin Studies
   in Contemporary Literature 8:454-58.
       A review of two books of criticism on Murdoch's
   work: A.S. Byatt's Degrees of Freedom and Peter
   Wolfe's The Disciplined Heart, saying that Murdoch
   read Byatt's book before publication and made suggestions. Finds Byatt's interpretations to be closely
   reasoned but complains that Wolfe's interpretations
   are farfetched and arcane.

2 BERTHOFF, WARNER. "The Enemy of Freedom is Fantasy."
   Massachusetts Review 8 (Summer):580-84.
       A review of The Time of the Angels that seeks to
   refute Denis Donoghue's charge that Murdoch is not a
   proper novelist. Admits the Gothic mannerisms and
   plotrigging of the novel but insists on its basic
   strength in the character of Carel and in the ideas
   absorbed into the narrative sequence. Asserts that
   Murdoch is part of major literary history.

3 _____. "Fortunes of the Novel: Muriel Spark and
   Iris Murdoch." Massachusetts Review 8 (Spring):
   301-32.
       Evaluates Spark and Murdoch as novelists of the
   "honorable second rank," writing within received conventions. Sees Murdoch working against the tyranny
   of masterpieces, portraying characters whose conceptions of themselves and others are shattered, revised,
   and reformed, a method that does not accommodate tidy
   resolutions. Admits problems with Murdoch's style
   but says she inspires readers to go along with her in
   her examination of contemporary problems.

4 BROICH, ULRICH. "Tradition and Rebellion: Zur
   Renaissance des pikaresken Romans in der englischen
   Literatur der Geganwart." Poetica 1 (April):214-29.

There is a renaissance in picaresque novel
writing in England as well as in Germany. In Under
the Net, Murdoch chooses a picaresque gestalt, assuming picaresque structure and motives. Jake Donaghue
is a fool and an outsider, as well as a parasite,
moving from friend to friend. His money comes from
accident, not work. Accident, related to contingency,
seems to be a controlling principle in the novel.
Instead of stream of consciousness, Murdoch uses first
person narrative. The use of the picaresque in this
decade is reactionary, as if Proust, Joyce, and Woolf
had never lived.

5   BUFKIN, E.C.   The Twentieth Century Novel in English:
    A Checklist.   Athens. University of Georgia Press,
    p. 89.
        List of Murdoch's novels from Under the Net (1954)
    to The Time of the Angels (1966).

6   BURGESS, ANTHONY.   The Novel Now: A Guide to Con-
    temporary Fiction.   London: Faber & Faber; New
    York: Norton, pp. 124-27, 128, 131, 137, 146.
        An account of Murdoch's career to date, naming
    The Bell her best novel and judging her great period
    over. Disparages The Italian Girl and The Red and
    The Green. Asserts that she may become simply a
    "popular woman novelist."

7   CRUTTWELL, PATRICK.   "Fiction Chronicle."   Hudson
    Review 20 (Spring):1760.
        A review of The Time of the Angels that depre-
    cates Murdoch's recent novels but says that in this
    new one the elements come out right: the characters
    and their world are alive and the imaginative creation
    is solid.

8   GARIS, ROBERT.   "Playing Games."   Commentary 43
    (March):97-100.
        Reviews The Time of the Angels and attributes
    Murdoch's troubles with her allegorical fiction to
    her writing so much. Asserts that her characters
    must be oddly assorted to define each other sharply
    but finds no galvanic meaning animating this novel.

9   GINDIN, JAMES.   "The Fable Begins to Break Down."
    Wisconsin Studies in Contemporary Literature 8
    (Winter):1-18.
        An article attacking recent critics' preference
    for fable over more realistic fiction. Criticises
    the fable as abstract, rigid, implying an unwanted
    metaphysics, and not hospitable to the theme of
    alienation, still a central problem in contemporary
    fiction. Mentions Murdoch as a writer of fables.

10 GRIFFIN, LLOYD W. Review of The Nice and the Good.
    Library Journal 92 (15 December):4524.
        Characterizes the novel as unusually compassionate
    for Murdoch, saying that it shows her keen intellect.
    Praises the characters' aliveness and recommends buy-
    ing the novel.

11 JONES, DOROTHY. "Love and Morality in Iris Murdoch's
    The Bell." Meanjin Quarterly 26 (Autumn):85-90.
        An interpretation of The Bell, calling it Murdoch's
    best novel and noting the two patterns of morality,
    the morality of rules and the morality of intuition.
    Sees the lifting of the bell as the stirring of sub-
    conscious emotions, and the community as unable to
    deal with the random and the animal in human nature.

12 KAEHELE, SHARON, and GERMAN HOWARD. "The Discovery
    of Reality in Iris Murdoch's The Bell." PMLA 82:
    554-63.
        An interpretation of The Bell that relates
    Murdoch's theories of characterization to the novel,
    saying the novel helps the reader understand the
    human personality and possesses the "self-contained
    form" of true art.

13 McKENZIE, VIRGINIA. Review of The Time of the
    Angels. Books Abroad 41 (Spring):221.
        States that Father Carel Marcus arrogantly dom-
    inated the lives of three women who live in isolation
    with him: Muriel, Elizabeth, and Pattie. The plot
    and the main characters are improbable, but Murdoch's
    descriptive powers and ability to create moods are
    sheer artistry. The lesser characters are so sturdy
    that their seeming reality lends credibility to the
    rest. Murdoch may be representing symbolically the
    world today with the current religious revival,
    violence, dissipation, and lack of sensitivity to
    spiritual values. The novel is bizarre, but its mes-
    sage is one of uncommon good sense.

14 MARTIN, F.X. "1916--Myth, Fact and History."
    Studia Hibernica 7:24.
        Asserts that Murdoch made an unexpected contri-
    bution to 1916 literature with The Red and the Green.
    The story centers around an Anglo-Irish family who
    are caught up in and divided by the conflicting
    emotions of Easter Week. Murdoch displays a sure
    touch in recalling the atmosphere and even details
    about Dublin in 1916. The novel's judgment on the
    men of Easter Week is that "they were inconceivably
    brave men."

15 MORRELL, ROY. "Iris Murdoch: The Early Novels."
    Critical Quarterly 9 (Autumn):272-82.

An analysis using Murdoch's monograph on Sartre
to illuminate The Sandcastle, The Bell, and Under
the Net with brief comments on A Severed Head and The
Flight from the Enchanter. Central concepts explained and applied include choice, bad faith, the world
of others, and the sickness of language. Judges The
Bell to be her best early novel.

16 PARRINDER, PATRICK. "Pastiche and After." Cambridge
Review 89A (4 November):65-66.
An account of a talk by Angus Wilson seeing
novelists' return to traditional techniques to be a
reaction against the extremism of Joyce, but Parrinder
rebukes the "pastiche novels" of Murdoch and others
as outdated, calling the techniques of the traditional
novel "facile."

17 RABINOVITZ, RUBIN. The Reaction against Experiment
in the English Novel, 1950-1960. New York and
London: Columbia University Press, 229 pp.
An assessment that groups Murdoch with other
novelists whose first novels were published between
1952 and 1955. Mentions Murdoch's ties with existentialism and calls her one of the best writers of her
time, an uneventful period for the novel.

18 SCHOLES, ROBERT. "Iris Murdoch's Unicorn." In
The Fabulators. New York: Oxford University Press,
pp. 106-32.
A demonstration of fabulation by discussing The
Unicorn as one of the finest modern allegorical
fictions, explaining how Murdoch transfers the reader's
interest from the characters to the ideas behind
their actions.
Murdoch is moving the reader from Gothic action
to Gothic allegory, teaching him how to read allegor-
ically. We see Hannah from the perspectives of
Marian and Effingham, the outsiders who are bridges
between the mystery and the reader's world. There is
a significant experience for the reader who, like
Marian, becomes involved in the events and who
imaginatively experiences good and evil.

19 SEEHASE, GEORG. "Kapitalistische Entfremdung und
humanistische Integration: Bemerkingen zum
englischen proletarischen Gegenwartsroman."
Zeitschrift für Anglistik und Amerikanistik 15:383-
400.
Study of capitalistic alienation and humanistic
integration in contemporary English proletarian literature. It asks whether capitalistic alienation is
a normal feeling in life or whether it is created by
a misanthropic social and political system and encountered daily. Murdoch, a popular contemporary author,

believes that capitalistic alienation is brought about
by an antagonistic class society, deepened by pervert-
ed masochism and encountered by people personally
every day.

20 STEVENSON, LIONEL. Yesterday and After: The
    History of the English Novel. New York: Barnes &
    Noble, 431 pp.
        A discussion of Murdoch's novels from Under the
    Net to The Time of the Angels, calling her first her
    most philosophical, The Bell her best, and the
    novels after A Severed Head lesser creations. Credits
    Murdoch with producing a complex fiction that epito-
    mizes earlier trends.

21 STIMPSON, CATHARINE ROSLYN. "The Early Novels of
    Iris Murdoch." Ph.D. dissertation, Columbia
    University, 366 pp. Abstract in DAI 28 (1968):
    5073A-74A.
        An examination of Murdoch's methods of character-
    ization, using her essays and articles to build
    Murdoch Man, "a theoretical moral agent." Character
    types include the questing male, the effeminate male,
    the magister, the enchanter, the strong woman, the
    ingenue, and the servant.

22 WIDMAN, R.L. "An Iris Murdoch Checklist."
    Critique 10:17-29.
        Includes novels and booklength works by Murdoch,
    followed by reviews, articles by Murdoch, general
    criticism of Murdoch in books, and significant crit-
    icism of Murdoch in articles and reviews. The scope
    is from 1953 and Sartre: Romantic Rationalist to
    1966 and The Time of the Angels; without annotations.

23 _____. "Murdoch's Under the Net: Theory and
    Practice in Fiction." Critique 10:5-16.
        Article proposing to review Murdoch's commentary
    and see how successfully she executes her own theory.
    Uses ideas from "Against Dryness" to critique Under
    the Net. States that the problem explored in the
    novel is Jake's attempt to know the reality of others.
    The novel parodies the father quest, the search for a
    lovemate, and the noble hero convention. Jake refuses
    to acknowledge the existence of another, Finn, and
    Murdoch's light treatment of the refusal is immoral.
    Her characters are not free because she is writing a
    roman bien fait and because many of the accidents are
    contrived or gratuitous.

1968

1 ARNAUD, PIERRE. "Les vertus du chiffre sept and le
   mythe de la dame à la licrone: Essai d'interpretation de The Unicorn d'Iris Murdoch." Les langues
   modernes 62 (March-April):206-10.
       Interprets the symbolism of the number seven and
   of the unicorn in Murdoch's novel. Seven is the symbol of the totality of numbers. Murdoch divided her
   story into seven parts. The number seven is also
   associated with penitence and expiation. Hannah is
   prisoner in the castle for seven years, expiating
   her sin. The story of the unicorn is that of the
   incarnation of Christ, and the heroine here is the
   Christ who has come on earth to spy out all sin.

2 BATCHELOR, BILLIE. "Revision in Iris Murdoch's
   Under the Net." Books at Iowa, University of Iowa,
   no. 8 (April):30-36.
       An account of Murdoch's revisions, seen in the
   Iowa manuscript of Under the Net. Finds an original
   manuscript and two separate revisions with changes
   made to achieve compression and concentration and
   stylistic excellence.

3 BEREK, P. "Adapting a Genre." New Leader 51
   (22 April):26.
       Praises the delightful wealth of character and
   incident in The Nice and The Good. Murdoch writes al-
   legories because in our society there is no agreement
   about the existence of free men and meaningful
   societies. The novel adapts the devices of Eliza-
   bethan stage comedy in which instantaneous love and
   sudden repentance affirm the importance of contingency. Complexity results from the ironic juxta-
   position of philosophical insight and ridiculous
   action.

4 BERGONZI, BERNARD. "Nice but Not Good." New York
   Review of Books 10 (11 April):36-38.
       A review of The Nice and the Good that judges it
   an unimportant book, trivial and pretentious. Charges that Murdoch relates to her characters only in
   acts of arbitrary sex or violence or in complicated
   physical activity. Implies her works are not part of
   serious literature.

5 BILLINGTON, MICHAEL. "Novel into Play." Play and
   Players 15 (March):26.
       An interview with James Saunders, coadapter with
   Iris Murdoch of the play The Italian Girl. Discusses
   their working habits, starting with Murdoch's adaptation, moving to Saunders' second draft, to a revision
   mutually written by Murdoch, Saunders, and Val May.

6 BRYDEN, RONALD. "Talking to Iris Murdoch."
Listener 79 (4 April):433-34.
    An interview with Murdoch for the Third Programme
with questions by Bryden and A.S. Byatt on the play
The Italian Girl and the novel The Nice and the Good,
with Murdoch declaring no need to experiment with the
novel.

7 BYATT, ANTONIA SUSAN. "Kiss and Make Up." New
Statesman 75 (26 January):113-14.
    A review of The Nice and the Good that finds it
richer and more formally successful than other recent
Murdoch novels. Calls it a novel with no mythical
center, with the ideas worked out through the characters. Sees in it the contrast between mechanical
facts and the individual consciousness.

8 CASSILL, R.V. "Hell Fires Banked for Home Use."
Book World, 7 January, p. 5.
    A review of The Nice and the Good that praises
the characters profusely, finding the author's comments memorable and sophisticated, but criticizes the
plot as lackluster and wayward.

9 "Characters in Love." Times Literary Supplement,
25 January, p. 77.
    A review of The Nice and the Good, characteriz-
ing Murdoch as confident and energetic and the novel
as a benevolent comedy. Sees the action to be desul-
tory but the writer to be giving serious attention to
moral problems.

10 DAVENPORT, GUY. "Frightfully Good, I'm Sure."
National Review 20 (9 April):350.
    Reviews The Nice and the Good as a happy story
about normal people with no monsters beneath the
surface, declaring the characters charmingly drawn.

11 DIAKONOVA, NINA. "Notes on the Evaluation of the
Bildungsroman in England." Zeitschrift für
Anglistik und Amerikanistik 4 (16 Jahrgang):341-51.
    An account of the development of the Bildungs-
roman in England, distinguishing Murdoch's novels
from the form in that Murdoch selects a critical
moment in the life of a character, with resignation
or disruption following the decisive events.

12 FREEMANTLE, ANNE. "The Probable and the Possible."
Reporter 38 (25 January):47-49.
    A review of The Nice and the Good that finds
Murdoch's intentions unclear but describes the novel
as immensely readable. Calls it an "Establishment
novel," of privileged characters who discover their
own evil.

13 GRIFFIN, LLOYD W. Review of Bruno's Dream. Library
     Journal 93 (15 December):4664.
         Recommends buying Bruno's Dream, comparing it to
     a Dickensian comedy with grotesque characters who are
     changed by conflict and love.

14 HALL, JAMES. "Blurring the Will: Iris Murdoch."
     In The Lunatic Giant in the Drawing Room: The
     British and American Novel Since 1930. Bloomington
     and London: Indiana University Press, pp. 181-212.
         A revision of Hall's 1965 article (1965.14)
     praising Murdoch for her continuing attempts to
     explore a changing view of wish and reality, for her
     talent to keep growing and raising new questions, and
     for her taking crisis as opportunity.

15 HALL, ROLAND. "British Books on Philosophy, 1962-
     67. Part II." British Book News 333 (May):321-26.
         A list and brief description of "significant"
     British books on philosophy. A.S. Byatt's Degrees
     of Freedom: The Novels of Iris Murdoch is noted as
     an exploration of the philosophical import of the
     novel.

16 HICKS, GRANVILLE. "By Love Possessed." Time 19
     (5 January):76, 79.
         A review of The Nice and the Good that character-
     izes it as well-written and well-meant, a story of
     lovers who love for the wrong reasons and go astray,
     a story of gentle irony.

17 _____. "Love Runs Rampant." Saturday Review 51
     (6 January):27-28.
         Reviews The Nice and the Good, discussing
     Anthony Burgess's charge that Murdoch is becoming
     just another popular woman novelist. Agrees that The
     Bell is her best novel but calls remarkable her gift
     for succinct characterization and her ingenious turns
     of plot. Disagrees with Burgess's final judgment.

18 HILL, W.F. "Fiction." America 118 (4 May):622.
         A review of The Nice and the Good, evaluating it
     as maybe Murdoch's best novel, praising the story,
     filled with incident and adventure and profundity.

19 JACKSON, KATHERINE GAUSS. "Books in Brief." Harper
     236 (February):100.
         A review of The Nice and the Good that judges it
     a jolly romp and a novel rich in characters, episodes,
     and reflections on love. Remarks especially on the
     climactic incident involving the caves.

20 JANEWAY, ELIZABETH. "Everyone Is Involved." New
York Times Book Review, 14 January, p. 4.
Reviews The Nice and the Good, calling it Murdoch's best and most exciting novel, asserting that
here she works with, not against, fictional devices,
using the conventions of the thriller to explore moral
problems. Complains, however, of no dramatic climax,
but only individual confrontations.

21 McCARTHY, MARGOT. "Dualities in The Bell." Contemporary Review 213 (17 December):313-17.
An analysis of The Bell, noting the opposing,
paired protagonists--Dora and Michael; the fraternal
pair, Nick and Catherine; the pair of community lead-
ers, Michael and James--and their opposed factions,
and the pair of bells, representing the actual religious experience and the indirect ecclesiastical experience.

22 MADDOCKS, MELVIN. "Iris Murdoch: Heartfelt Wit."
Christian Science Monitor, 11 January, p. 11.
A review of The Nice and the Good, asserting
that Murdoch is not just a player of Gothic games but
a novelist of feeling. Finds the ending of the novel
slightly clumsy but the exploration of character
imaginative and intense.

23 PALMER, TONY. "Artistic Privilege." London
Magazine 8 (May):47-52.
A review of The Nice and the Good that reproaches
what the reviewer sees as an individualistic bias in
the work, denying the claims of the social and denying
the artist's responsibility to others.

24 PONDROM, CYRENA N. "Iris Murdoch: An Existentialist?" Comparative Literature Studies 5 (December):
403-19.
An article that explores Murdoch's affinities
with French existentialists, delineating also her
differences. Using An Unofficial Rose, it establishes
four challenges to freedom--contingency of the world,
the established character of people, the gaze of the
other, and personal fantasies.

25 POORE, CHARLES. "Gods, Associate-Gods, and Sin-
ners." New York Times, 4 January, p. 35.
A review of The Nice and the Good that sees in it
an acceptance of the ridiculous. Names Octavian Gray
the god and John Ducane the associate god.

26 RABINOVITZ, RUBIN. Iris Murdoch. New York: Columbia University Press, 48 pp.

Monograph on Murdoch that interprets her books
from Sartre; Romantic Rationalist to The Nice and
The Good. Despite the fact that Murdoch's aim is to
keep academic philosophical concerns from intruding
on her novel writing, one of her greatest interests
is ethics. Her fictional characters often find themselves in moral dilemmas, unable to discover a solution because they believe in faulty ideologies.

Murdoch's compromise is to introduce ideas in
subtle forms, to provide alternatives for the ideas,
to introduce her own ideas through a minor or unsym-
pathetic character, and even to leave the reader with
problems that cannot be solved rationally. Sometimes
the reader feels uncertain about the moral positions
represented and does not grasp all of the import of
the action.

Murdoch constantly emphasizes the dangers of
subjectivity. She deprecates the degree of self-
knowledge needed to achieve morality or love. She
seems to feel that any introspection is a step on the
dangerous road to solipsism.

Murdoch misses being in the first rank of novelists because she does not seem to want to write the
great novel with universal themes. Her other faults
include drabness in some of the inferior novels like
The Sandcastle and a desire to fool the reader with
sudden twists of plot as in A Severed Head. Murdoch
belongs to the next rank, however, for her intelligent,
compassionate ideas.

27 RAVEN, SIMON. "Good News from Hades." Observer,
    21 January, p. 31.
    A review of The Nice and the Good, calling it
Murdoch's best novel since The Bell and possibly her
best of all. Claims that her depiction of humans in
relation to natural processes is surer and subtler
than that of any other contemporary novelist.

28 Review of The Nice and the Good. Choice 5 (April):
    196-97.
    Judges the novel to be first-rate, perceiving
Murdoch's style and plot to be a joke, reflecting
the arbitrary nature of life and the reader's desire
for neat meaning. Contends that the novel transcends
its material.

29 ROCKEFELLER, LARRY JEAN. "Comedy and the Early
    Novels of Iris Murdoch." Ph.D. dissertation, Bowl-
    ing Green State University, 237 pp. Abstract in DAI
    29:4018A
    Examines Murdoch's portrayal of characters,
asserting that her use of bitter satire in novels
from An Unofficial Rose on inhibited her creation of

of realistic characters and her finding a balance of
acceptance and judgment of her characters only in the
early novels.

30 ROSE, W.K. "An Interview with Iris Murdoch."
    Shenandoah 19 (Winter):3-22. Also published as
    "Iris Murdoch, Informally," London Magazine, n.s. 8
    (June):59-73.
        An interview with Murdoch, discussing her writ-
    ing, including her wish to be considered a realistic
    writer and her preference for writing novels, rather
    than plays.

31 ____. "Iris Murdoch, Informally." London Magazine,
    n.s. 8 (June):59-73.
        An interview with Murdoch affirming her alternat-
    ing closed novels with open novels and naming her main
    subject now not freedom but love. Characterizes her-
    self as no longer an existentialist but a Platonist.
    See 1968.30.

32 SEYMOUR-SMITH, MARTIN. "Virtue Its Own Reward."
    Spectator 220 (26 January):103-4.
        A review of The Sovereignty of Good over Other
    Concepts that calls it a useful guide to her inten-
    tions. Categorizes Murdoch as more of a philosopher
    than a novelist, crediting her intelligence and gener-
    al talent but asserting that her fiction is "dis-
    guised moral philosophy."

33 SIGGINS, C.M. Review of The Nice and the Good.
    Best Sellers 27 (15 January):402.
        Perceives The Nice and the Good as a provocative
    novel with ethical considerations worked into the
    characterization and subtle imagery woven into the
    story. Complains of an intricate plot, sometimes
    confusing.

34 SIMON, MARION. "Prose and Cons." National Observer
    7 (12 Febraury):21.
        Brief review of The Nice and the Good as an
    almost conventional novel with individuated characters
    and one or two pockets of black magic. Calls it a
    labyrinthine tale with Murdoch's usual amount of meta-
    physical musing. Commends it as a whopping good
    mystery tale in which love conquers all.

35 SOKOLOV, RAYMOND A. "Fleshly Rococo." Newsweek 71
    (15 January):73.
        A review of The Nice and the Good, comparing
    Murdoch to a minor master of nineteenth-century
    fiction for her prolificness and to Jane Austen for
    her social analysis of language, especially of the
    "nice" and the "good."

36 SPURLING, HILARY. "True Romance." Spectator 220
    (16 February):207.
       A review of the play The Italian Girl in London
    that finds the production "deliciously coherent."
    Asserts the genre to be farce, praising the comic
    device of having the action filtered through an ironic
    narrative consciousness.

37 TAUBMAN, ROBERT. "Not Caring." Listener 79
    (1 February):148.
       Reviews The Nice and the Good as a mixture of
    high culture and trash, comparing its enchantments to
    those of A Midsummer Night's Dream. Characterizes
    the novel as a comic strip with all of Murdoch's
    arts but spontaneity and satire.

38 THOMPSON, JOHN. "Old Friends." Commentary 45
    (January):65-67.
       A review of The Nice and the Good, calling it a
    learned fable of love that the reviewer is content
    with. Tells the reader to look up the novel.

39 TREVOR, WILLIAM. "Snobbery, Fun, Sex, and Sex."
    Manchester Guardian Weekly, 1 February, p. 12.
       A review of The Nice and the Good that finds it
    a game of rare skill, a story cunningly told, a feast
    of light satire, and a novel the reviewer loved.

40 WEEKS, EDWARD. "Nice Is not Always Safe."
    Atlantic 221 (February):135-36.
       Review of The Nice and the Good, lauding Mur--
    doch's portrayal of the young, the amusing interdepen-
    dence of the characters, and the author's enjoyment
    of her characters. Names it her most versatile novel.

41 WILLIAMS, DAVID. "New Novels." Punch 254
    (31 January):174.
       Calls The Nice and the Good a richly various
    book. Murdoch assembled a privileged crowd at every
    stage of human development, falling in or out of love.
    Her fecundity is a sign of her talent. Usually a
    satisfying observer of human character, Murdoch fails
    with Uncle Theo.

                          1969

 1 ALLEN, WALTER. Review of Bruno's Dream. New York
    Times Book Review, 19 January, pp. 5, 6, 34.
       Evaluates the novel as Murdoch's best since The
    Bell, praising the character of Bruno and Murdoch's
    making her device of the test here reveal truth.
    Ascribes passion and profundity to the novel.

2   ANDERSON, DAVID. The Tragic Protest: A Christian
    Study of Some Modern Literature. London:SCM Press,
    pp. 62-63, 135-36.
        A study that mentions Murdoch's book on Sartre
    and her discussion of the unique value of the human
    person. Also considers the adultery in A Severed
    Head as reflecting the problems of man-woman relation-
    ships in our time.

3   AVANT, JOHN ALFRED. Review of A Fairly Honourable
    Defeat. Library Journal 94 (15 December):4539.
        Extols the absorbing story and characters and
    the technical brilliance of the novel, pronouncing
    Murdoch an extremely moral writer.

4   BALDANZA, FRANK. "The Nice and the Good." Modern
    Fiction Studies 15 (Autumn):417-28.
        Asserts that although Murdoch's talents incline
    her toward the closed, tightly patterned myth, The
    Nice and the Good is looser in structure, crammed with
    little gems of minor relevance to the overall pattern.
    The structural openness is gained at the cost of
    greater diffusion and lack of concentration.
        A general movement of the sympathetic characters
    here is the overcoming of demons. The most intense
    focus is on John Ducane, the flawed, culpable,
    questing-learning male. He functions as a father-
    confessor to a crowd of accidental, separate, free
    characters. One of the paths of the double plot is
    the solution of the Radeechy suicide. It provides
    much moral anxiety for John Ducane in his belated
    process of growing up. The second path of the plot
    is the pairing off of the partners at the end. All
    of the pairings are between experienced partners,
    learning to live with past mistakes, discovering love
    as real contact with other real persons. A subsid-
    iary theme is a preoccupation with personal comfort,
    imaged as a rat that needs to be killed. The "nice"
    refers to the human love of the many pairings and the
    "good" to a selfless, transcendent spiritual love.

5   BLACKBURN, SARA. "Book Marks." Nation 208
    (27 January):124.
        Perceives in Bruno's Dream a gallery of gro-
    tesque characters and a series of zany relationships
    that Murdoch makes us care intensely about. Finds
    memorable characters in Bruno, Nigel, and two others,
    all first pitiful, then hilarious, and finally
    glorious.

6   "Briefly Noted: Fiction." New Yorker 44 (1 Feb-
    ruary):90.
        A review of Bruno's Dream that sees in it the
    triumph of the dark forces of nature, exemplified in

the death of Bruno. Describes the story as complex
and bludgeoning.

7 BYATT, ANTONIA SUSAN. "The Spider's Web."
   New Statesman 77 (17 January):86.
       A review of Bruno's Dream, describing it as a
   mix of black comedy and "metaphysical fantasy."
   Identifies the theme as oneness of love and death,
   both causing man to confront life's essentials.
   States that the novel is moving and humane, rendering
   precisely Bruno's consciousness.

8 CULLY, ANN, with JOHN FEASTER. "Criticism of Iris
   Murdoch: A Selected Checklist." Modern Fiction
   Studies 15 (Autumn).
       Lists general criticism of Murdoch's works and
   then criticism of specific novels, up to and including Bruno's Dream. Includes a chronology of Murdoch's
   novels and essays by and interviews with her.

9 CULLY, ANN. "Theory and Practice: Characterization
   in the Novels of Iris Murdoch." Modern Fiction
   Studies 15 (Autumn):335-45.
       An article that uses Murdoch's essays on aesthet-
   ics and ethics to determine Murdoch's theory of personality. Applies that theory to Murdoch's practice
   in her novels, discussing love, knowing, freedom,
   and the contingent as related to Murdoch's characters.

10 DAVENPORT, GUY. "Tables of Transformation."
   National Review 21 (11 Febrary):131-32.
       Reviews Bruno's Dream, calling the action brisk
   and delightful. Describes Bruno as a Beckett-like
   character and the novel as a romantic comedy, comparing Murdoch to Arnold Bennet crossed with the
   Italian surrealists.

11 DETWEILER, ROBERT. Iris Murdoch's "The Unicorn."
   New York: Seabury Press, 32 pp.
       Relates the characters and ideas to a religious
   framework, focusing on dilemmas of religious significance. The study discusses how the semiallegorical
   patterns in The Unicorn reinforce the idea of existential action and Christian belief. The novel works
   with three medieval tropes: the unicorn legend, the
   story of Sleeping Beauty and the prince, and the
   courtly love tradition. The freedom theme appears
   in the motifs of enchantment and imprisonment in all
   three tropes. The Unicorn calls for a Christian
   existential analysis based on Kierkegaard's terms.
   The language of Sartre's existentialism also reveals
   a valuable perspective on the novel. Murdoch suggests
   that we ask ultimate questions of ourselves and each
   other.

12 EMERSON, DONALD. "Violence and Survival in the
    Novels of Iris Murdoch." Transactions of the
    Wisconsin Academy of Sciences, Arts, and Letters
    57:21-28.
        An article taking examples from Under the Net,
    The Bell, An Unofficial Rose, and The Time of the
    Angels to demonstrate the changing function of violence
    in the novels from inconsequential violence in the earliest
    to consequential, evil violence in the latest.

13 FREEDMAN, RICHARD. "Dialogue as Trenchant as a
    5-to-1 Martini." Chicago Tribune Book World, 12
    January, p. 3.
        A review of Bruno's Dream, declaring it a
    triumph of intelligence and a major novel. Compares
    the novel to A Severed Head, praising the naturalness
    and warmth of the characters in Bruno's Dream.
    Commends the depiction of the slow death of Bruno.

14 FRIES, UDO. "Iris Murdoch: Under the Net. Ein
    Beitrag zur Erzah technik im Ich-Roman." Die
    Neueren Sprachen 68 (September):449-59.
        Discusses the contribution that Under the Net
    makes to the narrative technique of first-person
    novels.

15 GASKIN, D. BRUCE, ed. From "Lord Jim" to "Billy
    Liar": An Introduction to the English Novel in the
    Twentieth Century. London: Longmans, pp. 242-43.
        Excerpt from The Bell and brief introduction,
    calling that novel more complete and satisfying than
    Murdoch's earlier works. The total effect of A
    Severed Head and An Unofficial Rose is unconvincing
    and some of the later novels read like self-parody.
    Murdoch introduces obscure symbols and imprecise
    language, and she seems preoccupied with sexual devi-
    ation.

16 GERMAN, HOWARD. "Allusions in the Early Novels of
    Iris Murdoch." Modern Fiction Studies 15 (Autumn):
    361-77.
        Traces allusions in Murdoch's first five novels
    to show their existence and to suggest the particular
    relevance of the allusions. In Under the Net many of
    the details of Hugo's life are similar to Wittgen-
    stein's life as reported in Norman Malcolm's Ludwig
    Wittgenstein: A Memoir. Another source of allusions
    in the novel is the Aeneid. The basis for the paral-
    lel between Jake and Aeneas is their sharing an idea
    of fate or destiny. Jake is a romantic, always find-
    ing patterns in his life.
        Allusions in The Flight from The Enchanter
    reflect Through the Looking Glass, fairy tales by
    Grimm and Anderson, and myths and tales from the

mid-Eastern, Slavic, and Scandinavian countries. The
preoccupation with individual illusions in the novel
justifies the wealth of material from fairy tale and
myth.
     The Sandcastle may incorporate details from Bos-
well's Life of Johnson and from traits of other mem-
bers of Johnson's circle as well as from Romantic
poetry. There are also extensive parallels to Celtic
mythology and to the Romance of the Rose.
     A Severed Head takes its background from Oriental
mythology and from Dream of the Red Chamber, The Tale
of Genji, and The Love's Suicides at Amijima. In
asking whether Murdoch's background material inter-
feres with realism in her novels, German asserts
that the answer varies from work to work, naming The
Bell the most successful and The Flight from the
Enchanter the most criticized novel.

17 HALL, WILLIAM F. "Bruno's Dream: Technique and
    Meaning in the Novels of Iris Murdoch." Modern
    Fiction Studies 15 (Autumn):42-43.
         Analysis of Bruno's Dream that first relates
    Murdoch's novels to two large patterns in term of
    male form and female contingency. Declares that the
    body of Indian myth and legend permeates the novel
    with Nigel's mystic vision reenacting the Hindu
    creation myth and with Nigel a kind of Bodhisattva.
    Nigel symbolizes Eastern consciousness and Bruno the
    dying Western consciousness with his scientific
    interest and his preoccupation with money and posses-
    sions. Miles's wife Parvati is a benignant Great
    Mother, consort of Shiva, the paradigm for the lives
    of Lisa and Diana. Only Will and Adelaide live at an
    unexamined level of surface events and facts.

18 "Hanging by a Thread." Time 93 (21 February):84-85,
    p. E7.
         A review of Bruno's Dream that describes it as a
    subtle, rueful depiction of the art of dying, touch-
    ing and compassionate.

19 HICKS, GRANVILLE. "Literary 'Horizons.'" Saturday
    Review 52 (18 January):32.
         Reviews Bruno's Dream by comparing it to The
    Nice and the Good, determining the new novel to be
    better and more characteristic of Murdoch's work.
    Asserts that her novels are true in the way that
    dreams are true.

20 HILL, W.B. "Fiction: Review of Bruno's Dream."
    America 120 (3 May):538.
         A review that recounts the plot and then assesses
    Bruno's Dream as one of Murdoch's better efforts.

21 HILL, WILLIAM B.   Review of Bruno's Dream.   Best
    Sellers 28 (15 January):426.
       Important in Bruno's Dream are the gradually
    developing attitudes of people to other people with
    most of the action internal. The changes in the
    characters seem not only explicable but inevitable.
    Compares Murdoch with George Meredith, needing patient
    reading but satisfying; Murdoch is here at her formid-
    able best.

22 "Iris Murdoch Number."   Modern Fiction Studies 15
    (Autumn):225-457.
       Includes a bibliography by Ann Cully with John
    Feaster and articles by Frank Baldanza, Ann Cully,
    Howard German, William F. Hall, Peter Kemp, Alice P.
    Kenney, Linda Kuehl, William M. Murray, and Raymond J.
    Porter.

23 KAHRMANN, BERND.   Die idyllische Szene im
    zeitgenossischen englischen Roman.   Bad Homburg
    v.d.h., Berlin, 2nd Zurich: Verlag Gehten.
       Study of various modern British novels from
    James's The Ambassadors to nine of Murdoch's up to
    The Italian Girl in terms of several motifs: idyll,
    flight, liberation, and prettification. In the idyll
    there is a close connection between space, time,
    character, and action. The harmonious scene gives the
    illusion of time standing still. Idyll is not a
    flight from life but the creation of a perspective
    and opportunities for choice. The idyll can be a
    place where the character is freed from reality
    temporarily but eventually he will return to that
    reality.

24 KAPLAN, MORTON NEIL.   "Iris Murdoch and the Gothic
    Tradition."   Ph.D. dissertation, Columbia Univer-
    sity, 297 pp. Abstract in DAI 31:1232A.
       Asserts that Murdoch's closed novels are essen-
    tially Gothic and cannot be fully understood simply
    in terms of her philosophic ideas. Her closed novels
    include The Flight from the Enchanter, A Severed
    Head, The Unicorn, The Time of the Angels, and The
    Italian Girl. The novels are essentially Gothic in
    the primacy they give to terror and suspense evoked
    by the revelation of unsanctioned, usually incestuous
    sexuality. Other Gothic elements encompass the use
    of the supernatural, the frightening landscape, the
    imprisoning house, and the archetypal figures of the
    helpless heroine and the villain. Individual chapters
    examine in detail The Unicorn, The Time of the Angels,
    and The Italian Girl.

25 KAYE, HOWARD.   "Delight and Instruction."   New
    Republic 160 (8 February):19-20.

Review of Bruno's Dream that complains that some external system is moving the characters around like puppets. Murdoch, unwilling to commit herself to either the popular or philosophical mode, fails at both. Her spokesmen are Lisa, the realist, and Nigel, the voyeur and busybody, who is not God.

26 KEMP, PETER. "The Flight against Fantasy: Iris Murdoch's The Red and the Green." Modern Fiction Studies 15 (Autumn):403-15.
    Considers The Red and the Green a departure, characters clustered around an event, rather than an idea. The work has great formal neatness, restricted in time, place, and characters. The family is a microcosm with their fighting mirroring the national fighting and with Barney learning to respect the otherness of his fellows, in his story of suffering and degradation, leading to resurrection and a new life. As a novelist Murdoch has a strong desire to shape reality into meaningful, beautiful designs. As a philosopher she distrusts substituting necessity for contingency. Her characters are symbols, representing some state of mind or ideology. She remains a considerable paradox, losing the fight against fantasy.

27 KENNEY, ALICE P. "The Mythic History of A Severed Head." Modern Fiction Studies 15 (Autumn):387-401.
    Declares that the mythological dimension of A Severed Head provides a wealth of imagery, a highly complex structure, and a means of viewing the past. Explains the historical references relevant to the names of Martin Lynch-Gibbon, Antonia, Alexander, Georgie Hands, Palmer Anderson, and Honor Klein. Martin finds his way to Sir James Frazer's Golden Bough, where he learns the relationship between fertility and human sacrifice. With Martin's connection to history and Honor's to mythology, they have no words in common until Martin tries to understand her in her terms. Honor, trying to learn Martin's language, quotes Herodotus. The essay explains connections to Celtic mythology including the severed head and the goddess Medb as an earth goddess. The novel uses history to illuminate contemporary events. Antonia and Alexander flee to the past and Palmer and Georgie to the future, while Martin and Honor live in the present.

28 KOGAN, PAULINE. "Beyond Solipsism to Irrationalism: A Study of Iris Murdoch's Novels." Literature and Ideology 2:47-69.
    Murdoch's characters propagate her irrationalist outlook, and her fictions indicate the serious deterioration of bourgeois literature in the twentieth

century. She denies the possibility of knowledge of
life, locates the sources of social evils in solipsism, and proposes an irrational theory of love to
release the decadent bourgeoisie from self-centered-
ness. Her characters live in a society that does not
affect them but that functions only as a locale.
Irrational and ritualistic premonitions and even
witchcraft appear frequently. Words connoting the
mysterious and unknown dominate her novels.
     Materialist philosophy believes that the aliena-
tion of labor is the basis of all other forms of
alienation. Murdoch perverts the historical concept
of alienation into a universal condition of man and
offers in her novels an apology for twentieth-century
capitalism.
     The love that Murdoch offers as the basis of the
discovery of reality is irrational, and it undermines
the historical knowledge of their situation that
human beings have gained with the help of scientific
knowledge. Her solution is valuable only for the
middle-class intelligentsia. It indicates the break-
down of nineteenth-cnetury liberalism. Murdoch
belongs to the strong idealistic tradition that
defends the status quo and glorifies irrationalism.
She is reactionary.

29 KUEHL, LINDA. "Iris Murdoch: The Novelist as
    Magician, the Magician as Artist." Modern Fiction
    Studies 15 (Autumn):347-60.
         An analysis that first treats Murdoch's Gothic
    effects, achieved by shock and insinuation, and sub-
    sequently treats Murdoch's characterization, charging
    that by the characters' eccentricity, they are part
    of an antirational argument about personality. Con-
    tends that the characters are dwarfed by the Gothic
    settings.

30 _____. Review of Bruno's Dream. Commonweal 90
    (28 March):52-53.
         Reviews Bruno's Dream as an undistinguished
    novel of ideas with characters who are too abstract
    and who talk too much about metaphysics. Perceives
    the novel to be unexciting.

31 McGINNIS, ROBERT M. "Murdoch's The Bell."
    Explicator 28 (September):1, 3.
         A comparison of The Bell with Gerhart Hauptmann's
    Die Versunkene Glocke, asserting that Murdoch borrow-
    ed images and details and her treatment of the bell
    as a shifting symbol. Declares that both works por-
    tray the interaction between pagan dissidents and a
    Christian community.

32 MARSH, PAMELA. "Lights in the Shadow." Christian
    Science Monitor, 23 January, p. 11.
        Review of Bruno's Dream that empahsizes its
    dreamlike qualities. Murdoch's characters have a
    Dickensian immediacy and her scenes can be uncannily
    vivid. Only much later do the pairings and repair-
    ings of her characters seem fantastically unlikely.

33 MURRAY, WILLIAM M. "A Note on the Iris Murdoch
    Manuscripts in the University of Iowa Libraries."
    Modern Fiction Studies 15 (Autumn):445-48.
        Description of the eight manuscripts of twelve
    novels of Murdoch held at the University of Iowa
    Library. There are two holograph manuscripts for
    each of the following fictions: Under the Net, The
    Bell, A Severed Head (play), An Unofficial Rose,
    The Unicorn, The Red and the Green, The Time of the
    Angels, and Bruno's Dream. The manuscripts are com-
    posed of notebooks with the text in longhand. The
    second draft is usually slightly revised.

34 NARITA, SEIJU. "Tokyo no Iris Murdoch." Eigo
    seinen (Rising generation) 115:218-19.
        Account of a visit by Iris Murdoch to Japan,
    including a reception in Tokyo, a lecture at Waseda
    University on freedom and virtue in modern literature,
    and another lecture in Kyoto. Murdoch said that art
    is meant to be entertaining, but it is also a means of
    searching for what is human. Literature unmasks the
    unconscious side of the human mind and tries to ex-
    plain it. There are two kinds of literature: the
    existential and the mystical. Murdoch categorizes
    Under the Net as existential, but mostly she is
    interested in the moment when reality and spirit meet,
    a concern of mystical literature.

35 "Notes on Current Books." Virginia Quarterly
    Review 45 (Summer):xcii.
        A review of Bruno's Dream that calls it a strong
    novel that the reader will lose himself in, commend-
    ing the powerful writing.

36 PORTER, RAYMOND J. "'Leitmotiv' in Iris Murdoch's
    Under the Net." Modern Fiction Studies 15 (Autumn):
    379-85.
        Under the Net is a Bildungsroman in which Jake
    wants to encounter the world and find himself. In
    the beginning Jake has no entangling relationships,
    hates contingency, and projects on his friends his
    inaccurate subjective vision of reality. Murdoch's
    use of leitmotiv in the novel--diction, image, symbol,
    and phrase--has not yet been explored. Especially
    significant is the motiv of enchantment and reflec-
    tion. Jake projects his subjective vision on Anna

and Hugo with words like spell and fairytale. The
motiv of reflection is announced by the leitmotivs in
terms of mirrors and water. Jake's changes involve
water, life, renewal, and the breaking and reforming
of patterns. Actions concerning rivers, night storms,
swimming, and surrendering to the water all express
Jake's renouncing his demand for necessity.

37 PRICE, MARTIN. "Reason and Its Alternatives: Some
    Recent Fiction." Yale Review 58 (March):464-74.
        A review of Bruno's Dream that applauds the comic
    tone and its great tenderness, saying that the gener-
    osity of the book almost does the work of love.

38 SCHLEUSSNER, BRUNO. Der neopikareske Roman:
    Pikareske Elemente in der Struktur moderner
    englischer Romane 1950-1960. Abhandlungen zur
    Kunst-, Musik- und Literaturwissenschaft, 61. Bonn:
    Bouvier, pp. 137-45.
        After discussing the Spanish picaresque novel,
    the study examines Hurry On Down, Lucky Jim, and Billy
    Liar as neopicaresque fiction. Then it discusses
    picaresque elements, ideas, and structures in Under
    the Net, Room at the Top, and Saturday Night and
    Sunday Morning.

39 "Spiders and Flies." Times Literary Supplement,
    16 January, p. 53.
        A review of Bruno's Dream that praises the depic-
    tion of the central figure, Bruno, and the unsentimen-
    tal treatment of his dying. Notes thrilling moments
    in the narrative and the tragicomic climax.

40 THOMSON, P.W. "Iris Murdoch's Honest Puppetry--The
    Characters of Bruno's Dream." Critical Quarterly
    11 (Autumn):277-83.
        The convention of Bruno's Dream is not realistic.
    Instead, the setpieces like the duel and Nigel's
    lucubrations are openly ritualistic. The ritual
    events are enclosed by the Eros-Thanatos myth. The
    relationships whose alterations constitute the
    apparent dramatic activity of the novel for the most
    part could be contained within the frame of psych-
    ological realism. The novel's central action is the
    discovery by the three widowers--Bruno, Danby, and
    Miles--of death and the accompanying rediscovery of
    love. It is, however, the unsatisfactoriness of
    Nigel and the isolation of his notional importance
    from any psychological context that underlines the
    novels's mythic frame. On the last page Diana reveals
    Nigel's impact on her. Nigel is the angel of Eros
    and Thanatos. He is the interpreter of Bruno's
    dream, the go-between carrying the transforming
    myth to the psychological world of social transactions.

41 TUBE, HENRY. "Women's Rites." Spectator 222
    (17 January):79-80.
        A review of Bruno's Dream, contending that Mur-
    doch has only two types of male characters and two
    types of female, which she uses again in this novel.
    Assesses Under the Net as her best novel.

42 WAIN, JOHN. "Women's Work." New York Review of
    Books 12 (24 April):38-40.
        Declares that one assents to Bruno's Dream as
    wisdom-literature for saying two things strongly:
    Intense suffering transforms people and prepares
    them for joy. Death strips away the confusions of
    life. Murdoch has affinities with someone like
    William Golding who also sees life in apocalyptic
    terms. Her vision is not frivolous, but some symbolic
    events and characters like Nigel do not fit well with
    solidly realized characters like Danby.

43 WASSON, RICHARD. "Notes on a New Sensibility."
    Partisan Review 36:460-77.
        Links Murdoch, with Robbe-Grillet, Barth, and
    Pynchon, as reacting against the modernist notions of
    metaphor as superational truth and of myth as a prin-
    ciple of order. "The Sublime and Beautiful Revisited"
    presents Murdoch's objection to the picture of man
    alone in the universe with his own consciousness.
    Robbe-Grillet rejects the world of nature, objects,
    and other people always appropriated to the subjec-
    tivity of the hero and the author. Barth's mytho-
    therapy suggests that if one turns life into a
    symbolic drama, one eliminates his sense of respon-
    sibility to others. Pynchon sees metaphor trans-
    forming the human into the animate.
        Contemporary writers seem to think that modern-
    ist literary concepts violate the indifferent nature
    of things and the unique otherness of separate
    people. Literary language should restore particulars
    and incompleteness, man coping spontaneously with
    contingency.

44 WEATHERHEAD, A.K. "Backgrounds with Figures in
    Iris Murdoch." Texas Studies in Literature and
    Language 10 (Winter):635-48.
        Sets out to describe the singularity of Murdoch's
    feeling for human nature and the peculiar use she
    makes of a person's environment. The paradigm behind
    the novels is that of a character entering into the
    orbit of an enchanter and then withdrawing. Often
    a background used for atmosphere has a grotesque or
    ironic tinge. A background can be given a life of
    its own or endowed with human qualities. Murdoch
    seems to see personality as residing partly in

people's physical environments. Sometimes an enchanted character responds to another's setting as Martin
Lynch-Gibbon falls for Georgie when he sees her bed.
A character in bad faith may think of another as
merely part of a setting. Clothes and even the body
may be thought of as an extension of the self.

45 WEEKS, EDWARD. Review of Bruno's Dream. Atlantic
    223 (February):129.
        Judges the novel to be dreary and disappointing,
    comparing it to The Nice and the Good, which was
    animated and gay.

46 WILLIAMS, DAVID. "New Novels." Punch, 15 January,
    p. 106.
        Review of Bruno's Dream as Murdoch's best since
    Under the Net, noting the formidable intelligence
    behind the extravagence of her work. She is strong
    in her belief in love.

1970

1   ANDERSON, THAYLE KERMIT. "Concepts of Love in the
    Novels of Iris Murdoch." Ph.D. dissertation,
    Purdue University, 223 pp. Abstract in DAI 31:
    5385A-86A.
        In Murdoch's essays she defined love as the
    difficult realization that something other than one-
    self is real. This definition, studied in the con-
    tex of her fiction, becomes persuasive. She presents
    a myriad of love relationships to emphasize that
    such attachments are as various as individuals are.
    Although her characters often fail in the difficult
    task of loving, Murdoch still retains a strong faith
    in the possibility of human love.

2   BALDANZA, FRANK. "The Murdoch Manuscripts at the
    University of Iowa: An Addendum." Modern Fiction
    Studies 16 (Summer):201-3.
        Brief note to correct two "misleading" statements
    in William M. Murray's bibliographic description of
    the Murdoch manuscripts at the University of Iowa in
    Murray's MFS 1969 article. Murray says that there
    are chapters in the second drafts of An Unofficial
    Rose and The Unicorn that are not in the first drafts.
    Baldanza says that material in the first drafts was
    rearranged into new chapters for the second drafts.
    The point for Baldanza is that Murdoch envisions most
    of her material in advance and seldom adds any large
    blocks of new material.

3   BERGONZI, BERNARD. The Situation of the Novel.
    London: Macmillan & Co., pp. 47-51, 75.

Discusses the concept of character that Murdoch in "Against Dryness" and John Bayley in The Characters of Love share. The great novels of the nineteenth century offer a full sense of the mysteriousness and uniqueness of the human personality. Since The Bell, Murdoch has, however, failed to put into practice these ideas about the primacy of character. Her later novels have become myths or fantasies in which the manipulative will of the writer subdues contingency.

Murdoch lacks the essential traits of sympathy, insight, and true imagination. Her characters relate to each other only in some complicated physical activity, some act of violence, or some arbitrary sexual encounter. Since 1961 Murdoch has made her ideas about the novel conform more to her own practice. In 1968 she affirmed the importance of a beautiful shape or form for a novel.

Bergonzi agrees with Bayley and Murdoch about the supremacy of character in the novel, but the human future may be anti-individual, collectivist, and totalitarian. The past idea of character may be lost.

4 BRONZWEAR, W.J.M. Tense in the Novel: An Investigation of Some Potentialities of Linguistic Criticism. Groningen, The Netherlands: Wolters-Nordhoff, pp. 81–116.

Linguistic analysis of The Italian Girl based on its use of tenses. The novel employs a number of devices to differentiate the character-I from the narrator-I. The narrator uses a straightforward tense-system with the present and perfect tenses referring to his present time frame, the preterite to his past time frame, and the pluperfect to his anterior past. The present tense is his zero tense. As soon as the narrator becomes involved in the action of the story, however, he becomes a character in it. This second I uses the preterite as his zero tense to refer to the present time frame. The novel is a study of the "I's" psychological and moral development. Besides tracing the use of tenses, this chapter also examines the use of the free indirect style and of certain lexical patterns that form associative fields.

5 CULLIGAN, GLENDY. Review of A Fairly Honourable Defeat. Saturday Review 53 (February 7):37–38.

Perceives in the novel a set of antitheses about love, commends the bold plot, and names the novel a dark comedy of manners. Discerns beneath the authentic surface a theorem, while comparing Murdoch to Euclid, Pascal, and Jane Austen.

6 "The Donkeys." Time 95 (9 March):69–70.

A review of A Fairly Honourable Defeat, asserting

that the novel moves from comedy through melodrama to
tragedy and that Murdoch is a moralist and a magician.

7 FAST, LAWRENCE EDGAR. "Self-Discovery in the Novels
   of Iris Murdoch." Ph.D. dissertation, University
   of Oregon, 232 pp. Abstract in DAI 31:5397A
      An examination of the process of self-discovery that
   illuminates the novels of Murdoch. The study includes
   thirteen novels, her philosophical essays, and criticism. The first two chapters describe the loss of
   self in modern literature, while the next four chapters concern themselves with Murdoch's concepts of
   freedom, love, and involvement as they relate to the
   process of self-discovery. For a person to find his
   true self, he must acknowledge others as independent
   individuals and must permit them to make their own
   decisions. He must also recognize and accept contingency. Individuals must escape the bonds of con-
   vention, the pleasures of fantasy, and the dreams of
   the past to confront the real world and discover
   themselves.

8 FIELD, J.C. "The Literary Scene: 1968-1970."
   Revue des langues vivantes 26:658-60.
      Reviews The Nice and the Good as curiously
   un-Murdochian with less obtrusive symbolism and a less
   contrived tangle of sexual relationships than usual.
   In the novel Murdoch achieves a new control with a
   diffusion of ideas through the action and an
   impressive thematic unity. She suggests that real
   evil is in our power to hurt both others and ourselves,
   not in black magic. Her characters are particularly
   striking, managed with no sense of authorial manipulation until the ending. John Ducane's sense of
   moral rectitude and his uneasy questioning of his role
   in life make him an effective focal point. The scene
   in the cave, however, is used as a crudely symbolic
   watershed. The strongest thing is the genre, an
   adventure story that includes the suicide and the
   scene of entrapment in the cave. Murdoch maintains
   suspense skillfully, presents cliff-hangers with
   panache, and cleverly switches from a climax in the
   suicide plot to the domesticity of the group in Dorset.
   She fuses her story and her philosophy extraordinarily
   well. The novel is entertaining and stimulating.

9 GRAY, PAUL EDWARD. "New Books in Review." Yale
   Review 60 (Autumn):102-3.
      A review of A Fairly Honourable Defeat that calls
   it witty and fascinating, but not one of Murdoch's
   best novels. Regards her as one of the most impressive contemporary novelists.

10 McDOWELL, FREDERICK P.W.   "Recent British Fiction:
    Some Established Writers." Contemporary Literature
    11:421-24.
        A review of Bruno's Dream, declaring it incisive,
    subtle, and persuasive. Contends that Murdoch drama-
    tizes ideas so that her novels are not usually
    allegorical but rather symbolic.

11 MACNIVEN, C.D. "Analytic and Existential Ethics."
    Dialogue 9 (June):1-19.
        Analyzes the encounter between existentialism
    and analytic moral philosophy by examining the
    writings of two critics of them, E.A. Gellner and
    Iris Murdoch. Both critics draw on existentialism to
    attack certain forms of analytic moral philosophy.
    In Sartre: Romantic Rationalist, Murdoch charges
    that analytic philosophy is dry and prosaic. She
    remarks on its lack of concern for the difficult moral
    problems that often confront the involved human being.
    Murdoch asserts that the analysts want to remain
    morally neutral, while Sartre desires to change the
    lives of his readers. Murdoch sympathizes with the
    particularist view of morality.
        Murdoch dramatizes most of these criticisms of
    analytic ethics in Under the Net. In the novel she
    has Jake criticize Dave Gellman, an academic linguis-
    tic analyst.
        In a talk, "Metaphysics and Ethics," Murdoch
    contends that existential and analytic philosophers
    both share the liberal viewpoint of extreme individ-
    ualism. There is some truth in Murdoch's claim. Her
    final criticism is that analytic moral philosophers
    have failed to produce a universal model of their
    own society's current morality, just liberal individ-
    ualism in a new guise. Murdoch attacks analytic
    moral philosophers because they haven't provided an
    analysis of moral language. They fail to consider
    that some moral differences are differences of con-
    cept as well as choice.
        Murdoch is probably right in suggesting that
    there are many affinities between Sartre's earlier
    existential and Hare's analytic ethics. The encount-
    er between analytic and existential ethics demon-
    strates that ethical theory is unavoidably bound up
    with our moral lives.

12 MUTIS, C. GUIDO. "El mundo arquetipico de Iris
    Murdoch: El viaje y el descenso al infierno en
    Flight from the Enchanter. Estudios filologicos
    6:229-89.
        Several of Murdoch's fictions use as structural
    background certain mythical plots like the journey
    and the descent into hell, which constitute an
    essential part in the life of the mythic hero. Such

mythic plots parallel the psychological process of
individuation. The Flight from the Enchanter is
structured around a series of dualities: light and
darkness, youth and age, masculine and feminine, good
and evil, human and animal, and fantasy and reality.
The final stages of the Return imply the reconciliation of opposites and the acceptance that the two
worlds (the infernal and the real) are two different
dimensions of the same reality. The novel centers
itself around the second mythic stage, the descent
into hell. Through the journey, the characters attain
a degree of freedom and individuation, which allows
them to accept reality with fewer distortions. In
order to maintain that grasp on reality, however, the
characters must continue to struggle.

13   PRITCHARD, WILLIAM H.   "Senses of Reality."
     Hudson Review 23 (Spring):162, 165-66.
        Reviews A Fairly Honorable Defeat as another of
     Murdoch's explorations into the complexities of love.
     Questions the reality of Julius as anything more than
     a sinister convenience with which to move around
     various other characters. Events are presented
     through the voice of a dead-pan omniscient narrator,
     not adequate to enlighten serious novelistic action.
     The serious ends to which the comedy is supposedly
     employed seem to be nonexistent.

14   RABINOVITZ, RUBIN.   "Iris Murdoch's Thirteenth
     Novel, about Evil."   New York Times Book Review,
     8 February, pp. 1, 28.
        A review of A Fairly Honourable Defeat that finds
     it enjoyable and interesting, pronouncing it an
     exploration of the problem of evil. Criticizes the
     lack of integration between the gloomy theme and the
     comic incidents.

15   "Re-Run for the Enchanter."   Times Literary Supple-
     ment, 29 January, p. 101.
        A review of A Fairly Honourable Defeat, assess-
     ing Julius as the least plausible character, lacking
     the density of Bruno in Bruno's Dream. Lauds the
     intelligent dialogue and the inventive story, but
     perceives the novel as academic, lacking feeling.

16   Review of A Fairly Honourable Defeat.   Choice 7
     (June):545.
        Highly recommends the novel as one of Murdoch's
     best performances. Sees in it her inventiveness, her
     Gothic imagination, and her gift for melodrama and
     suspense. She creates a world that becomes an effec-
     tive vehicle for her moral vision. Mentions some
     wildly contrived and comic scenes and some dialogue
     possessing philosophical subtlety.

17 REYNOLDS, STANLEY. "Artful Anarchy." <u>New Statesman</u>
    79 (30 January):157.
        A review of <u>A Fairly Honourable Defeat</u>, appreci-
    ating it as a funny, artful comedy once the reader is
    past the first twenty pages. Asserts that Murdoch
    mocks the privileged and pretentious.

18 RICKS, CHRISTOPHER. "Man Hunt." <u>New York Review
    of Books</u> 14 (23 April):37-39.
        Ten years ago Murdoch asserted the need for a
    reinstatement of character, but her advocacy remains
    advocacy. The whole novel here is redolent of
    puppet-mastery. Murdoch annually rewrites the same
    novel. She keeps saying "a sort of " like a nervous
    tic. The thinness of the minds and hearts of the
    characters in this novel results in an artistic
    thinness.

19 SULLIVAN, ZOHREH TAWAKULI. "Enchantment and the
    Demonic in the Novels of Iris Murdoch." Ph.D.
    dissertation, University of Illinois at Urbana-
    Champaign, 142 pp. Abstract in <u>DAI</u> 32:458A.
        Murdoch's novels demonstrate an interest in
    enchantment that progressively deepens into an obses-
    sion with the demonic. In <u>Under the Net</u>, man's
    unchecked fantasy creates illusory heroes and comic
    misunderstandings. In her later novels, it creates
    powerful manipulators and demons. The study treats
    in detail <u>The Flight from the Enchanter</u>, <u>The Unicorn</u>,
    and <u>The Time of the Angels</u>. Like the solipsistic
    existential hero, the demons begin as rebels desiring
    to be free from the real, messy modern world. Murdoch
    annually rewrites the same adventure of isolated
    romantic figures who pursue an unreal totality of
    form. The central claim is that Murdoch sees the
    demonic as an automatic result of conceptual and
    imaginative inadequacy in an age of power and solip-
    sism.

20 THOMAS, EDWARD. "Veteran Propellors." <u>London
    Magazine</u> 10 (April):100-3.
        Reviews <u>A Fairly Honourable Defeat</u>, noting con-
    ventions of Shakespeare plays and West End comedy.
    Murdoch examines people's feelings in a philosophical
    and not the more common psychological way. Discusses
    the success of Julius King in manipulating the other
    characters. In so far as they are puppets in their
    folly and vanity, they uphold a mechanistic psych-
    ology. In so far as they understand their experience
    and consciously strive for something better, they
    reaffirm the notion of the good.

21 VINCE, THOMAS L. Review of A Fairly Honourable
    Defeat. Best Sellers 30 (April):12-13.
        Labels the novel "a rare reading experience,"
    commending its excellent writing, witty repartee, and
    brisk plot. Declares that Murdoch's novels combat the
    aridity of most contemporary fiction.

22 ZIMMERMAN, PAUL D. "Poor Fools." Newsweek 75
    (16 February):100A
        A review of A Fairly Honourable Defeat that notes
    Murdoch's slashing irony, calling the book a tragedy
    of manners. Accuses her of sadistically destroying
    her characters.

1971

1 BERTHOFF, WARNER. "Fortunes of the Novel: Muriel
   Spark and Iris Murdoch." In Fiction and Events:
   Essays in Criticism and Literary History. New
   York: Dutton, pp. 118-54.
       Spark and Murdoch are two of the most admired
   and most productive of English novelists to appear
   since the 1950s. Each has created a substantial fictional world, recognizable from novel to novel. Each
   has helped keep the novel alive as a creative, serious
   form. Neither is likely, however, to transform the
   novel or alter consciousness to the same extent as
   Joyce or Faulkner. And neither will probably produce
   a masterpiece. Murdoch's emphasis is on the
   writer's persistence in her work rather than on the
   competition of masterpieces. She accepts Sartre's
   idea of a moral imperative at the heart of the artistic enterprise. Her complex stories concern such
   moral phenomena as love, intention, individuality,
   sincerity, and choice. Her characters face crises in
   which they act on wrong conceptions, see them shattered, and then revise and reform them.
       In the classic line of English moral fiction,
   her central subject is love and its shocks. The
   energy and self-assurance of her fictional world
   attest to her inclusion in the mainstream of literary
   history. Her philosophical ideas are ingenuously
   embodied in the train of events. In it the secrets
   of the moral life are disclosed by the complex
   language of movement. That movement finds its mirror
   image in the violence of surprise. reversal, and inward shock of the characters and their actions.

2 "Change of Life." Economist 241 (6 November):vi-
   vii.
       Suggests that Murdoch seems to be mellowing with
   her characters less bizarre and more recognizable as
   human beings. Formerly a teller of glittering fairy

tales with complicated sexual couplings, Murdoch late-
ly is more interested in the destructive facets of
human relationships. An Accidental Man is a study in
vampirism with only the teeth marks missing. In it
Austin is responsible directly or indirectly for five
of the seven deaths recounted. Murdoch shows the monster beneath the skin. As an interpreter of contemporary social issues (for instance, in Ludwig and his
surprisingly tough fiancée), Murdoch is a sizeable
class above Mary McCarthy.

3 COVENTRY, JOHN. Review of The Sovereignty of Good.
   Heythrop Journal 12 (April):202-3.
       Murdoch's essays are truly spiritual reading.
   She gives body to a true moral vision against the
   empty existentialist will in a world meaningful only
   to science or to a shrinking mind that would try to
   be authentic by looking mainly at itself. In art she
   discerns the discipline imposed on the human agent by
   the vision of the good. She explores the possibility
   of refusing the consolation of fantasy and having the
   strength to attend to reality with all its chance and
   mortality.

4 CUMMINGS, PHILIP W. Review of The Sovereignty of
   Good. Library Journal 96 (15 April):1372.
       Asserts that Murdoch seems to have gotten back
   to the ethical core of Plato's thought, with a gen-
   uine apprehension of the idea of the good, but complains of some obscurity and a view difficult to
   judge by modern standards.

5 DAWSON, S.W. "New Scrutinies, I: Iris Murdoch or,
   Anyone for Incest." Human World 2:57-61.
       Reviewers imply that in her novels Murdoch has
   thought of her characters carefully, but she has not
   been possessed by them. Her absorption in individual
   characters lacks creative enthusiasm. Nevertheless,
   Murdoch still gets substantial attention from the
   reviewers. Under the Net was a lively first novel with
   few pretensions, but her whimsical sentimentality
   reduces much of her writing to the level of the
   woman's magazine. The Bell displayed self-indulgence
   that is essentially sentimental. In The Red and the
   Green Murdoch manipulates her characters blatantly
   to fit in with her conceptual scheme. She fails in
   her attempts to suggest depths beyond the farcical.
   The Abbey in The Bell and Honor Klein in A Severed
   Head are contrived and boring symbols. Her novels
   have become a closed system, and her ideas do not
   touch our lives.

6 DOWNEY, Brother BERCHMANS. Review of The Sovereignty of Good. Best Sellers 31 (1 April):8-9.

Calls the book very thoughtful, criticizing the
existentialist-behaviorist look at mankind. States
that Murdoch connects freedom with clear vision with
man's effort to be loving and just.

7 GERMAN, HOWARD. "The Range of Allusions in the
   Novels of Iris Murdoch." Journal of Modern Literature 2 (September):57-85.
        Examines Murdoch's five novels from An Unofficial
   Rose to The Time of the Angels for covert allusions
   to other literary works and myths in details describing character, setting, or action. An Unofficial
   Rose contains allusions from the folklore of Northern
   Europe in references to elves, sprites, and fairy
   women. The references to myth and fantasy are rele-
   vant to the theme because the characters are depicted
   as creating fantasy worlds.
        The Unicorn contains allusions to La princesse
   de Cleves, Jocelyn Brooks's The Scapegoat, The
   Oresteia, and Sartre's The Flies. The novel also
   evokes the atmosphere of the Gothic novel, especially
   through the works of Sheridan Le Fanu.
        The Red and the Green draws heavily on the work
   of the Irish writers: George Moore, Oliver St. John
   Gogarty, James Joyce, W.B. Yeats, and Jonathan Swift.
   Most of the allusions to the works of Gogarty and
   Moore relate to the character Barney. The works of
   Yeats pervade the novel. Many of the animal images
   convey a repugnance to the body like that of Stephen
   Daedelus. Some details from Swift's Battle of the
   Books and his "On Madness" appear.
        The Time of the Angels contains allusions to the
   lives and works of André Gide, Graham Greene, and
   Vladimir Nabokov. The works of the Irish writers
   used in The Red and the Green seem to spill over into
   this later novel. When certain images reappear in
   several novels, they become enriched and more precisely defined.

8 GINDIN, JAMES. Harvest of a Quiet Eye: The Novel
   of Compassion. Bloomington: Indiana University
   Press, pp. 346-48.
        Examines Murdoch's work in relation to Gindin's
   "novel of compassion," a novel that achieves openness
   by destroying its own form in order to approach human
   experience more closely. In her work the fable is
   handled ironically, often ruining those who believe
   in it. In Murdoch's first four novels, the abstract
   pattern is shown to be foolish, and the characters
   are left in chaos. A Severed Head is even more skeptical. The characters create false gods out of the
   other characters and then are destroyed by their worship. In novels like The Unicorn and The Time of the
   Angels, Murdoch depicts the intrusion of the strange

and unknowable into human lives. A Fairly Honourable
Defeat shows that no generalization about humanity can
remain unchallenged for very long. The Nice and the
Good and Bruno's Dream employ highly sophisticated
articles and frequent ironies to reverse expectations.
It has become a means of confronting the complexities
of history and human relationships to play one character against another. Then the novels attack their
own premises and demolish rationality and conscious
control. Murdoch employs philosophical terms to demonstrate the inadequacies of abstract philosophy. In
her best work, the message struggles against the form,
and the mode is philosophical. Her less philosophical
novels are sentimental. She seems to need to undercut
philosophical structures to create strength and
excitement in her novels. Murdoch's fiction displays
an attitude of compassion.

9 GINDIN, JAMES. "Well beyond Laughter: Directions
   from Fifties' Comic Fictions." Studies in the Novel
   3:357-64.
      In the 1950s writers like Kingsley Amis, John
   Wain, John Braine, Keith Waterhouse, Iris Murdoch,
   Angus Wilson, and Alan Sillitoe were seen as a group
   involved in social protest. Actually, almost all of
   the fiction is comic, satirizing man's pretensions.
   The comic iconoclasm attacks social institutions as
   well as individuals. Frequently it reverses itself
   and affirms slightly insular localism. Murdoch and
   Angus Wilson depict their characters as unable to
   deal with all the complexities, enchantments, and
   international aspirations they can imagine and encounter. But both writers implicity endorse the
   resiliancy of the plain Englishman.
      Despite charges by critics that the British nov-
   elists of the Fifties refused to take literary risks,
   the novelists did experiment with form. Murdoch set
   up bizarre comic structures as mirrors of human effort
   that she then subverted. Her recent fiction combines
   comic fabrications with an ethical preoccupation.
   The Nice and the Good and Bruno's Dream still convey
   an iconoclastic attitude while they strive to define
   ethical good.

10 HOPE, FRANCIS. "Really Necessary?" New Statesman
    82 (22 October):561.
       Review of An Accidental Man that finds it cur-
    iously bloodless despite its arcane eventfulness.
    The characters seem to be there to illustrate the
    business of solving problems. Austin, the central
    figure, is an accident-prone person whose misfortunes
    substitute for strength and whose persistent helpless-
    ness becomes a purpose. His self-pity destroys others.
    However, the pure core of invention, not contrivance,

is missing. The novel presents oddly second-hand
observation and second-hand comedy in the passages of
party chatter.

11 "I'll Move Mine If You Move Yours." Times Literary
    Supplement, 22 October, p. 1305.
        Compares Murdoch's novels to a game of chess with
predetermined confrontations arranged in the variety
of possible combinations. An Accidental Man questions
the causality of human behavior, but in the end all of
the characters except perhaps Austin fulfill their
roles in the moral scheme. Murdoch teases the reader
with the possibility of chaos and free will, but she
reimposes the ordered destinies of the characters.
        It seems as if Matthew's ability to rescue the
accidental victims will break the spell of bad luck
or wickedness. Yet he is partly the cause of the
tragic happenings, and he refuses to love and be
involved. The apparatus of letters and quick fire
dialogue is sometimes glib and unsubtle. What redeems
Murdoch's novels is the sudden gleam of her philosopher's wit. She often, however, tantalizes the
characters and the reader with red herrings.

12 JANSING, GEORGE WILLIAM. "Iris Murdoch as a Moral-
    ist." M.A. thesis, University of Louisville, 100
    pp. Abstract in Masters Abstracts 10:76.
        Comparison of Murdoch's beliefs with those of
Jean Paul Sartre. For Sartre, the only real virtue is
sincerity. On the other hand, Murdoch believes in
moral progress through a loving respect for others.
Her characters achieve their existence through experi-
encing fundamental evil, resulting in an affirmation
of Platonic goodness.

13 KENNY, ANTHONY. "Luciferian Moralists." Listener
    85 (7 January):23.
        A review of The Sovereignty of Good, identifying
it as three essays pointing out wrong directions taken
by moral philosophy. Asserts that Murdoch uses Plato
as a corrective, affirming that moral activity is the
effort to conquer illusion and to apprehend reality.

14 ____. Review of The Sovereignty of Good over Other
    Concepts. Notes and Queries, n.s. 18 (October):
    389-90.
        Declares that Platonism in morals is not dead.
In The Sovereignty of Good, Murdoch argues that Plato's
theory of the Idea of Good in The Republic is a profoundly accurate metaphor. Like Plato, she believes
that the task of moral philosophy is to make us
better. The consummation of moral theory must be a
contemplation of the Good, an attempt to look away
from the self. She believes that value is discerned

by the attention of the purified intellect. Ignoring
this, contemporary moral philosophy has deified man in
the image of Milton's Lucifer. In her challenge to
other philosophers, Murdoch writes with sharpness and
lucidity and with a warmth and color rare in moral
philosophy.

15 KERMODE, FRANK. Modern Essays. London: Fontana,
      pp. 261-67.
        States that Murdoch's interesting views on what
novels should be like are hard to reconcile with the
novels she writes. Bruno's Dream, though, is perhaps
her best novel yet. Unlike her chosen model, Tolstoy,
Murdoch adores plot and patterns. Beneath the surface
of her novels are deep speculations about ethics,
language, fiction, and reality. In Bruno's Dream,
the pattern does not overwhelm the fiction. Instead
the ending is surprising but apt. Both Miles and
Nigel express the theme: the ability to deal with
necessity requires self-abnegation, seeing love as
death. But Nigel is a phoney, and Miles is unlovable.
A strength of the fiction is that Murdoch never
makes us see these old and aging people confronting
love and death as absurd. Instead, at the point of
death, the point of love is clear. The novel is entertaining and seriously intelligent.

16 KLEINIG, JOHN. Review of The Sovereignty of Good.
      Australasian Journal 49 (May):112.
        Asserts that the themes of the three essays over-
lap and it would be better to have a single, extended
essay. The essays lack clarity of expression and a
sight argument. Murdoch's endeavor is to present an
alternative to the image of man in the writings of
Hampshire, Ryle, Hare, and Ayer. The image they offer
is behaviorist in its connecting the meaning of action
with the publically observable. It is existentialist
in eliminating the substantial self and emphasizing
the solitary will. It is utilitarian in assuming
that morality is concerned with only public actions.
Instead morality is a matter of seeing things justly
and lovingly. The behaviorist-existentialist view
of man fails to come to grips with fallenness. The
final essay explores Plato's cave analogy and relates
various aspects of Good to it. The book draws attention to the paucity of much contemporary philosophy,
but it offers a highly idiosyncratic alternative.

17 LODGE, DAVID. The Novelist at the Crossroads and
      Other Essays on Fiction and Criticism. Ithaca,
      N.Y.: Cornell University Press, pp. 6-9.
        Discusses the possibility that the synthesis of
the novel between realism, romance, and allegory is
disintegrating, an allegation in Robert Schole's

The Fabulators (1967). Scholes holds up for admira-
tion Murdoch who has enjoyed a higher reputation
abroad than in England. Scholes interprets The
Unicorn as an elaborate and multifaceted allegory in
Gothic terms about the conflict of secular and religious attitudes. Reading The Unicorn following
Schole's interpretation, one understands more clearly
what Murdoch was up to. Scholes does not, however,
convince Lodge that the ideas, or the melodramatic
plot, or the process of abstracting the ideas from
the plot yield any great pleasure or instruction.

18 MARTZ, LOUIS. "Iris Murdoch: The London Novels."
    In Twentieth Century Literature in Retrospect.
    Edited by Reuben A. Brower. Cambridge, Mass.:
    Harvard University Press, pp. 65-86.
       Contends that in her London novels Murdoch is
the most important heir to the Dickens tradition.
The Dickensian use of London scenes that marked
Murdoch's first novel was not a dominant feature in
the next nine, but in the last three and especially
in Bruno's Dream and A Fairly Honourable Defeat the
Dickensian vein has strongly reemerged. Both writers
employ a great particularity of detail because they
present so many of their London characters as inseparable from the London setting. Murdoch's London
novels grow a deep, instinctive affection for the
London setting, and that affection for man's habita-
tion derives from the theme of love, the redemptive
element in the novels.
       In Under the Net, Jake misunderstands all the
human characters, but he is rooted, and he can finally
perceive the truth about himself. In Bruno's Dream,
Diana's new grasp of particulars at the end signifies
that she is rescued from her barren existence by her
affectionate care of Bruno, redeemed in Danby's house,
in Bruno's room, in Bruno's dream. That other people
exist must arise from a recognition that our surround-
ings consist primarily of other men, a basic theme of
Murdoch's. Murdoch has established herself as the
most significant novelist now in England.

19 "Paying Attention." Times Literary Supplement, 26
    February, p. 241.
       Reviews The Sovereignty of Good as brilliantly
perceptive and expressed in memorable phrases. Yet
at points the reader is baffled. The three papers
support each other well. The main theme--that we
need to cultivate an awareness of others and of the
world around us--is timely. We tend to live in
selfish fantasy. The corrective, which is a vision of
things as they really are, can be found in great art,
especially in great literature.

Murdoch, however, discounts the need for effort
and a disciplined will. Also her adaptation of religious notions like transcendence and grace are of
doubtful value. She is a much better preacher than a
philosopher or a novelist.

20 PEREZ-MINIK, DOMINGO. "Amigos y amantes, la comedia
    y la metafisca de Iris Murdoch." Insula 26 (Feb-
    ruary):6.
        The Nice and the Good is a simple narrative with
    the intrigue of Restoration drama. It is easy read-
    ing, not needing any metaphysical background. The
    characters are ordinary middle-class people who ex-
    change sexual partners without their marriages suffer-
    ing. The novel is entertaining without any grandiose
    pretensions.

21 ROME, M.R. "A Respect for the Contingent: A Study
    of Iris Murdoch's Novel The Red and the Green."
    English Studies in Africa 14:87-98.
        Asserts that in The Red and the Green, Murdoch
    successfully combines the seemingly incompatible tech-
    niques of naturalism and allegory, capturing the indi-
    vidual. The physical atmosphere is evoked in two
    ways: in the naturalistic description of Dublin and
    in the presence of the two women, Frances and Millie.
    Although Frances is the structural and thematic pivot
    of the novel, we look into her mind and heart only at
    the end. In contrast, the anarchic Millie typifies
    everything wrong with Ireland. Between Frances's and
    Millie's standards of moral conduct are placed three
    men--Andrew, Patrick, and Barney--all searching for
    identity. Their stories, although told in a natural-
    istic manner, form part of the allegorical pattern.
    Their personal agony is echoed in the struggle of
    Ireland against England. Ireland is a microcosm of
    the world.

22 SALE, RICHARD B. "An Interview in New York with
    Walter Allen." Studies in the Novel 3 (Winter):
    405-29.
        A discussion with Allen on the contemporary
    British comic novel, with Allen deploring Murdoch's
    repetition of the same pattern in her novels. Con-
    tends that her novels move from formal comedy to
    mystery at the end. States that Murdoch has the eye
    of a novelist.

23 SHEED, WILFRID, ed. "Iris Murdoch: The Red and
    the Green." In The Morning After: Selected Essays
    and Reviews. New York: Farrar, Straus, & Giroux,
    pp. 286-98.
        Criticizes Murdoch as a permanently promising
    writer who delivers a little less each time. Her new

book is a serious attempt to write a public novel,
but these Anglo-Irish are the same emotional acrobats,
redefining themselves with a freedom that doesn't
arise for most people. Her preoccupation with family
relationships including incest is a metaphor for a
congealed society where a small group conspires to
act as if nobody else existed. The labels attached
to Murdoch's novels--intellectual, witty, cold, and
unreal--have been attached to other Irish outsiders
from Swift to Shaw and Wilde.

24 STINSON, JOHN JEROME. "The Uses of the Grotesque
and Other Modes of Distortion: Philosophy and
Implications in the Novels of Iris Murdoch, William
Golding, Anthony Burgess, and J.P. Donleavy." Ph.D.
dissertation, New York University, 283 pp. Abstract
in DAI 32:1533A
Each of the four writers has a strong tendency
toward grotesque forms including fantasy and mixed
modes. All employ the grotesque as a radical critique
of some form of excessive or naively inadequate
rationalism. They use it to protest against various
dehumanizing forces that deny the emotional and spiritual components in man. The study analyzes at some
length Murdoch's theory of the formal and the contingent.

25 "This Week." Christian Century 88 (31 March):410.
A review of The Sovereignty of Good that says it
presents Murdoch as the philosopher, rather than the
novelist, discussing love of the good.

26 VICKERY, JOHN B. "The Dilemmas of Language:
Sartre's La nausée and Iris Murdoch's Under the Net."
Journal of Narrative Technique 1 (May):69-76.
The modern philosophic novel is epistemic, problematic, and ironic. Two highly instructive examples
of the contemporary novel are La nausée and Under the
Net. Both raise important questions. Under the Net
reads like a commentary on La nausée, dramatising the
inadequacies of Sartre's argument about the nature of
existence and the individual.
The two novels use a first-person narrator. They
each include a hero who is a reluctant questioner of
reality and a heroine who combines enigma and wisdom.
Both use music as the hero's temptation to transcendence. Both employ the ordinary man's discovery of
the relevance of philosophical thinking to his life.
The two novels focus on the issue of the philos-
ophizing activity itself, the nature of human nature,
and the redefinition of language. It is through the
interaction of these three motifs that the dilemma
of language emerges as the controlling existential
and aesthetic problem in both Sartre and Murdoch.

Both seize the same theme--man's raising of philosophical questions as the result of his personal
experiences--but they elaborate it in radically different ways.
In the two novels, the characters, themes, and
actions of the plots all assist in the redefinition
of language. When Roquentin and Jake become disen-
chanted with history and translation and aspire to
literature, they portray their consciousness of the
importance of language itself. Both also realize,
however, the uncertainty and instability of language.

27 WARNOCK, G.J. "The Moralists: Values and Choices."
    Encounter 36 (April):81-84.
         A review of The Sovereignty of Good that notes
Murdoch's criticism of the romantic picture of modern man at the center of a valueless world. Contends
that Murdoch's idea of Good, like Plato's, may need
some metaphysical scaffolding.

1972

1 ADELMAN, IRVING, and RITA DWORKIN. The Contemporary Novel: A Checklist of Critical Literature on
   the British and American Novel since 1945.
   Meutchen, N.J.: Scarecrow Press, pp. 376-85.
        General criticism and then criticism about spe-
cific novels from Under the Net (1954) to The Nice
and the Good (1968), but not including criticism on
Bruno's Dream (1968). Not annotated.

2 AVANT, JOHN ALFRED. Review of An Accidental Man.
   Library Journal 97 (15 January):215.
        Calls the novel a disappointment because of the
worthless characters with no possibility of redemp-
tion. Describes the novel as small and cruel.

3 BELL, PEARL K. "In a Tangle of Crashing Symbols."
   Christian Science Monitor, 27 January, p. 10.
        Reviews An Accidental Man as oddly wearying
because Murdoch has done this better several times
before. The characters are an incongruous group of
Londoners who are either related to or pathologically
dependent on one another. Matthew is the part-sinis-
ter, part-godlike enchanter figure. Though he means
to be a healer, he sets off a chain reaction of
suicide attempts, accidental death, broken engagements,
failed promises, and musical beds. The message of the
novel is that men cling to the illusion of free will
in the face of an ethically neutral destiny, but Murdoch fails to dramatize the thesis adequately. The
compassion and wit of her past novels depicting the
complexities of love are missing.

4 BORKLUND, ELMER. "Iris Murdoch." In Contemporary
   Novelists. Edited by James Vinson. New York:
   St. Martin's Press; London: St. James Press, pp.
   911-15.
        Biographical information, bibliography, and essay
   of critical interpretation, primarily in terms of her
   intellectual position. Murdoch's activity as a novelist reflects an implied criticism of the limits of
   philosophical discourse. At the center of her work is
   a pessimism. She accepts the definition of man as an
   accidental creature adrift in a contingent universe.
   Her persistent concern is the nature of ethical behavior.
        In the novels an archetypal plot is at work in
   which a character is forced by some violent or irrational event to realize his lack of freedom and his
   ability to know or to love. The complexities of the
   plots usually spring from Murdoch's surrounding the
   central action of discovery with a host of comic or
   serious variations in which the other characters
   learn or fail to learn the same lesson.
        The ending of Under the Net illustrates the par-
   ticular attractiveness of Murdoch's best work, a kind
   of joyous acceptance of things as they are. The Bell,
   perhaps the finest of her novels, traces the disintegrating relationships among characters who seek a
   retreat from human frailty. Their failures involve a
   failure to love. A Severed Head is a splendid comic
   version of the quest for liberation and maturity.
   Murdoch and Angus Wilson are the most accomplished
   British novelists to come to maturity since the close
   of World War II.

5 "Briefly Noted: Fiction." New Yorker 47 (12 February):102.
        A review of An Accidental Man that sees in it
   extremes and very little middle ground. Compares
   Murdoch's puzzles to Kierkegaard's.

6 BROYARD, ANATOLE. "Adding Quiddity to Oddity."
   New York Times, 18 January, p. 29.
        Declares that in An Accidental Man Murdoch has
   reformed from being a metaphysical practical joker.
   Her characters still behave oddly but for better
   reasons. She puts her characters in extreme situations because only in them can people be jolted into
   extreme action. She has found a natural way to poise
   her characters on the brink of that predicament.
   Murdoch has become a complete novelist. She knows
   exactly how to dramatize this thinking, to make the
   words flesh.

7 BUFKIN, E.C. "Book Reviews." Georgia Review 26
   (Spring):103-5.
        A review of The Nice and the Good, remarking on
   the splendid scenes and Murdoch's exuberant invention
   and identifying the action as several characters
   trying to free themselves from constricting love
   relationships.

8 CLEMONS, WALTER. "Booby Traps." Newsweek 79 (24
   January):68, 72, 72A.
        A review of An Accidental Man that describes
   Murdoch's comic vision as unnerving and calls Austin
   the least likely hero, who copes with change and
   contingency, while continuing to be an unrepentant
   swine.

9 COOKE, MICHAEL. "New Books in Review." Yale Review
   61 (June):599.
        Reviews An Accidental Man, criticizing it for
   lacking substantive action and characters who care
   about doing and being. Instead finds the world of the
   novel too concerned with language, with explanations
   and analysis.

10 DEGNAN, JAMES P. "Fiction Chronicle." Hudson
    Review, pp. 334-35.
        Reviews An Accidental Man as competent, readable,
    and funny but not up to the author's best. The novel
    is an ambitious one that contains some splendid
    writing, but Murdoch's narrative method has the story
    told from too many points of view. There is a good
    deal of needless repetition, and at times her charac-
    ters all begin to sound the same. Her powers of
    description are as devastating as ever. Her talent
    for creating brilliantly comic conversations combines
    perfectly the absurd and the realistic.

11 D., M. "Little England." Time 99 (7 February):7,
    86.
        A review of An Accidental Man praising Gracie as
    a realized character and praising the suspense
    created by cutting from one character to another.
    Asserts that the novel puts on display smug Britishers.

12 GOSHGARIAN, GARY. "From Fable to Flesh: A Study
    of the Female Characters in the Novels of Iris
    Murdoch." Ph.D. dissertation, University of Wis-
    consin, 354 pp. Abstract in DAI 33:3583.
        Murdoch satirizes the false mystique of woman-
    hood. She creates male characters who hold inflated
    images of the women they adore. These inflated images
    presuppose the opposite view of women as possessions.
    The novels exhibit some feminist values and attitudes.
    In the early novels, the few female characters fail

because they are too heavily weighted with symbolic
meaning. In the later novels, they are presented more
realistically as moral agents parallel to the men.
Murdoch also becomes less contemptuous of her male
characters. The study closely analyzes six novels to
show the changes in the treatment of the female characters.

13 GRIFFIN, JAMES. "The Fat Ego." Essays in Criticism
    22 (January):74-83.
        Reviews The Sovereignty of Good, saying that it
makes clearer Murdoch's conception of the kinship
between art and moral philosophy. She believes very
strongly, however, in a mystical monism, and at
points her language becomes very abstract.
        Murdoch thinks that the chief enemy in morality
is personal fantasy. The enemy is "the fat relentless
ego." We can penetrate the obscurity of other persons
only by the exercise of attention, a just and loving
gaze at reality. It is doubtful, however, that true
vision always leads to right conduct. We may be able
to see the reality of someone and still not love him.
The failure of my treating other people's interests
equally with my own may stem from selfishness.
        Much of what Murdoch says about arts seems un-
deniable. Good art brings us into contact with
something outside ourselves. But she also says that
good art helps us pierce the veil that the ego casts
over the world. If all good art puts us in contact
with the world, how does Murdoch account for nonrep-
resentational art? Murdoch's thesis about art needs
restrictions and qualifications.

14 GUNTON, COLIN. Review of The Sovereignty of Good.
    Religious Studies 8 (June):180-81.
        States that one persistent theme of the book is
an attack on philosophers who see the moral person as
just an autonomous choosing will. Kantians come
under relentless fire. The reader wonders why such
a one-sided view of man ever became accepted. Murdoch
avoids the pitfall of reductionism. The detailed
argument begins convincingly but trails off into
vagueness.
        When it comes to a description of the reality of
which the moral agent attends, the account is less
satisfactory. Murdoch becomes mystical in her
search for a new naturalism. The Good is there, but
access to it is through the insights of intellect
and imagination, especially through art.

15 HAUERWAS, STANLEY. "The Significance of Vision:
    Toward an Aesthetic Ethic." Studies in Religion
    2 (Summer):36-49.
        Critical analysis of the philosophical ethics of

Murdoch to emphasize the importance of vision for the
moral life and the inadequacy of the image of man as
self-creator. By making man's will the source of all
value, we have turned away from the classical insights
of philosophy and Christianity. Murdoch explores our
using past formulations of the truth as a defense
against the constant struggle to perceive the living
truth. She will put her own philosophy into the mouth
of a character so that it becomes false in that particular context. For Murdoch, most of our loving is
not a recognition of the other, but an assertion of
self, imposing our own preconceived image of him on
the beloved. Men differ not just by their choices
but because they see different worlds based on their
individual experiences. Virtue is the self's cor-
responding to reality. Murdoch believes that transcendence becomes possible as we see and affirm the
contingency of our lives. We must center our attention on the Good to overcome our subjectivity.

Love is the difficult recognition that something
other than ourselves is real. The beginning of the
moral life may be the recognition of an inanimate
object in all its particular detail because it turns
our vision outward. Murdoch's novels are full of
realistic descriptions of places and nature because
to notice the beauty of everyday things is important
to moral experience. Art can enlarge the consciousness and enliven the imagination by drawing us away
from self-absorption. The artist at work is the
paradigm of the moral man who lovingly lets others
exist through him.

What is the significance of Murdoch's thought
for Christian ethical reflection? When the Christian
life is understood as the life of attention, the
emphasis is placed squarely on the everyday. The
moral significance of our lives depends on our willingness to work at being human through the particularity
of our lives.

16 HEBBLETHWAITE, PETER. "Feuerbach's Ladder: Leszek
    Kolalowski and Iris Murdoch." <u>Heythrop Journal</u>
    13 (April):143-61.
        Much of contemporary theology is a continuing
    debate with Feuerbach, who provided a powerful
    attack on Christianity, suggesting that the idea of
    God is only the projection of man's ideal. Feuerbach's
    ladder is the idea of God, reason, and man as three
    stages of human thought. In <u>The Sovereignty of Good</u>,
    Murdoch sees that a way to deal with real problems is
    to reinvigorate some important theological concepts,
    such as fallenness. She aims to broaden our moral
    vocabulary to achieve a more accurate picture of man.
    She also stresses attention as a way to combat the
    assertiveness of the self. Attention to the Good leads

away from fantasy toward a more realistic assessment
of the world. Murdoch is one of the heirs of Feuerbach in her illuminating exposition of secularized
religious concepts.

17 HERBERT, HUGH. "The Iris Problem." <u>Manchester
    Guardian</u>, 24 October, p. 10.
        Interview with Murdoch at the opening of her play
<u>The Three Arrows</u> at the Cambridge Arts Theatre. She
says that if there's anything wrong with the play, the
fault will be in the text, not the production. She
has been cutting some of the political meditation
from the text. The play concerns the nature of
power and sovereignty, the hierarchial system and
freedom.
        Murdoch says that the difference between writing
novels and plays is similar to that between painting
in oils and watercolors. With a novel, you can
deepen it, brighten it, change the characters. With
a play, you have to block it all in very quickly and
have to get the structure right from the start.
        Murdoch says that she would like to change the
novel's heavy dependence on a protagonist. She is
constantly trying to expel the center, but it drags
everything in towards it. She would like to write a
novel in which the peripheral characters carry the
story. She says that being a novelist is the lone-
liest art.

18 HILL, W.B. "Fiction." <u>America</u> 126 (20 May):549.
        A review of <u>An Accidental Man</u> that finds the
profusion of characters well portrayed and the ending reflecting T.S. Eliot's influence.

19 HIRSCH, FOSTER. "Ruled by Some, Not Benign."
    <u>Nation</u> 215 (24 July):59-60.
        Calls <u>An Accidental Man</u> a grimly ironic account
of the entangled histories of a large and bumbling
cast of characters. A cosy familiarity is the source
of the novel's uninsistent charm. As an arbiter of
destiny, Matthew fails in his two grand schemes: to
destroy his brother Austin and to claim as his own
Ludwig Leferrier. The characters are paired off in
other sibling hostilities for tidy thematic doubling.
They all enact recurring patterns of betrayal. Murdoch's cruel sense of humor protects the characters
from our sympathy. Particularly successful are the
exchange of letters and the party scenes of uniden-
tified speakers. The characters are rooted in the
ordinary as social beings, and they are plagued by
metaphysical anxiety about their lives. At the brisk
comic level, Murdoch is a perceptive observer of
universal human insecurities.

20 HOLBROOK, DAVID. "The Charming Hate of Iris Mur-
    doch." In The Masks of Hate. Oxford: Pergamon
    Press, pp. 147-58.
       Discusses The Flight from the Enchanter as man-
    ifesting the nihilistic and schizoid modes Murdoch
    takes from European culture. Like Kingsley Amis and
    Ian Fleming, she shows no feeling for human inner
    realities and no symbolic depth. Murdoch's novels
    stir one's primitive anxieties and unconscious hate.
    Rosa's relationship with the two Polish characters is
    an example of the multiple object phantasy found in
    clinical histories, caused by a fear of relationships.
    We can also find an infantile preoccupation with the
    primal sex scene and the imago of the castrating
    mother. Murdoch's books, consciously or unconsciously,
    are based on violence and hatred of human nature. Her
    play on primitive hate suggests a distrust of and
    denial of feeling.

21 HOSKINS, ROBERT. "Iris Murdoch's Midsummer Night-
    mare." Twentieth Century Literature 18 (July):
    191-98.
       Asserts that several of Murdoch's later novels,
    including The Nice and the Good and An Unofficial
    Rose, abound with references to Shakespeare. Her
    technique of allusion has apparently changed. A
    Fairly Honourable Defeat has extended parallels with
    A Midsummer Night's Dream. Julius King mirrors
    Oberon who stages a little drama involving two vic-
    tims who are made to believe they love each other.
    Murdoch's technique is parody-inversion. It is
    serious parody because the sustained parallels are
    employed in a tragic rather than a comic structure.
    It is inversion because the moral structure implicit
    in a stable world is turned upside-down.
       Murdoch uses A Midsummer Night's Dream to
    underscore the importance of the collapse of spiritual
    authority and social structure by depicting it in
    terms of the fall of an epic world. Through her
    ironic comparison, she dramatizes effectively the
    loss of stable moral referents.

22 KANE, PATRICIA. "The Furnishings of a Marriage:
    An Aspect of Characterization in Iris Murdoch's
    A Severed Head." Notes on Contemporary Literature
    2:4-5.
       An analysis of Martin's compulsive naming of his
    furniture with the implication that he cares more
    about objects than people, a behavior that changes
    whn Martin meets Honor Klein.

23 KARL, FREDERICK R. A Reader's Guide to the Contem-
    porary English Novel. Rev. ed. New York: Farrar,
    Strauss, & Giroux, pp. 260-65, 338-43.

Extends Karl's 1962 discussion with a "Postscript 1960-1970." Murdoch's achievement remains puzzling despite her productivity. She is adroit at social comedy, at witty dialogue, and at suggesting existential situations for ordinary people. She displays a kind of puppet show for our amusement, based on existential concepts of freedom and necessity. But styles clash, and something is distorted. She uses fastidious controlled language to present sordid actions. Murdoch's most meaningful novels are A Severed Head, An Unofficial Rose, and The Unicorn, in which she combines symbol or myth with intellectual discussions of freedom and bedroom farce.

24 KEATES, LOIS SILVER. "Varieties of the Quest-Myth in the Early Novels of Iris Murdoch." Ph.D. dissertation, University of Pennsylvania, 323 pp. Abstract in DAI 33:1730A.
Murdoch attacks the use of myth in the modern novel, saying that real people destroy myth, but her own early works are romances. Her novels depict the point at which one's beliefs and feelings are seen to be discontinuous with the self. For Joseph Campbell this is the beginning of the quest. For Northrop Frye it is a theme of the ironic mode. The influence of the religious existentialists on Murdoch strengthens her use of the "double reality" principle, which is central to the quest myth: the realm of the gods parallel to the realm of men. The examination of Murdoch's novels shows that the modern hero can achieve selfhood in harmony with the outside world if he invokes the old mythic patterns. Her novels are ironic fables that organize existence to portray the process of rebirth.

25 KENNEDY, EILEEN. Review of An Accidental Man. Best Sellers 31 (1 March):530.
Reviews the novel, criticizing the plot and narrative technique but commending the intellectual energy and the probing of moral stances. Names Murdoch a significant comic novelist.

26 KERMODE, FRANK. "The British Novel Lives." Atlantic 230(July):85-88.
Contends that much that seems to be wrong with the contemporary British novel is really wrong with the publishing trade and the general literature scene. Reviews An Accidental Man as perfectly readable as fun, as a plot game, as a virtuoso exposition, and more. Compared to Muriel Spark, Murdoch is more ready to think with the story and to use its many-layered complexities as an instrument of discovery. The ethical issue--of what stands in for God who used to oversee ethical contracts--is embedded in a great

tangle of plot. Austin is a destroyer and exploiter; his brother Matthew is kind and solves people's problems. The two represent the ambiguities of spirit in the modern world. In contrast, Gracie's family has no spiritual dimension. The novel announces in its incompleteness the imperfection of a search into necessity and grace.

27   LEMON, LEE. "Some English Fiction." Prairie Schooner 46 (Fall):266-67.
     Assesses An Accidental Man as one of Murdoch's most complex novels in the variety of character relationships but also as one of her least profound. Austin, the accidental man, is a walking disaster, brooding masochistically on his misfortunes. The chapters of letters and conversations from different points of view that interrupt the narrative are technically interesting. The brittle wit is fun to read, but the novel goes on for too long.

28   LERNER, LAURENCE. "Metaphysick." Encounter 38 (June):73-74.
     A review of An Accidental Man, accusing it of pretentiousness but praising Murdoch's technique, including an ingenious plot and lively dialogue. Credits her with being not boring.

29   MAJDIAK, DANIEL. "Romanticism in the Aesthetics of Iris Murdoch." Texas Studies in Literature and Language 14:359-75.
     Essay that describes the ways in which Murdoch's concern with the influence of Romanticism is reflected in her aesthetics and that analyzes two of her novels--The Time of the Angels and The Bell--to see how this concern is reflected in her art. Murdoch believes that the modern image of man is usually a Romantic Kantian one, an image derived from Milton's Lucifer in his assertion of freedom and his will to power. The picture of the eternally suffering rebel was used to change the idea of death into the idea of suffering. She wants to revitalize Coleridge's distinction between imagination and fantasy. Imagination is sympathetic, able to see the reality of others. She believes that we must expand the sympathies of the imagination and abandon the Romantic quest for unity.
     Two of Murdoch's most successful novels--The Time of the Angels and The Bell--demonstrate the influence of Romanticism on her. The two special aspects of Romanticism incorporated are the connection between sex and spirituality in Romantic thinking and the idea that transcendence of Romantic dilemmas may be achieved through the improvement of Romantic insights. In The Time of the Angels Carel is Murdoch's

most extreme example of the ambiguity of the spiritual world. In The Bell, character and symbol are
kept in proper relation. In attending to Romanticism,
Murdoch rejects much of it, but she has absorbed much
as well.

30 MALLET, GINA. Review of An Accidental Man. Satur-
    day Review 55 (29 January):68
        Reviews the novel as a collection of bizarre
    incidents that overwhelm the characters, for whom
    Murdoch seems to feel distaste. Asserts that the
    menace is cumbersomely rendered.

31 MANO, K. KEITH. "Enormous Trifles." National
    Review 24 (14 April):408-9.
        Review of An Accidental Man that sees it as
    comedy seeded with unfortunate events and accidents,
    swirling around the accidental man, Austin. The
    novel is an extensive and unfairly weighted indictment
    against the free will theory. The funniest things in
    it are the sets of party dialogue in which ideas and
    opinions fade and pop up again recostumed. The
    novel should have been shorter with fewer characters.

32 MILLER, KARL. "The Sisterhood." New York Review
    of Books 18 (20 April):19-20.
        States that An Accidental Man involves a welter of
    loves, bereavements, and troubles affecting an assort-
    ment of decayed gentlefolk. Finds it hard to grieve for
    the characters as much as they grieve for themselves.
    Combined with the comedy is a theology lesson on the way
    decisions are validated. The number of calamities and
    the flow of abstractions make the book seem callous.

33 "Notes on Current Books." Virginia Quarterly
    Review 48 (Summer):c.
        A review of An Accidental Man stating that it
    alternates philosophical musing with party chatter,
    expressing a vision of randomness. Calls the novel
    Murdoch's wittiest since Under the Net.

34 OATES, JOYCE CAROL. "So Many People!" Chicago
    Tribune Book World, 23 January, p. 3.
        Asserts that An Accidental Man would have been
    a suspenseful and entertaining novel if it had not
    been stretched out to such lengths. The fictional
    world is doomed by too much magic and talk and too
    many haphazard loves. Murdoch invents more characters
    than she has interest in. The reader grows less
    enchanted with each novel.

35 OSTERMANN, ROBERT. "Religion Gets Its Lumps in
    An Accidental Man." National Observer, 12 February,
    p. 23.

Reviews the novel first as a criticism of traditional organized religion. States that Murdoch portrays man especially here as a fascinating enigma.
Asserts that she stimulates and provokes the reader.

36 Review of An Accidental Man. Choice 9 (April):215.
Judges that Murdoch's largest novel to date is
not up to par. It lacks the wit of her earlier novels. The device of letters catching us up on the
current moods of her cast is unconvincing. Still
libraries should have a complete set of Murdoch's
works.

37 SAYRE, NORA. "A Poet's Journal, a Strange Western,
a Novel of Quest, a Philosopher's Fantasy." New
York Times Book Review, 23 January, pp. 7, 10.
A review of An Accidental Man that characterizes
Murdoch's continuing theme to be the idea that no
one is necessary to anyone else. Calls this novel
better written than many of her novels and lauds
Murdoch's dramatic visual images.

38 WATRIN, JANY. "Iris Murdoch's A Fairly Honourable
Defeat." Revue des langues vivantes 38:46-64.
An interpretation that applies Murdoch's ideas
from "The Sublime and the Beautiful Revisited" and
"Against Dryness" to her practice in A Fairly Honourable Defeat. Judges it to be an effective blend of
formalism and naturalism, treating its few characters
in depth.

39 WOLF, NANCY CONNORS. "Philosophical Ambivalence in
the Novels of Iris Murdoch." Ph.D. dissertation,
University of Connecticut, 214 pp. Abstract in
DAI 33:2959A.
The purpose is to inquire whether Murdoch's
theory of the autonomy of personality is seriously at
odds with the dark comedy she writes. The study
identifies three groups of novels. The first, social
novels of sensibility, are books that fulfill the
moral and aesthetic demands she sets down for the
density of human experience. The novels of sensibility include lesser books, too, without the scope of
coherence of the larger novels. A second group is
the comedies of moral education in which the first-
person narrators suffer a comic initiation into a new
state of awareness. In the third group, the severely
ironic tales, the characters suffer demoralization
and confusion. Three novels are chosen for close
reading: The Italian Girl, The Red and the Green,
and The Time of the Angels.

1973

1 AMIS, MARTIN. "Alas, Poor Bradley." New Statesman
  85 (23 February):278-79.
    Reviews The Black Prince as an attempt to synthe-
  size Murdoch's earlier existential style with her
  later allegorizing style. While Bradley presents his
  love as an escape into life, he remains a man who
  lives by words. The editor presents the postscripts,
  which distort the narrative and accuse it of distortion. Murdoch is distancing herself from her work
  with the artifice of the surrounding framework.

2 ARNAN, GABRIELE. "Hamlet on the Central Line."
  Listener 89 (22 February):249-51.
    Asserts that the story of The Black Prince is
  ambiguous and somewhat tortuously told. The editor's
  foreword is part of the novel, which is a novel about
  a novel, and a posthumous autobiographical one. From
  this trompe-l'oeil frame, Bradley pops out now and
  then to comment directly to Loxias on the other characters, the story, the way it is written, novel writing in general, art, the creative process, love,
  mysticism, and religion. The chief clue is the title:
  Hamlet is the black prince. Loxias--Apollo, another
  black prince--presides over the creative struggle,
  which is what the book is about. This novel is Murdoch's most inventive and involuted exercise. La
  Rochefoucauld hovers like another dark presence over
  her tragicomic dissection of the human condition.
  Murdoch's attitudes are not very Anglo-Saxon.

3 AVANT, JOHN ALFRED. Review of The Black Prince.
  Library Journal 98 (1 June):1844.
    Reviews the novel as amazingly satisfying, warmer
  and richer than Murdoch's previous fictions, with a
  remarkable thematic interplay.

4 BALDANZA, FRANK. "The Manuscript of Iris Murdoch's
  A Severed Head." Journal of Modern Literature 3
  (February):75-90.
    The manuscripts of A Severed Head give an inti-
  mate view of Murdoch's writing process. She makes
  few major changes once the first draft is underway.
  She usually writes two drafts, sometimes preceded by
  working notes and tables of contents with one sen-
  tence chapter summaries.
    Although the finished draft of the novel is set
  in London, the early setting was largely in the country. At an early stage, Murdoch meant to include a
  brother of Georgie Hands and some other minor characters. There are fewer abandoned plot ideas. Baldanza then discusses symbolic and thematic material,
  some used in the final version, and some abandoned.

5   BRADBURY, MALCOLM.   "'A House Fit for Free Charac-
    ters': Iris Murdoch and Under the Net." In Possibil-
    ities: Essays on the State of the Novel. London:
    Oxford University Press, 1973.
        Since Under the Net, Murdoch has been recognized
    as one of the most brilliant and intelligent of the
    British novelists. The novel with its picaresque
    structure is a superb exercise in male impersonation
    with its outsider hero, Jake. The novel presents a
    sharp, accurate sense of contemporary life and a
    knowledgeable account of London.
        Murdoch is prolific, producing a distinctive
    version of the novel of sentiments that incorporate
    unusual metaphysical and emotional speculation. The
    idea of love as a mysterious apprehension of the other
    is the context for her rococo plots with their power
    figures and bewildered followers. A difficulty in
    Murdoch's novels concerns her view of reality and
    character in fiction. Sometimes by reality she seems
    to mean a sense of density and social texture and
    sometimes a sense of otherness or mystery. Her anti-
    symbolist theory means to protect individuality or
    character in fiction.
        The Red and the Green roots its characters in a
    dense, contingent society and personal milieu. But
    the coincidence of four central male figures going to
    see Millie on the same night creates a certain kind
    of stylish classic farce. Distillation is part of
    the method of the novel, and Millie is a charismatic
    agent involved in the idea of culmination.

6   BROMWICH, DAVID.   Review of The Black Prince.
    Commentary 56 (September):88-90.
        Reviews the novel, questioning the antagonism
    against Murdoch's work, calling it a philosophical
    conversation. Compares Murdoch favorably to Doris
    Lessing and Vladimir Nabokov. Commends the complex
    imagination of The Black Prince.

7   CLEMONS, WALTER.   "Writers, Lovers, Killers."
    Newsweek 81 (18 June):99, 102.
        A review of The Black Prince, saying that Murdoch
    has got it all together in her best novel since
    The Bell. Calls it an entertaining dark comedy, re-
    flecting her philosophical and moral concerns.

8   DRESCHER, HORST W., and BERND KAHRMANN.   The Con-
    temporary English Novel: An Annotated Bibliography
    of Secondary Sources. Frankfurt am Main: Anthenaum-
    Verlag, pp. 135-47.
        Attempts to mirror international research on the
    contemporary English novel from 1954 to the 1979s with
    a substantial entry on criticism of Murdoch's novels.

9 DUECK, JACK. "Uses of the Picaresque. A Study of
   Five Modern British Novels." Ph.D. dissertation,
   University of Notre Dame, 142 pp. Abstract in DAI
   34:4255A.
        Study demonstrates that the picaresque novel is
   a viable vehicle for some modern British novelists.
   These modern novels depict picaresque chaos in the
   contemporary scene and use picaresque elements to
   illustrate an alternate reality. Hurry on Down,
   Lucky Jim, Under the Net, Herself Surprised, and
   Murphy are examined as picaresque. Under the Net
   portrays a picaresque world at first and then intro-
   duces an alternate vision, creating a dialectic
   between the two modes. It combines features of the
   Bildungsroman with those of the picaresque. It
   presents a substantially reflective hero with a picaresque plot, combined with philosophical themes. The
   novel works with the oppositions of imagination and
   fantasy, communion and detachment, creative love and
   nets, the reality of others and romantic sincerity,
   and miracle and fracture.

10 FRASER, KENNEDY. "Ordinary Human Jumble." New
   Yorker 49 (30 July):69-71.
        A review of The Black Prince that complains that
   Bradley and the commentators at the end all write in
   Murdoch's quirky style. Uneasy that she resolves
   moral problems by jokes and grotesque accidents.

11 GILLIGAN, JOHN T. "The Fiction and Philosophy of
   Iris Murdoch." Ph.D. dissertation, University of
   Wisconsin-Milwaukee, 347 pp. Abstract in DAI 35:
   1099-1100A
        Analysis of the evolution of Murdoch's thought
   and techniques within the context of her art and
   philosophy. The first chapter discusses her criticism
   of contemporary moral philosophy and outlines her
   synthesis of morality and art. The next chapters
   trace the evolution of some of her major themes--power
   and freedom, Eros and Thanatos, and art and morality
   synthesized through love. They examine her use of the
   techniques of irony and pathos, melodrama and farce,
   and comedy and terror. Murdoch's early novels explore
   ideas of Jean-Paul Sartre, Friedrich Nietzsche, Ludwig Wittgenstein, and Sigmund Freud. Later novels
   use religious metaphors in the Gothic mode. Her
   latest novels combine a neo-Platonic Good with a
   naturalistic point of view on art. She uses the figure of the loving artist as hero. Her novels have a
   strong mimetic strain that produces a realistic atmosphere with surrealistic intensity. Murdoch uses
   coincidence and contrivance with highly imaginative
   and gripping taletelling. Her novels embody a tension
   between naturalistic detail and philosophical fantasy.

12   GORDON, JAN B.   Review of The Black Prince.
     Commonweal 99 (14 December):300-1.
         Reviews the novel as questioning history itself,
     comparing it to Gide's The Counterfeiters and Barth's
     The Sotweed Factor.   Calls The Black Prince a dis-
     tinguished work.

13   GOSHGARIAN, GARY.   "Book Briefings."   Christian
     Science Monitor, 27 June, p. 9.
         Asserts that The Black Prince is Murdoch's most
     compassionate study of the hazards of human love.   As
     a writer, self-absorbed Bradley has two fundamental
     problems: he has nothing to write about, no love,
     ecstasy, ordeals, or suffering.   And other people
     suddenly intrude on his life.   Bradley's love for
     Julian teaches him that art needs experience to be
     meaningful.   The reader is encouraged to play detec-
     tive and reevaluate Bradley's interpretation of his
     story.   The novel is dazzling, perhaps Murdoch's best.
     It is inventive, witty, and elegant.   What makes the
     novel a major accomplishment is its clear perception
     of characters who are trying to perceive each other.
     The characters are fascinating and free.

14   GRAVER, LAWRENCE.   "A New Novel by Bradley Pearson
     (his last) in a New Novel by Iris Murdoch (one of
     her best)."   New York Times Book Review, 3 June,
     pp. 1, 12, 14.
         A review of The Black Prince, judging it Murdoch's
     best novel in years, for making plot and symbolism be
     more closely a function of character.   Calls the novel
     an "epistemological detective story."

15   "Hitlerian Parallels."   Times Literary Supplement,
     23 November, p. 1418.
         A review of "The Three Arrows" and "The Servants
     and the Snow" that calls the plays novice work, too
     didactic, with The Three Arrows a better play for its
     humor.

16   HOPE, FRANCIS.   "Strange and Unnatural."   Observer,
     25 February, p. 36.
         Declares that The Black Prince is pretentious, a
     strange mixture of slick plotting, intellectual weight,
     and swooming adjectives.   Murdoch has never been so
     grim and savage in the portrayal and in the fates of
     her characters.   The novel moves too slowly, and it
     is decked out with ambiguous artifice like the post-
     scripts.   Yet the writer's passion for passion and its
     numinous power for good and evil come through, along
     with the violence of marriage and the thin crust
     between everyday life and the appalling flames below.

17 "Letting Others Be." Times Literary Supplement, 23
    February, p. 197.
        A review of The Black Prince that sees in it
    Murdoch grappling with her crucial questions and
    casting them in a remarkable fictional form, questions
    about art and the moral life. States that the novel
    asks is Bradley another "Accidental Man" or an
    artist?

18 LINDROTH, JAMES R. Review of The Black Prince.
    America 129 (1 September):130-31.
        Reviews the novel as another achievement by one
    of Britain's most impressive writers, one with closely
    crafted point of view. Identifies the theme as the
    sin of solipsism, with the wicked ignoring the results
    of their actions.

19 LURIE, ALISON. "Wise-Women." New York Review of
    Books 20 (14 June):18-19.
        States that The Black Prince is a very good book,
    serious and funny. But it does not seem to be taking
    place in the modern world. The form of the book with
    its forewords and postscripts seems old-fashioned,
    and the style seems Edwardian. Much of what Murdoch
    has to say about writing, art, sexual love, and
    human psychology is perceptive. But the book is a
    romantic melodrama. In important ways Murdoch's
    novels are less serious than those of Doris Lessing.

20 MADDOCKS, MELVIN. "Wild Minuet." Time 101 (18
    June):84.
        A review of The Black Prince that lauds it for
    conveying the immediate texture of being in love.
    Asserts that the novel brings Murdoch's fiction to
    a high point, exploring connections between art, love,
    and death.

21 "Notes on Current Books." Virginia Quarterly Review
    49 (Autumn):cxxxvi-cxxxvii.
        Reviews The Black Prince as a fitting vehicle for
    Murdoch's concern about the interrelationships be-
    tween art and life. Names Bradley her most fully
    realized character and identifies the novel as Mur-
    doch's celebration of Shakespeare, Hamlet, and love.

22 OSTERMANN, ROBERT. "Life Entangles, Imprisons a
    Writer in Search of Truth and a Masterpiece."
    National Observer, 21 July, p. 25.
        A review of The Black Prince, comparing it to
    "The Turn of the Screw" for its shocking climactic
    scene. Sees erotic love as fate upsetting the orderly
    patterns of the characters' lives. The novel is en-
    grossing.

23 PALMER, HELEN, and ANNE JANE DYSON. English Novel
    Explication: Criticism to 1972. Metuchen, N.J.:
    Scarecrow Press, pp. 211-19.
        Notes criticism on twelve of Murdoch's novels
    from Under the Net (1954) to Bruno's Dream and The
    Nice and the Good (1968). Not annotated.

24 PRICE, MARTIN. "New Books in Review." Yale Review
    63 (October):80.
        A review of The Black Prince that finds it artful
    and humane, noting the powerful portrayal of Bradley's
    transformation. Remarks that Bradley is both seen
    through and seen with.

25 RABAN, JONATHAN. "Books and Writers." Encounter
    40 (May):84-85.
        A review of The Black Prince, commending it as
    depiction of evil, executed by Murdoch with relish.
    Describes the novel as ambitious enough to afford
    its failures.

26 RAYNOR, VIVIEN. "Something Keeps One Reading."
    Washington Post Book World, 17 June, pp. 4-5.
        Reviews The Black Prince and complains of its
    Restoration plot and artificial quality, while con-
    tending that Bradley's passion is convincing.

27 Review of The Black Prince. Choice 10 (September):
    1981.
        Judges the last novel to be one of Murdoch's
    best, containing the usual dollops of sex, passion,
    and violence mixed in with disquisitions on meta-
    physics and aesthetics. The work is serious and
    amusing.

28 "Rich Bitches." Economist 246 (10 March):118.
        A review of The Black Prince, calling it a good
    yarn and Murdoch an elegant writer. Asserts that it
    distinguishes between a woman dependent on her husband
    and one with money of her own, in a funny social
    fable.

29 SWINDEN, PATRICK. Unofficial Selves: Character
    in the Novel from Dickens to the Present Day.
    New York: Harper & Row, pp. 247-56.
        Declares that Murdoch's highly patterned, sophis-
    ticated novels give us a renewed sense of the dif-
    ficulty and complexity of the moral life. Her critics
    emphasize her remarks on character and ignore her
    points about the enrichment of moral concepts. Few
    of her characters are opaque or seem mysteriously
    alive and free. Instead her plots are the principal
    means by which Murdoch communicates her ideas about
    freedom, reality, truth, and goodness. She manipulates

concepts so that the reader may understand the mystery
and opacity of persons. The idea that dominates the
novels is the final fallibility of concepts. Characters are repeatedly discovered transforming reality
into fantasy.
     In her novels, patterns are made up of actions,
not motives or intentions, actions that create their
own connections. The disjunction between intention
and the effects of actions derives from Murdoch's
skepticism about patterns. At the center of each
novel, a character discovers his identity and the
artificiality of plots and roles. The reader is led
to move from the action to the characters, not, as is
more usual, the other way around. The characters may
not find a pattern in which they comfortably fit or
discover the shape of their lives.

30 WEEKS, EDWARD. "The Peripatetic Reviewer."
    Atlantic 232 (July):101-2.
         Reviews The Black Prince, focusing on the critic-
    al friendship between the two authors Bradley Pearson
    and Arnold Baffin. When Bradley falls in love with
    Julian, his behavior is as brilliantly characterized
    as is his envious antagonism for her father. The two
    men are superbly drawn and when they berate each
    other, their talk crackles. How Bradley gets into
    prison is one of Murdoch's most readable and ingen-
    ious stories.

31 WILEY, PAUL. The British Novel: Conrad to the
    Present. Northbrook, Ill.: AHM Publishing, pp.
    88-90.
         Bibliography of Murdoch's texts, bibliographies,
    critical and biographical books, and selected critical
    essays about Murdoch's works, with the essays cited
    mainly concerning Under the Net and The Bell.

                              1974

1   ACKROYD, PETER. "Iris Is No Pupil." Spectator,
    23 March, pp. 363-64.
         Reviews The Sacred and Profane Love Machine,
    calling it too stylish for a cautionary tale. Compli-
    ments Murdoch's descriptions, not her dialogue, and
    praises her rendering of the reality of passion by
    indirection.

2   ALLEN, DIOGENES. "Two Experiences of Existence:
    Jean Paul Sartre and Iris Murdoch." International
    Philosophical Quarterly 14 (June):181-87.
         Comparison of Roquentin's nausea at tree roots
    in Sartre's La nausée with Effingham Cooper's blessing
    of the world in Murdoch's The Unicorn, seeing it as

a counterscene and an answer to Gabriel Marcel's
question: "Why does Sartre find the contingent over-
abundance of the world nauseating rather than glor-
ious?" For Sartre, fluid man seeks completeness and
is threatened by the contingency of things. For
Murdoch, stable but egotistical man distorts things
until he can give up his desire to control them,
possibly like Cooper in the face of death. Prefers
Murdoch's presentation of the problem.

3 AMIS, MARTIN. "Queasy Rider." New Statesman 87
   (22 March):414.
        Censures the drawn-out scenesetting in The
   Sacred and Profane Love Machine and the melodramatic
   ending. Complains about Murdoch's elevation of profane love. Charges that the novel lacks a verbal
   center of gravity, that Murdoch's prose is careless,
   and that the novel is overextended. Calls for Murdoch
   to write less and find out how good she is.

4 ASHDOWN, ELLEN ABERNETHY. "Form and Myth in Three
   Novels by Iris Murdoch: The Flight from the
   Enchanter, The Bell, and A Severed Head." Ph.D.
   dissertation, University of Florida, 186 pp.
   Abstract in DAI 35:5334.
        The study examines the relation of form and myth-
   ology in three of Murdoch's novels. In her essays,
   Murdoch sees myth as antagonistic to the life she
   wants to create in fiction. But according to Joseph
   Campbells' creative mythology, myth can be a liber-
   ating form that encompasses life fully. Actually,
   Murdoch's novels use myth pervasively. Because she
   sees life as continuous process, she fears that too
   much form will stultify that process. But form itself
   can be seen as an expression of the rhythm of creation
   and destruction. Mythology gives fiction immediate
   contact with awesome spiritual energy.

5 BALDANZA, FRANK. Iris Murdoch. New York: Twayne
   Publishers, 189 pp.
        Overview of Murdoch's novels from Under the Net
   to The Black Prince that sees her "transcendental
   realism" concerned primarily with the concepts of
   love, power, and freedom.
        Baldanza traces Murdoch's use of the artist-saint
   dichotomy in several novels and her use of the alien-
   god figure. He discusses her development as an artist
   and her changing thematic emphases. Although he
   surveys her essays in aesthetics and ethics, he does
   not treat Sartre: Romantic Rationalist. He concludes
   that astonishingly productive, Murdoch ranks among
   the top five British novelists of the day. She is
   reviving the traditional realistic novel with its

elaborated social context, intricate plotting, and
fully realized characters, despite her natural tendency toward the crystalline allegory. In her novels,
she achieves wonder and mystery through rich fantasy,
emerging out of the realistic context.

6   BETSKY, CELIA. Review of The Sacred and Profane
    Love Machine. New Republic 171 (14 September):28-
    29.
        Finds the novel very human in contrast to earlier
    overcerebral ones. Perceives Murdoch working with
    doubleness, opposites, and ambiguity, noting the
    frightening dream lives of the characters. Senses a
    criticism of British middle-class life and the theme
    of people learning through insecurity, shock, and
    violence.

7   COOPER, SUSAN. "Fiction: Vintage, Intricate Mur-
    doch." Christian Science Monitor, 23 October, p. 13.
        Review of The Sacred and Profane Love Machine,
    commending its technical skill and its compelling
    characters. Regards Murdoch as better than most cur-
    rent novelists but misses in this book her ability to
    engage the reader's subconscious.

8   C.,W. Review of The Sacred and Profane Love Machine.
    Newsweek 84 (11 November):1200-21.
        Calls tricky the novel's premise--a psychologist
    with a double life. Judges the novel not as enter-
    taining as usual but very acute about the selfish
    demands of supposedly selfless lovers.

9   DICK, BERNARD F. "The Annual Murdoch." Sewanee
    Review, Fall, pp. xc-xcii.
        Views the subject of The Sacred and Profane Love
    Machine to be a typical but diverting Murdoch subject:
    the mating dance. Asserts that she is using myth to
    portray the irrational. Characterizes the novels as
    fictions of comic existentialism, pushing the phil-
    osophy to its limits.

10 DOHERTY, PAUL C. "The Year's Best in Paperbacks,"
    America 130 (9 February):93.
        Briefly reviews A Fairly Honourable Defeat,
    praising it and noting the irony of Alex, the most
    intelligent and charitable character, having to hide
    his feelings.

11 DRABBLE, MRAGARET. "Gothic Hollywood." Listener
    91 (17 January):89.
        Review of The Servants and the Snow and The
    Three Arrows, two of Murdoch's plays, as missing the
    complexity and density of her novels. Recognizes

her familiar themes on a smaller scale. Declares that
her scenic effects work better in her novels than in
theatrical sets.

12 FALLOWELL, DUNCAN. "Plotting the Emotional Course."
    Books and Bookmen 19 (June):85.
        Criticizes The Sacred and Profane Love Machine as
    superficial, like a well-crafted television series or
    a paperback thriller. Accuses Murdoch of writing too
    much and too frequently.

13 "First Books of Christmas." Book World, 8 December,
    p. 1.
        Brief review of The Sacred and Profane Love
    Machine, noting the intricacy and ambiguity of the
    relationships and the question of which loves are
    sacred.

14 GAILEY, PAUL. "Naming Love." Manchester Guardian
    Weekly, 6 April, p. 22.
        Calls The Sacred and Profane Love Machine sur-
    prising and interesting, remarking on the stylized
    talk and the sense of performance and artifice.
    Extols Murdoch's "mordant observations" on human folly.

15 GOSHGARIAN, GARY, "Feminist Values in the Novels of
    Iris Murdoch." Revue des langues vivantes (Brussels)
    40:519-27, 597.
        Discovers a strong feminist attitude in Murdoch's
    fiction in her critique of male fantasies and romantic
    projections about women, turning them into objects
    and into the extremes of lowly creatures or exalted
    mystic beings. Applies Murdoch's ideas from "Against
    Dryness" and Sartre: Romantic Rationalist. Analyzes
    male characters who deform female characters by fan-
    tasy, including Cooper in The Unicorn, Mor in The
    Sandcastle, Martin in A Severed Head, Miles in Bruno's
    Dream, and Randall in An Unofficial Rose. Judges the
    male characters to be solipsistic, denying female
    reality.

16 GRIGSON, GEOFFREY. "A Captured Unicorn." In The
    Contrary View: Glimpses of Fudge and Gold. London:
    Macmillan Press; Totowa, N.J.: Rowman & Littlefield,
    pp. 30-33.
        Scathing general denunciation, discussing the
    symbol of the unicorn and accusing Murdoch's characters
    of being like Disney cartoons, jerkily animated. Con-
    siders her fiction to be histrionic and vulgar, fudge
    not gold.

17 HENDERSON, GLORIA ANN MASON. "Dionysus and Apollo:
    Iris Murdoch and Love." Ph.D. dissertation, Georgia
    State University, 235 pp. Abstract in DAI 36:902A.

Murdoch describes love as a central element in art and in moral philosophy. Love is the main theme in her novels. This study examines her statements about love and then studies the love relationships in the novels, focusing on the progress from Dionysian to Apollonian love and the increase in lasting love relationships. It analyzes three novels to see the Dionysian aspects of love: The Bell, The Unicorn, and and The Time of the Angels. They demonstrate the failure of characters to attain lasting love and the destructive power of love not tempered with reason. In the novels published from 1968 to 1974, at least one love relationship in each promises to last. The Dionysian element is, however, still strong. The Apollonian element is particularly emphasized in The Black Prince with P. Loxias as the final love of Pearson.

18 HILL, WILLIAM B. Review of The Sacred and Profane Love Machine. America 131 (16 November):301.
     Briefly reviews the novel, lauding Murdoch's singular genius, especially in the development of minor characters.

19 "In a Recognizable World." Times Literary Supplement, 22 March, p. 281.
     Review of The Sacred and Profane Love Machine, rating it much below The Black Prince. Asserts that the novel concerns irreconcilable desires and the possibility of renouncing desire. Calls the author imaginative and gifted, stimulating readers' minds with her provocative ideas.

20 LEHMANN-HAUPT, CHRISTOPHER. "Another Iris Murdoch Machine." New York Times, 19 September, p. 41.
     Calls The Sacred and Profane Love Machine an absurdly symmetrical machine, working with Freudian-like dreams and classical allusions. Finds the purpose difficult to express but concludes that the novel works.

21 LEMON, LEE T. "All You Need Is What?" Prairie Schooner 48 (Winter):366-67.
     Judges The Sacred and Profane Love Machine to be deeply moving, with complex characters having plausible emotions, each character motivated by different kinds of love.

22 MELLORS, JOHN. "Ladies Only." London Magazine, June-July, pp. 135-39.
     Review of The Sacred and Profane Love Machine as a magnificent novel, praising Murdoch's descriptions of setting and her vigorous narrative, packed with

moral observations and insightful paradoxes. Compares her to Dickens for her individual set of novels and her creation of eccentric characters.

23 O'HARA, T. Review of The Sacred and Profane Love Machine. Best Sellers 34 (1 October):297-98.
     Asserts that Murdoch is displaying the foibles of the British upper-middle class with eccentric touches. Calls this novel her most impressive since The Flight from the Enchanter, dramatizing the clash between instinctive and civilized behavior in a philosophical, psychological, mythic thriller.

24 OSTERMANN, ROBERT. "Drama Created for the Mind's Eye." National Observer, 13 July, p. 19.
     Review of The Three Arrows and The Servants and the Snow, suggesting that Murdoch is an accomplished writer in any form with her authority and intelligence. Asserts that her subject matter is language, revealing the vitality of words.

25 RABAN, JONATHAN. "Lullabies for a Sleeping Giant." Encounter 43 (July):73-75.
     Praises Murdoch's easy, natural writing, her formidable intelligence, and her fertile imagination in a review of The Sacred and Profane Love Machine. Appreciates the mirroring and doubling, the symmetries and divisions. Discusses the relation of Titian's "Sacred and Profane Love," a puzzle painting, to the novel. Sees an opposition between the importance of convention and the chaotic mess of existence. Defends Murdoch's style as having unexpected weight in context, reflecting people's scruffy lives.

26 Review of The Sacred and Profane Love Machine. Booklist 71 (1 December):367.
     Mentions the complicated plots and authorial detachment and the dualistic imagery.

27 Review of The Sacred and Profane Love Machine. Economist 251 (13 April):73.
     Compares the novel negatively to The Black Prince, calling it melodramatic but entertaining.

28 Review of The Sacred and Profane Love Machine. Kirkus Review 42 (15 July):761.
     Contends that the novel is minor Murdoch, dealing with an interrelated group of characters who are not as moral as they seem or as didactic as they sometimes sound. The characters trespass on our patience without incurring our sympathy in Murdoch's usual clever fashion.

29 Review of The Sacred and Profane Love Machine.
    New York Times Book Review, 1 December, p. 70.
        Brief mention of the novel, naming Murdoch a
    major writer and the subject a man torn by desire and
    duty.

30 Review of "The Three Arrows" and "The Servant and
    the Snow." Choice 11 (July-August):762.
        Thinks The Three Arrows the more successful play
    but sees them both as convincing microcosms of the
    corrupting effects of power.

31 SALE, ROGER. "Winter's Tales." New York Review of
    Books 21 (12 December):18, 22.
        Evaluates The Sacred and Profane Love Machine as
    a dreadful mess, despite some fine scenes. Character-
    izes the cast as kinky misfits and the last half as
    long and boring.

32 SCHNEIDERMEYER, WILMA FAYE. "The Religious Dimen-
    sion in the Works of Iris Murdoch." Ph.D. disserta-
    tion, University of Southern California, 204 pp.
    Abstract in DAI 35:3113A.
        In the Sovereignty of Good, Murdoch posits ration-
    al principles, which finally, however, appeal to the
    Good, a transcendent idea. Her idea of the Good
    functions much like a religious ideal. Religious
    aspects of her thought pervade all of her novels.
    This study examines the theme of suffering as a source
    of moral refinement in The Bell, An Accidental Man,
    The Unicorn, and Bruno's Dream. Enlightenment through
    suffering is a way to counteract illusion and an
    egotistical view of the world.
        Murdoch depicts art as a spiritual activity in
    Under the Net, The Sandcastle, Bruno's Dream, and
    The Black Prince. Art is fundamental to the moral
    life because it instructs us in how to picture the
    human situation. In three other novels, Murdoch por-
    trays the process of moral enlightenment: An Unoffic-
    ial Rose, The Time of the Angels, and The Nice and the
    Good. Central to her portrayal of good people is
    their devotion to moral ideas and their capacity to
    love.

33 SKOW, JOHN. "Uncouples." Time 104 (23 September):
    97-98.
        Review of The Sacred and Profane Love Machine,
    comparing it to a Victorian tale of morality, a blend
    of soap opera and farce. Declares that the book
    explores the mechanistic side of love.

34 STUBBS, PATRICIA. "Two Contemporary Views on Fic-
    tion: Iris Murdoch and Muriel Spark." English
    23 (Autumn):102-10.

Compares Murdoch's and Spark's attitudes to fiction, finding both to have tension between their fictional ideals and their natural tendencies, their ideals reinforcing their weaknesses. Declares that Murdoch's central concern is with the writer recording truth but reports her work criticized for unreality. Notes her opposition to crystalline fiction but her attraction to myth, rather than to stories of obstreporous "real" characters, and simple experience. Asserts that writing novels of character, Murdoch's writing is strained and tense.

35 THWAITE, ANTHONY. "Chapter of Accidents." Observer, 24 March, p. 39.
    Commends the verve and fluency of The Sacred and Profane Love Machine, calling it readable, funny at times, and somewhat absurd.

36 VAIZEY, JOHN. "A Sense of Doom." Listener 91 (21 March):379-80.
    Reviews The Sacred and Profane Love Machine, perceiving as interesting the concern with the supernatural and the mythic and the attention to moral questions. Sees an opposition between the world of dreams and the world of surfaces, each vying for importance.

37 WAIN, JOHN. "Iris Murdoch Novel about One Man and Two Women." New York Times Book Review, 22 September, pp. 1-2.
    Recommends The Sacred and Profane Love Machine, saying that Murdoch makes an old subject seem fresh in her compassionate view. Lauds her deep analysis of character.

38 WEEKS, EDWARD. Review of The Sacred and Profane Love Machine. Atlantic Monthly, November, p. 120-22.
    Describes Murdoch as original, skilled at portraying a strained domestic situation, here creating vivid, fresh characters.

1975

1 ACKROYD, PETER. "On Top of the World." Spectator 234 (26 April):514.
   Review of A Word Child that characterizes it as melodrama at its best or fable, rather than realistic fiction. Praises its social humor and exact descriptions but criticizes it wordiness.

2 ADAMS, PHOEBE. "Short Reviews." Atlantic 236 (September):85.

Calls A Word Child a superior novel, elegant,
witty, and amazingly believable.

3 ALLEN, BRUCE. "Fragments of Truth." Saturday
   Review 2 (9 August):40-41.
        Finds A Word Child to be densely woven and dra-
   matic with suggestive symbols woven into the action.
   Sees the novel as criticizing the worship of the individual.

4 BANNON, BARBARA. "PW Forecasts." Publishers
   Weekly 207 (16 June):73.
        A brief review that declares Murdoch's irony
   brilliant, acclaiming the evocation of the London
   setting, in A Word Child.

5 BELLAMY, MICHAEL O'NEIL. "The Artist and the Saint:
   An Approach to the Aesthetics and the Ethics of Iris
   Murdoch." Ph.D. dissertation, University of Wiscon-
   sin-Madison, 291 pp. Abstract in DAI 36:6110A
        Murdoch tries to write novels that are contingent
   by being obscure and that are quasi-allegorical. The
   two poles are represented by the figures of the saint
   and the artist. Her artist figures crave necessary
   form, while her saints show a high tolerance for
   contingency. Murdoch keeps searching for the right
   balance through the dramatic interaction of these
   two types of characters. The conflict between artist
   and saint is made clearer in each novel. In A
   Fairly Honourable Defeat, she depicts the proper sub-
   ordination of the artist to the saint almost allegor-
   ically. In The Black Prince, the conflict between
   the artist and the saint is subsumed in a preoccupation with mysticism that incorporates ethics and art.
   Also The Black Prince radically explores the form of
   the novel itself, using even devices of the antinovel.
   It implies that solipsism can be overcome by the
   artist's desire to communicate.

6 BERTRANDIAS, BERNADETTE. "Vision fantastique et
   vision mythique dans The Unicorn d'Iris Murdoch."
   Confluents 2:13-37.
        Hannah is a steady image out of time, an ideal,
   Circe, the unicorn, a trap. Marian tries to rationalize the mystery of Hannah, while Effingham accepts
   the mystery and exalts it. In Hannah's committing
   adultery and breaking her image, she remains a legend
   although Nature is thereby introduced into the drama.
   Gaze or vision is the heart of the story. The text
   is a gaze itself. To rationalize the irrational or
   to idealize primordial instincts is impossible and a
   dead end. But in the second part of the novel,
   imagination will reappear with poetic vision. We may

interpret Hannah as a romantic manifestation of the
excesses of consciousness and its search for what it
is not.

7 BROMWICH, DAVID. "Iris Murdoch's New Novel and Old
   Themes." New York Times Book Review, 24 October,
   pp. 21-22.
        Asserts that A Word Child raises questions about
   Murdoch's constant imitation of herself. Names her
   persistent theme the search for a passion beyond the
   self. Commends her ear for ordinary speech and her
   vivid character sense.

8 BROYARD, ANATOLE. "Peeving with Thought." New
   York Times 124 (8 August):25.
        Reviews A Word Child as freshman philosophy with
   Hilary talking on and on with only flashes of the
   writer's intelligence.

9 C., A. "Bye Bye Burde." Newsweek 86 (25 August):66.
        Judges A Word Child not Murdoch at her best,
   censuring it as contrived melodrama.

10 DE FEO, RONALD. "Mechanical Murdoch." National
   Review 27 (28 March):356.
        Review of The Sacred and Profane Love Machine
   that perceives its theme as the unpredictability of
   love and human nature. Criticizes Murdoch's use of
   adjectives and of trivial characters.

11 EGREMONT, MAX. "Inner Circle." Books and Bookmen
   21 (October):60.
        Compares A Word Child to The Black Prince as
   both celebrations of the power of love, calling the
   new novel a considerable literary event.

12 "Fiction Reprints." Publishers Weekly 208 (1 September):72.
        Brief review of The Sacred and Profane Love
   Machine as one of her most entertaining novels, wise
   and amusing.

13 GERSTENBERGER, DONNA. Iris Murdoch. Bucknell, Pa.
   Bucknell University Press, 85 pp.
        Discusses Murdoch's fiction in a series on Irish
   writers in terms of her general accomplishment, the
   novel The Red and the Green, and Murdoch's Irish
   connections. Justifies the general look at her fiction by the difficulties many readers have in understanding her contribution to modern fiction. The
   main roots of Murdoch's fiction seem to be English,
   rather than Irish.
        The Red and the Green expresses a self-conscious
   ambivalence about Ireland. Murdoch's determination

to view the subject from every possible facet results
in a distancing from the subject, but certain emotional responses inherent in the Irish situation militate
against the formula of meaning through objective multiplicity.

The real question of Murdoch's Irishness would
address her own consciousness of national materials
and her attitudes toward them. The Irish characters
in her fiction usually show up as servants, simple
and automatically colorful. The idea of Irishness in
the English world of the novels carries with it a
definite class status. Martin Lynch-Gibbon, the
Anglo-Irish protagonist of A Severed Head, is part of
a completely different class structure.

Murdoch's debt to her Irish connection includes
her use of setting, her sense of the value of the
individual difference in characters, and her tolerance
for eccentricity as a means of achieving individual
difference. The force of her Irish background is
felt if only indirectly. Murdoch is an important contemporary writer to students of Irish literature.

14 GINDIN, JAMES. "Ethical Structures in John
    Galsworthy, Elizabeth Bowen, and Iris Murdoch."
    In Forms of Modern British Fiction. Edited by Alan
    Warren Friedman. Austin: University of Texas
    Press, pp. 15-41.
        Asserts that many critics value most highly
    fiction that expresses a fundamental entity of human
    personality or creates a consistent cosmos with a
    discernible metaphysics. Besides the metaphysical,
    another well-established line of fiction is closer to
    verismilitude, communicating through the texture of
    ordinary experience. The authors who devote their
    attention to ethical questions demonstrate an interest
    in the complexity of human relationships.
        The study examines as ethical fiction the works
    of John Galsworthy, Elizabeth Bowen, and Iris Murdoch.
    Murdoch's early novels are primarily existential
    statements in which characters try to fabricate
    abstractions and live by them. They display worlds in
    which ethical consciousness is generally self-defeat-
    ing. In Murdoch's novels, characters reveal themselves
    through the quality of their impositions and their
    deliberate connections with other people.
        In its immediacy and its willingness to comment
    directly on problems in human experience, the novel
    with an ethical focus risks sentimentality and banal-
    ity. The novel with an ethical focus, however, gains
    immediacy, and for some readers it can be as powerful
    as metaphysical fiction in its appeal to closeness
    and to differences.

15 HUNT, LESTER H. "Generosity." <u>American Philosophi-</u>
    <u>cal Quarterly</u> 12 (July):235-44.
       Discussion of the nature of generosity, distin-
    guishing it from justice or charity. Criticizes
    several general ethical theories and attempts to
    establish what generosity itself is. Mentions Mur-
    doch in passing. The generous intention is gratuitous.
    As generous, the way the deed is done can be justified,
    but that it is done cannot. We have here an example
    of what Murdoch calls "Luciferian freedom"--that free-
    dom in which we either lack or do not need a ground
    for what we do.

16 KENNARD, JEAN E. <u>Number and Nightmare: Forms of</u>
    <u>Fantasy in Contemporary Fiction.</u> Hamden, Conn.:
    Shoestring Press, pp. 155-75.
       Despite her existentialist terminology, Murdoch
    differs fundamentally from existentialist and post-
    existentialist novelists of number. Ihab Hassan has
    distinguished between the language of number, which
    creates a world of arbitrary order, and the language
    of nightmare, that of confusion and multiple reference.
    For Murdoch, contingency, although brute and nameless,
    is valuable and must be respected for its otherness.
    Murdoch's view of the uniqueness of the individual
    opposes Sartre's view of identity as nothingness.
       Murdoch has been accused of failing to create
    free characters because of certain recurring types in
    her novels. Nineteenth-century realist novels created
    the appearance of free characters by establishing a
    clear connection between motives, choices, and
    consequences. Because she wants to show the restric-
    tions on man's freedom and the mysteriousness of
    others, there can be no clear link between events and
    characters' motives. Through her suprarealistic tech-
    niques, Murdoch moves the reader to perceive and re-
    spect the mystery of reality.

17 KENNEY, EDWIN J., Jr. "Psychoanalyst Heal Thyself."
    <u>Nation</u>, 29 March, pp. 377-79.
       Review of <u>The Sacred and Profane Love Machine</u>
    that sees the novel as psychoanalytical in method,
    language, and situations, portraying "absurd misery."
    Hopes that Murdoch will return to comedy.

18 KERMODE, FRANK. "Leader to a Vacuum." <u>Listener</u> 93
    (17 April):516.
       Reviews <u>A Word Child</u> as portraying the relation
    of education to goodness and guilt. Criticizes
    Hilary for saying too much and feeling too little.

19 NORDELL, RODERICK. "Iris Murdoch Shows Words Can
    Do--Or Undo--Events." <u>Christian Science Monitor</u>,
    12 September, p. 27.

Review of A Word Child that sees London's subways
like Dante's Inferno. Notes some bizarre coincidences
but applauds the few "characters of uncommon decency."

20 OBUMSELU, BEN. "Iris Murdoch and Sartre." ELH
    42:296-317.
        Declares that although Murdoch's criticism of
existentialism have become harsher, she remains in
the existentialist camp. The world reflected in her
novels is lonely and absurd. Commentators have noted
how closely Under the Net resembles La nausée.
Her novel, however, echoes Sartre's only to contradict
it. While Roquentin aspires toward Being as a refuge
from the formlessness of Becoming, Jake accepts art as
a humble activity in the realm of Becoming. While
Roquentin chooses, Jake obeys. While Roquentin aspires
to the radiance of Platonic forms, Jake descends into
the mundane.
        Murdoch's main criticism of Sartre is that he
makes the lonely will morally normative. The problem
of solipsism relates to An Unofficial Rose, which
contrasts Randall's egotism and Ann's self-denying
submission to contingency. Murdoch's demand for real
persons and things, her nostalgia for particulars,
are in fact, a legacy of existentialism. And in the
novel she may be aiming at relating character to
social circumstances, but the promise is not completely fulfilled.
        Murdoch's responses to moral life arise usually
from her contact with existentialism. Often her work
can be seen as a revision of Sartre. In Kafka and
later existentialist novels, Murdoch found her models
for the symbolic melodrama.

21 OSTERMANN, ROBERT. "Murdoch." National Observer
    14 (30 August):19.
        Reviews A Word Child, praising its lack of mechan-
ical contrivance. Finds the characters deeply felt
and the theme commanding, questioning what mature
behavior consists of.

22 PEARSON, GABRIEL. "Fearful Symmetry." Manchester
    Guardian Weekly 112 (3 May):22.
        Notes the Peter Pan symbols, the Inner Circle
allusions, and the clock motifs in A Word Child as
overexplicit. Finds words, ideas, and dreams but
little realism.

23 PENDLETON, DENNIS. Review of A Word Child. Library
    Journal 100 (1 October):1845-46.
        Endorses the novel as one of Murdoch's most com-
pelling, construing Peter Pan as a symbol of immature
spirituality.

24   Review of A Word Child.   America, 15 November, p.
     332.
          Praises Murdoch's characterization and dialogue
     but finds her work disturbing.   Sees the theme of sin
     and possible redemption.

25   Review of A Word Child.   Booklist 72 (15 September):
     114.
          Regards the novel as social tragicomedy, delineat-
     ing class lines precisely and tracing tangled emotion-
     al ties.

26   Review of The Sacred and Profane Love Machine.
     Choice 12 (March):76-77.
          Judges it one of Murdoch's best with vivid,
     engaging characters but calls the plot resolution
     melodramatic.

27   Review of A Word Child.   Kirkus Review 43 (15 June):
     678.
          States that in the novel Murdoch gives us all the
     machinery in the most perverse, contradictory, and
     surreal complexity.   It is a universe in which moral
     impasses stubbornly continue to exist and to have
     consequences.   After Hilary's horror at causing the
     death of another man's wife, he undergoes a decade of
     grotesque self-thwarting.   Hilary and his small circle
     perceive in contradictory terms the moral imperatives
     of his intrigue with Gunnar's second wife.   The famil-
     iar Murdoch materials are here, bu the total is less
     than triumphant.

28   SAGE, LORNA.   "No Time for Perfection."   Observer,
     20 April, p. 30.
          Reviews A Word Child as embodying the theme of
     not growing up and as maintaining that people can't
     possess things but only words.   Declares Murdoch's
     works not objects for contemplation but for consump-
     tion, although rich consumption.

29   SCHWARTZ, LYNNE SHARON.   "Grammarian of Human
     Relations."   Nation 221 (11 October):343-45.
          Calls the outstanding achievement of A Word Child
     the reader's utter absorption in it, the novel ground-
     ed in feeling and consciousness.   Finds in Murdoch's
     recent novels "a steady increase in density and tex-
     ture."

30   SPACKS, PATRICIA MEYER.   "New Novels: In the Dumps."
     Yale Review 64 (June):590-92.
          Alleges that The Sacred and Profane Love Machine
     avoids emotional commitment.   Says that Murdoch manip-
     ulates characters in exploring resemblances between
     the mechanisms of love and of fiction.

31 SULLIVAN, ZOHREH TAWAKULI. "Enchantment and the
    Demonic in Iris Murdoch: The Flight from the
    Enchanter." Midwest Quarterly 16 (Spring):276-97.
        States that in The Flight from the Enchanter on
    a psychological level, the characters reveal such
    devices of fantasy as illusion, bad faith, and the
    schizoid tendency to split the person into disem-
    bodied mind and deanimate body. The enchanter is that
    power of mind that fragments reality. As social
    commentary, the novel may be seen as an allegory of
    power, a study of demonic energy that emanates from a
    central figure who embodies the will to power. On a
    mythic level, the world of the novel is typical of
    Northrop Frye's demonic world, held together by
    loyalty of pharmakoi to a tyrant leader. Here the
    leader is Mischa Fox, whose power dehumanizes.
        In Murdoch's novels a recurring theme is the
    struggle of goodness and love against the many forms
    of evil. The Flight from the Enchanter introduces a
    psychological investigation of enchantment and
    demonic power, an investigation that is continued in
    The Unicorn and The Time of the Angels.

32 UPDIKE, JOHN. "Topnotch Witcheries." New Yorker
    50 (6 January):76-81.
        Reviews The Sacred and Profane Love Machine as
    Murdoch's best since A Severed Head, both treating
    the fluctuations of erotic love. Compares Murdoch
    to Muriel Spark with both being intelligent and
    fluent, creating dark comedies of enchantment and
    deception. Calls Murdoch more Prospero than Shake-
    speare.

33 WALL, STEPHEN. "The Grammar of Guilt." Times
    Literary Supplement, 18 April, p. 416.
        Judges A Word Child a dazzling embodiment in
    experience of ideas about language, accident, responsi-
    bility, and salvation. Sees in it tragic power and
    moral forces. Asserts that the first-person narrator
    intensifies the reader's involvement.

34 WARNOCK, MARY. "Inner Circles." New Statesman 89
    (18 April):519-20.
        Review of A Word Child that praises the uniformly
    wintry setting. Objects to the fantasy and implausi-
    bility that surrounds the "central Jamesian" situation.

35 WEEKS, BRIGITTE. "First Degree Murdoch." Book
    World, 7 September, p. 4.
        Perceives A Word Child as a book about moral
    choices and turning points, calling the characters
    believable but the novel as a whole troubling and
    puzzling.

36 WILSON, FRANK. Review of <u>A Word Child</u>. <u>Best</u>
    <u>Sellers</u> 35 (October):190-91.
        Finds in the novel the continuing Christian
    themes of sin and redemption.

<u>1976</u>

1 ABERNATHY, PETER, CHRISTIAN J. KLOESEL, and
   JEFFREY R. SMITTEN. <u>English Novel Explication</u>,
   <u>Supplement I</u>. Metuchen, N.J.: Shoestring Press,
   pp. 171-73.
       List of selected criticism of Murdoch's work
   arranged alphabetically by novel and then by critic's
   name from <u>Under the Net</u> (1954) to <u>The Black Prince</u>
   (1973).

2 BLOW, SIMON. "An Interview with Iris Murdoch."
   <u>Spectator</u> 25 (September):24-25.
       Murdoch emphasizes her being a reflective,
   rather than a philosophical novelist. Asserts that
   her greatest problem is character portrayal, revealing
   psychological battles within a closely knit group.
   Declares that she tries to break patterns of fantasy
   to reveal character.

3 "Books of the Year." <u>Observer</u>, 12 December, p. 26.
       Brief review of <u>Henry and Cato</u> by Stephen Spender,
   commending its wit and intelligence.

4 BROCKWAY, JAMES. "Catching Up with Murdoch."
   <u>Books and Bookmen</u> 22 (December):46-47.
       Review of <u>Henry and Cato</u>, rating one Murdoch
   novel as worth six of most other contemporary British
   novels. Commends her plot for conveying ideas about
   human behavior.

5 BYATT, A.S. <u>Iris Murdoch</u>. London: Longman Group,
   42 pp.
       States that although Murdoch's novels have always
   sold extemely well, critics find her achievement problematic. In the mid-1950s, she was classified with
   the Angry Young Men, but what she has in common with
   John Wain and Kingsley Amis is an interest in fast-
   paced comedy and in the farcical episodic novel. Reviewers are suspicious of the artificial world of
   her novels and the probability of her characters'
   sexual behavior.
       The first novels, <u>Under the Net</u> and <u>The Flight</u>
   <u>from the Enchanter</u>, are philosophical fables, using a
   range of characters and dramatic incidents to illustrate a central theme. The theme of the first is the
   necessity and danger of using concepts and forms in
   thought and action. The theme of the second concerns

119

the proper and improper employment of power. Both
novels take up Sartrean issues of freedom, art, the
individual, and the nature of language. They do not,
however, offer Sartrean answers.

The Sandcastle attempts to respond to the erosion
of the reality of characters in contemporary fiction,
a concern in John Bayley's two critical studies. The
Bell and An Unofficial Rose dramatize characters'
efforts to apprehend the distinct being of other people. Both use paintings to symbolize the authority
of the Good and human attempts to invest life with a
sense of form.

In A Severed Head, The Unicorn, and The Time of
the Angels, the individual characters have less aesthetic power than the structures do. The sexual
shifts in A Severed Head represent how we are puppets
of incomprehensible forces. The Unicorn and The Time
of the Angels are both fantasies of the spiritual life.
Murdoch's use of the Gothic is part of her interest
in primitive forces and forms.

Readers and critics have trouble with the tension
between realism and more artificial ways of writing
in Murdoch's fiction. Such critics see Under the Net
as her most successful novel. A Severed Head fuses
several styles and subject matters. The Bell is her
most successful attempt at social and emotional realism. Undeniably, Murdoch has admirable aesthetic
courage. She produces comic metaphysical adventures
of a high order.

6 CAUTE, DAVID. "To the Life." New Statesman 92
   (24 September):420.
      Discusses Murdoch's theme in Henry and Cato as
the relationship between possession and power, with
the upper-middle class preoccupied with ownership of
real estate, sexual objects, and God.

7 CHARPENTIER, COLETTE M. Le thème de la claustration
   dans "The Unicorn" d'Iris Murdoch: Etude lexique et
   semantique. Paris: Didier, 216 pp.
      Study combining thematic and formalist criticism,
asserting that the central themes of Murdoch's romantic work are confinement, jail, and freedom. After
a statistical analysis of words indicating confinement,
jail, and freedom, Charpentier uses a semantic model
to find the articulation of these themes. She also
discusses the existential tradition and the relationship between morality and freedom in Murdoch's works.

The image of man in Murdoch's novels is that of
a hostile, grasping creature, living in darkness, not
knowing how to love. Selfish, he lives in confinement.
Beauty is all around, but he is blind to it. He is
tempted to fill in the vacuum with fantasy. In Murdoch's world, anguish does not lead to love but to

alienation. Charpentier tries to find a relationship between the conceptual and referential metaphors in Murdoch's writing.

8 DE FEO, RONALD. "Unlikely Possibilities." National Review 28 (20 February):167-68.
   Reviews A Word Child as one of Murdoch's better recent novels. Praises its many fine comic scenes and the descriptions of London streets. Suggests that the first-person narrator helps create a more substantial world. Judges as strength and weakness Murdoch's attraction to unlikely events.

9 DOHERTY, GAIL, and PAUL DOHERTY. "Spring Paperback Parade: Literature." America 134 (20 March):230.
   Calls The Sacred and Profane Love Machine clever and intelligent. Finds the suggestions, secrets, and surprises to comprise a more than fine plot.

10 GLOVER, STEPHEN. "An Interview with Iris Murdoch." New Review 3 (November):56-59.
   States that Murdoch started writing when she was nine, and she wrote her first complete novel when she was about twenty. She didn't publish anything until later, partly because the war took seven years out of her life.
   She thinks that the English novel tradition is very strong and sees no reason to leave that tradition. It is a marvelously versatile form. In it a lot of experiment can take place without the reader being necessarily disturbed.
   She hopes that she does not impose her philosophical theories on her novels. Philosophy and fiction are different disciplines with different modes of thought and aims. But a little theory may come in just for fun and because a character may hold that theory.
   Murdoch does not think that she is a pessimist in the novels. Of course, we may be doomed, but we have lots of fun along the way. She thinks that her later novels are more profoundly funny than her earlier ones.
   The tone of the dialogue matters very much. She is not a very good detailed mimic, but she tries to imply speech patterns of a different sort without going into much detail. She has in her own life two different sort of speech patterns, the Oxford English one and the Irish. So if she wants to portray an alien character, she can make him implicitly or explicitly Irish.

11 HAYMAN, RONALD. The Novel Today 1967-1975. Essex: Longman Group, pp. 5, 13-17, 29.

States that some critics believe that none of
the contemporary British novelists are great but names
Murdoch as one of ten who are often mentioned as con-
tenders. Her best work is antirational even though it
has roots in the nineteenth-century novel. Shake-
spearean elements in her work include the power of
structuring, the suggestive effects of the rhythms,
the grouping of characters in accord with moral
criteria, and the cluster of images that take on symbolic significance in connection with the plot.
      Murdoch says that she has tried to create many
people who are not her, but sometimes the myth of the
work draws the people into a spiral, reflecting the
form of the writer's mind. The Black Prince is the
best novel Murdoch has yet written: the most ingen-
iously structured and the most experimental. She
writes fiction which is also literary criticism.

12 JONES, DAN. "Arms against Absurdity." Times
    Literary Supplement, 24 September, p. 1198.
          Review of Henry and Cato that sees it concerned
    with reconciling the absurdity of human life with the
    possibility of living a Christian life. Asserts that
    the most absorbing part of the novel is the discus-
    sion between the priests about faith.

13 KALSON, ALBERT E. "A Severed Head from Novel to
    Play: Coarsening as the Essence of Adaptation."
    Ball State University Forum 17 (Autumn):71-74.
          When Murdoch attempted to dramatize A Severed
    Head for the stage, her first version was unwieldy so
    she and J.B. Priestley decided to collaborate on the
    play. Priestley said that adaptation reveals the
    coarseness of the dramatic form. A play must be
    coarse to evoke a communal response from a group of
    spectators whereas a novel leads one reader at a time
    through it. The coarsening of Murdoch's novel makes
    the play easier to follow. Its patterning and mythic
    background are deemphasized in the play. On the stage,
    it becomes more sharply a comedy of manners and not
    so intellectual. The two provided witty lines to
    evoke more laughter. Unlike the novel, which shifts
    about in locale, the action of the play occurs in
    three residences. The adaptors expanded some speeches
    to make motivations clearer and the dialogue less
    ambiguous. The most vivid moment of the play--Honor's
    severing the head of a bust--makes clear for the audi-
    ence the meaning of the title.

14 KELLMAN, STEVEN G. "Raising the Net: Iris Murdoch
    and the Tradition of the Self-Begetting Novel."
    English Studies 57 (February):43-50.
          The self-begetting novel is a major subgenre of
    this century. Its paradigm is Marcel Proust's

À la recherche du temps perdu: simultaneously an
account of its own birth and the rebirth of its protagonist as a novelist. It is an intensely reflexive
novel, keeping the reader conscious of the problematic
status of art. Murdoch's Under the Net is a remarkable instance of this French tradition transposed to
British soil. Like other self-begetting novels, this
one has a cast of artist figures. Of course, the most
important artist is Jake. Jake's development as a
novelist is inseparable from his growth as an individual.

When Jake sees the Siamese kittens and says that
it is just one of the wonders of the world, the
comment indicates Jake's progress as a human being and
artist in embracing the untidy dappledness of the
world. The sense of rebirth and liberation at the end
of the novel derives from the promise of an artistic
work that will succeed in understanding the contingent world and uttering what is completely particular.

15 KERMODE, FRANK. "To Be Taken Seriously." Manchester
    Guardian Weekly 115 (10 October):21.
        Reviews Henry and Cato as containing not just a
    story but a vision. Notes the alternation of rapid
    dialogue with long discussions of the spiritual life.
    Praises the depiction of the ordinary universe.

16 PENDLETON, DENNIS. Review of Henry and Cato.
    Library Journal 101 (15 November):2394.
        Sees the novel as exploring the relationship
    between love and freedom. Calls it elaborately plot-
    ted, enlivened with compassion and humor.

17 "Pick of the Paperbacks." Observer, 11 December,
    p. 28.
        Brief review of The Sacred and Profane Love
    Machine that pronounces it sexy and disturbing.

18 PRITCHARD, WILLIAM H. Review of A Word Child.
    Hudson Review 29 (Spring):157.
        Asserts that the novel is Murdoch's best since
    A Severed Head or The Bell. Acclaims the solid sur-
    face and her accuracy in depicting the particular.

19 RABINOVITZ, RUBIN. "Iris Murdoch." In Six Contem-
    porary British Novelists. Edited by George Stade.
    New York: Columbia University Press, pp. 271–332.
        Extension of his monograph in the Columbia Essays
    on Modern Writers Series (1968). Adds discussions of
    Bruno's Dream, A Fairly Honourable Defeat, An Acciden-
    tal Man, The Black Prince, the plays The Three Arrows
    and The Servants and the Snow, and The Sacred and Pro-
    fane Love Machine.
        Bruno's Dream demonstrates again the instability

of love relationships, but the rapid metamorphoses of
the characters and their relationships undermine and
erode the novel's verismilitude. A Fairly Honourable
Defeat also relies too much on sudden turns of plot
and melodramatic devices. An Accidental Man has a
number of shrewd and original characterizations, but
it too has perfunctory analyses of complicated ethical
and psychological situations.
    A lack of contingency undermines Murdoch's later
fiction. Fragile plots and thinly disguised moraliz-
ing convey a sense of authorial manipulation. Con-
tradicting her earlier philosophical essays, Murdoch
tries to instruct the reader, instead of merely showing the underlying truth of things.

20 RANDALL, JULIA. "Against Consolation: Some Novels
    of Iris Murdoch." Hollins Critic 13 (February):1-
    15.
        Murdoch's novels from Under the Net to A Word
    Child show no major change in preoccupation or tech-
    nique. Interprets An Accidental Man favorable but
    complains of flat, inexact writing. The Sacred and
    Profane Love Machine is found to be flawed in depict-
    ing love as a machine, compromising human freedom.
    Murdoch's work is forgettable because her characters
    are funny, grotesque, and ordinary.

21 Review of Henry and Cato. Booklist 73 (15 December):
    588.
        Characterizes the novel as social comedy but
    criticizes the action for petering out.

22 Review of Henry and Cato. Kirkus Review 44
    (15 November):1237
        Finds Murdoch not at her best but still recogniz-
    able. The same sterile self-bound characters invite
    indignities and humiliations. Present is the usual
    fastidiousness, even fussiness, of style with those
    surprising small errors. The plot is predictably
    unpredictable as the lives of Henry and Cato inter-
    sect. Only two characters get the gift of happiness.

23 Review of Henry and Cato. Publishers Weekly 210
    (1 November):66.
        Pronounces the novel feverish with ironic twists,
    outrageous situations, and bizarre characters.

24 SAGE, LORNA. "Englishmen's Homes." Observer, 26
    September, p. 25.
        Declares that Henry and Cato has all the elements
    of Murdoch's mature fiction but slightly out of joint
    and forced. No one in her books is allowed to opt out
    of the culture although the two main characters in
    this one try. Henry wants to revenge himself on his

family by getting rid of the estate. Cato's war with
his inheritance involved his conversion and priesthood,
aimed at foiling his natural father's insistent
rationalism. Then the pressures of instinct, accident,
and inertia reassert themselves, and each shrinks into
his own limited destiny.

25   TENNANT, EMMA. "The Strong and the Weak." Listener
     96 (23 September):379.
        Reviews Henry and Cato, regarding the character
Beautiful Joe as unreal and a failure. Censures the
speeches as too long and the dialogue as lacking
sparkle.

26   TOMINAGA, THOMAS T., and WILMA SCHNEIDERMEYER.
     Iris Murdoch and Muriel Spark: A Bibliography.
     Metuchen, N.J.: Scarecrow Press, pp. 3-91.
        Includes biographical list and chronology of
major publications with sections for biographies, bibliographies, critical books and parts of books, dissertations, critical essays, interviews, reviews and
translations of novels, all through A Word Child.
Lists critical essays by Murdoch, plays and reviews,
stories and book reviews by Murdoch. Only occasion-
ally annotated.

27   TOTTON, NICK. "The New Learning." Spectator 237
     (25 September):19.
        Assesses Henry and Cato as a major, mature work
of Murdoch's, showing her increasing confidence in
solving moral and technical problems. States the
theme to be that knowledge and certainty will never be
grasped.

28   WALL, STEPHEN. "Disparate Measures." New Review
     3 (November):54-55.
        Review of Henry and Cato, comparing it unfavorably
to A Word Child because of the thinness of its heroes,
Cato and Henry, and of its villain, Beautiful Joe.
Complains that the world of the novel lacks density.

                            1977

1   ALLEN, BRUCE. "Henry and Cato by Iris Murdoch."
    New Republic 176 (19 February):25-26.
        Reviews Henry and Cato as a dramatization of the
failure of two ideals: Henry's nonmaterialism and
Cato's nonviolence. Praises Murdoch's use of secon-
dary characters and symbolic associations in support
of the theme that no pattern is consistent and no
ideal can be fully realised.

2 B., E.B. Review of Bruno's Dream. Kliatt Paperback Book Guide 11 (Spring):7.
       A brief review that recommends the novel to
   sophisticated readers, calling it well written and
   very readable.

3 BAKER, ROGER. "Iris Murdoch." In Contemporary
   Dramatists. Edited by James Vinson. 2d ed.
   London: St. James Press, pp. 578-80.
       After a short biography and a list of publica-
   tions, a discussion of Murdoch's novels adapted for
   the stage--A Severed Head and The Italian Girl--and
   of her plays--The Servants and the Snow and The Three
   Arrows. Asserts that the dramatic adaptations clarify
   the purposes of the novels.

4 BELLAMY, MICHAEL O. "An Interview with Iris Murdoch."
   Contemporary Literature 18:129-40.
       Murdoch says that in her fiction she focuses on
   how consciousness and conduct are changed. Other
   topics include the novel as a comic form, her iden-
   tification with men, and the conflict in her novels
   between the form-maker and the truthful, formless
   figure.

5 BRADBURY, MALCOLM, ed. Introduction to The Novel
   Today. Manchester: Fontana, pp. 7-20 .
       The book is an anthology of essays by some impor-
   tant novelists and critics of the novel writing
   today, including Murdoch's "Against Dryness." There
   is a fascinating critical debate about the novel in
   recent years, and a serious aesthetic shift is taking
   place with a new era of style. In contemporary
   English fiction, the liberal novel has persisted in
   its attempt to sustain the idea of character and
   other elements of realism, despite challenges.
   Important writers of realistic fiction include Murdoch,
   although her career has been less realistic than mythic. "Against Dryness" is an important statement that
   defends contingency against form or absurdism. It
   emphasizes that we are not isolated free choosers, a
   postexistential position. With the experiments in
   the late sixties and early seventies, the novel now
   has a new range of possibilities. The theorizing
   concerns a central form for English literary experience.

6 BROWNJOHN, ALAN. "The Long and the Short."
   Encounter 48 (March):81-82.
       Review of Henry and Cato that credits Murdoch's
   work with invention and intelligence but complains
   that the credibility of the characters does not match
   the serious themes. Criticizes Murdoch's labeling

the characters with explicit adjectives. Names her strong point her communicating "the suddenness of things."

7 BROYARD, ANATOLE. "Books of the Times." New York Times 126 (7 January):C 19.
    Commends the major characters of Henry and Cato for being successful, after the novel's beginning badly. Asserts that the last few Murdoch novels have followed a formula--with the characters tested in a maturity rite. Affirms that the characters experience the ideas in her novels: faith, love, art, tradition, and discontinuity.

8 FLOWER, DEAN. Review of Henry and Cato. Hudson Review 30 (Summer):307.
    Defends Murdoch's writing novel after novel as her spiritual craving to communicate the mystery of freedom and the opacity of people. Criticizes the crystalline plot of Henry and Cato for undercutting the moral concerns.

9 FORREST, ALAN. "A Year's Good Reading." Books and Bookmen 22 (January):57.
    Brief review of Henry and Cato that calls it disappointing, accusing Murdoch of rewriting the same book again and again.

10 FROEB, JEANNE RINEY. "The Fiction of David Storey, John Fowles, and Iris Murdoch." Ph.D. dissertation, University of Tulsa, 296 pp. Abstract in DAI 38: 1378A.
    Despite their claims, all three novelists are not committed primarily to the depiction of character and society, to the aims of the realistic novel. David Storey presents speculative, not social philosophy. John Fowles sets out aesthetic and ethical concerns. And Murdoch creates characters who are foils for the philosophical debates that the plots are designed to display. All three show that their aesthetic positions are extensions of their moral thinking. They all distrust the symbolist emphasis on subjectivity, on the imagination's construction reality, and on art as prescription. All portray in their fiction the idea that symbolist dogmas lead to sterile art and unethical or destructive behavior.

11 "Fury and Technique." Philosophy 52:377-79.
    Reviews The Fire and the Sun as Murdoch externalizing her conflict between her talent for fiction and her talent for philosophy. States that Plato castigated poets because they were rivals in finding and

and telling the truth. Asserts that an important
theme to Murdoch is "jumble": the untidiness of human
existence.

12 GOSSMAN, ANN. "Icons and Idols in Murdoch's A
    Severed Head." Critique: Studies in Modern Fiction
    18 (April):92-98.
        Explication of A Severed Head that discusses the
    head of Medusa and the "head-hunting" of the charac-
    ters. The study perceives a sequence of religious
    images, signifying idolatrous worship, and explores
    cave imagery. Sees Georgie as the most sacrificial
    character and Honor as an assassin with Martin having
    little chance to survive or become good in his attrac-
    tion to Honor.

13 HAMPSHIRE, STUART. "The Platonic Ideal." Observer,
    31 July, p. 29.
        Review of The Fire and the Sun as an admirable
    description of Plato's temperament and his fear of
    anarchy. Says that Murdoch may have understated the
    political motives for Plato's pessimism. Finds ten-
    tative Murdoch's answer, based on the Romantic distinc-
    tion between imagination and fantasy.

14 HELLER, AMANDA. "Short Reviews." Atlantic 239
    (February):96.
        Reviews Henry and Cato, asserting that Murdoch is
    dishonest in dealing with England's problems with
    money, crime, and loss of faith. Enjoys the intricate
    plot and the neat pairing of the characters.

15 HOFFMAN, ROBERT. Review of The Fire and the Sun.
    Library Journal 102 (1 November):2264.
        Explains that the book relates Plato's aesthetic
    theory to his metaphysics. Calls Murdoch's compari-
    sons of Plato with Aristotle, Freud, Kant, and Tolstoy
    illuminating. Characterizes as discerning her final
    remarks on the relation of art to life.

16 KENNER, HUGH. "Plato and Those Poets." New York
    Times Book Review, 20 November, p. 28.
        Reviews The Fire and the Sun, complaining that by
    not mentioning Eric Havelock's Preface to Plato, it is
    part of a "literary power game." Finds the book
    impossible to summarize with no governing thesis.

17 KUEHL, LINDA. "Books in Brief." Saturday Review 4
    (8 January):47.
        Considers Henry and Cato as evidence of Murdoch's
    loyalty to the nineteenth-century novel. Notes the
    ironies, surprises, and contrivances and the familiar
    pattern of her plot.

18 MAY, DERWENT. "Nice or Good?" <u>Listener</u> 98 (27
    October):548-49.
        Reviews <u>The Fire and the Sun</u>, contending that
    Murdoch discusses Plato's charges against the artist
    but not just as an academic exercise. Murdoch justi-
    fies the artist as aiding in the journey from appear-
    ance to reality, by helping us see truth.

19 MOHAN, ROSE ELLEN. "Through Myth to Reality: A
    Study of the Novels of Iris Murdoch." Ph.D. dis-
    sertation, Purdue University, 235 pp. Abstract in
    <u>DAI</u> 39:874A.
        The study employs a structural approach and ex-
    amines Murdoch's use of traditional mythology as a
    thematic framework. It also analyzes her philosophi-
    cal and aesthetic position as it affects her choice
    of theme. When the theme derives from the mythic
    structure, her novels are more successful. When the
    mythic allusions are not an organic part of the
    structure and theme, her novels are less successful.
    Chapter 1 summarizes the controversy about Murdoch's
    work and establishes her aesthetic and philosophical
    stance. Chapter 2 analyzes her early novels and finds
    myth functioning usually as comic parody to indicate
    the distance between the real and the ideal. Chapter
    3 analyzes <u>The Unicorn</u> and <u>Bruno's Dream</u> in which myth
    symbolizes a transcendent reality, unattainable but
    worth attending to. Chapter 4 finds that in <u>A
    Fairly Honourable Defeat</u> and <u>The Sacred and Profane
    Love Machine</u>, myth indicates the deterioration of the
    moral referent in contemporary society. Chapter 5
    evaluates Murdoch's canon and her progress as a novel-
    ist and a moral philosopher.

20 ORR, CHRISTOPHER. "Iris Murdoch's Critique of
    Tragedy in <u>The Black Prince</u> and <u>A Word Child</u>." <u>Bul-
    letin of the West Virginia Association of College
    English Teachers</u>. 4:10-18.
        Examines <u>The Sovereignty of Good</u> as a guide to
    Murdoch's novels, saying that it relates the sense of
    mortality to the comic, a relation that Murdoch devel-
    ops in <u>The Black Prince</u> and <u>A Word Child</u>. Middle-
    aged male civil servants whose mistakes about women
    are catastrophic narrate both novels. <u>The Black
    Prince</u> follows the tragic pattern of a fall, punish-
    ment, and resolution, but <u>A Word Child</u> sets up and
    then frustrates its own tragic expectations.

21 PACKER, P.A. "The Theme of Love in the Novels of
    Iris Murdoch." <u>Durham University Journal</u> 69 (June):
    217-24.
        Begins by comparing Murdoch's novels to those of
    Thomas Love Peacock, finding similarities in settings
    and in the limited social and intellectual canvas.

Distinguishes Murdoch from Peacock in her psychological depiction of personal relationships. Murdoch is
an outstanding writer for her understanding of life
and of the aspirations of men. Her novels present a
deep sense of the reality of the Good.

22 PRESCOTT, PETER S. "Wordly Goods." Newsweek 89
(10 January):67.
Reviews Henry and Cato, complaining that Henry
is put into unreasonable predicaments and treated
like a character in a farce. Finds the only sense of
a real human dilemma in the debates between Cato and
the other priest. Wants to feel that the characters
matter and the story matters.

23 PRITCHARD, WILLIAM. "The Bleakest of Lords: Murdoch's Eighteenth." New York Times Book Review, 16
January, pp. 4, 24.
Criticizes Henry and Cato for not sounding new
and fresh. Declares that Murdoch is interesting and
lively page by page but the pages together don't add
up to much.

24 PURCELL, H.D. "Faust Lives O.K." Books and Bookmen 23 (November):52.
Critiques The Fire and the Sun, by saying that
Murdoch and Plato are both puritans, presumably for
valuing art that leads people to the good. Asserts
that Plato is more like Jung than like Freud to whom
Murdoch compares him, Murdoch saying that both Plato
and Freud believed that the source of the unlimited
in art is repressed egotism.

25 Review of The Fire and the Sun. Booklist 74
(1 November):449.
States that in the book Murdoch examines Plato's
hostility to art and considers the danger artists
pose to a stable society, with Murdoch finally defend-
ing both art and Plato.

26 Review of Henry and Cato. Choice 14 (April):202.
Declares that fans will find it one of Murdoch's
best novels, gripping, with "detective-story" turns
and characters the reader cares about.

27 Review of Henry and Cato. Publishers Weekly 212
(22 August):64.
Briefly recommends the novel with its ironic
twists, bizarre characters, and trenchant satire.

28 ROSENHEIM, ANDREW. "Moderate Ambitions." Nation
224 (January):24, 26.
Reviews Henry and Cato and The Takeover by Muriel

Spark, comparing the two writers. Calls Murdoch's
novel ambiguous and ultimately unsatisfying, as if
Murdoch couldn't decide which characters to focus on.
Deplores the absence of risk, unlike American novels.

29 SAGE, LORNA. "The Pursuit of Imperfection."
      Critical Quarterly 19 (Summer):60-68.
        Finds in Henry and Cato much that is different
but nothing completely new. This novel is a particularly visual book, dominated by pictures and concen-
trating on the problem of making people see. In this
bold allegory, there is sharp moral humor from the
contrasting careers of the two heroes. The two are
at different stages: Cato is losing his certainties
as Henry is finding his. The reversals of fortune
demonstrate the characters' lack of freedom. In Cato's
being forced to see that Joe has a reality of his own,
the illusion of the autonomy of the hero is shattered.
These plots turn the pattern back on itself. The
Flemish tapestry focuses the questions about why one
should cling to the texture of English life. For
Henry without that English life, his separate identity
would be lost. Murdoch suggests that it is arrogant
to think that anyone can be cultureless.

30 SCANLAN, MARGARET. "The Machinery of Pain: Roman-
      tic Suffering in Three Works of Iris Murdoch."
      Renascence 29 (Winter):69-85.
        Examines Murdoch's critique of romantic suffering
and of romantic love in The Sovereignty of Good, An
Accidental Man, and The Sacred and Profane Love
Machine. The basis for her critique is that goodness
is a selfless respect for reality, especially for the
painful reality of death. Her principal contentions
about the relationship between suffering and moral
behavior are explored in An Accidental Man. Her
critique of suffering centering on Austin is effective,
but less effective are the attempt to show the moral
value of contemplating death and the attempt to show
that human love is too possessive to create vision.
The Sacred and Profane Love Machine is more interesting, better dramatized, and better at illustrating
the ambiguities of Murdoch's concepts. The novel
reexamines whether a great love (between Blaise and
Emily) can be the measure of all things in terms of
the suffering it causes. Monty articulates many of
the novel's main themes, and Edgar embodies most of
the Murdoch virtues. The novel confirms at least a
negative vision of The Sovereignty of Good.

31 SCHLUETER, PAUL. Review of Henry and Cato. Best
      Sellers 37 (May):40.

Regards Murdoch as a thoughtful writer, worth a
careful reading. Considers her characters and their
dilemmas to be believable.

32 SCRUTON, ROGER. "Through Fictions to Reality."
    Times Literary Supplement, 25 November, p. 1382.
        Reviews The Fire and the Sun, finding it academ-
    ically and popularly useful, as a good introduction to
    Plato's thought. Wishes that Murdoch's suggestive
    assertions were more clearly distinguished from Plato's.

33 SKOW, JOHN. "Metaphysical Props." Time 109
    (17 January):71-72.
        Criticizes Henry and Cato as a religious melo-
    drama only half serious. Finds it to be derivative
    of Graham Greene.

34 STURROCK, JUNE. "Good and the Gods of The Black
    Prince." Mosaic 10:133-41.
        Murdoch's fullest elaboration of the nature of
    art related to sexual love and moral action is found
    in The Black Prince. Pearson's work of love is made
    possible through his love. Shadowy figures of gods
    (who merge into one figure)move behind the action.
    Pearson feels that the same force is working in his
    art and in his love for Julian. His narrative is
    addressed to P. Loxias, Apollo the crooked or ambig-
    uous.
        Murdoch says that art and love are instances of
    attention, leading to the good. The reader gets a
    sense of the agony of the human condition with
    Pearson in prison, but no demonstration of his more
    loving attitude to people. The novel testifies to the
    value of love and attention, but it shows only fantasy
    and ego. This flaw derives from the overactivity of
    Murdoch's comic gifts and her final pessimism about
    human actions.

35 SULLIVAN, ZOHREH T. "The Contracting Universe of
    Iris Murdoch's Gothic Novels." Modern Fiction
    Studies 23 (Winter):557-69.
        Murdoch's waifs, refugees and demons all share
    an isolation, a loss of community. She associates
    this loss of community with the inadequacies of
    empirical and existentialist thought that depends on
    self-centered standards of individual consciousness
    rather than on other-centered values of love and
    imagination. The psychological distortion of solip-
    sism can be cured only by an act of imagination
    that Murdoch identifies with love. Her characters in
    a fantasy world can redeem themselves only by discov-
    ering new ways of perceiving reality.
        The essay examines Murdoch's handling of two
    forms of man-made order that substitute for community:

work and rooms. Work substitutes for community in
three ways. The vocation of a character sometimes
reflects his psychological inadequacy. The work might
reflect a character's demonic need to control and
exert power. Work might also serve as a means for the
protagonist to redeem himself and to progress towards
self-discovery.

Rooms and houses function metaphorically to
define the relationships within them. Enclosures can
reflect the ailments of interiority of the characters
and their erotic and often incestuous relationships.
The essay focuses on three Gothic novels: The Flight
from the Enchanter, The Unicorn, and The Time of the
Angels.

36 _____. "Iris Murdoch's Self-Conscious Gothicism:
   The Time of the Angels." Arizona Quarterly 33
   (Spring):47-60.
      Explication of The Time of the Angels, applying
Leslie Fiedler's analysis of the Gothic to Murdoch's
novels, saying that in it Murdoch reexamines the
Gothic form. Discusses Carel, its demonic hero, as
a solipsistic existentialist, who tries to make others
fit his private formula. Perceives three pairs of
antithetical characters in the novel: dark, evil
Carel and light, good Eugene; dark, good Patti and
light, evil Elizabeth; and evil Leo and good Muriel.
Murdoch's closed Gothic novels display her negative
romanticism, criticizing solipsism that alienates man
from the other and criticizing the emotional and moral
failures of the contemporary world.

37 TYLER, ANNE. "The What-Ifs Enliven an X-Shaped
   Novel." National Observer 16 (5 February):19.
      Reviews Henry and Cato as a flawed book, still
possessing Murdoch's cool clarity. Calls Murdoch a
master puppeter and finds life in the characters
surrounding Henry and Cato.

38 WALTERS, RAY. "Paperback Talk." New York Times
   Book Review, 20 November, p. 69.
      Brief review of Henry and Cato, describing Mur-
doch as a skilled maker of traditional novels with a
satiric outlook.

39 WILLIAMS, BERNARD. "The Nice and the Good." New
   Statesman 94 (5 August):182.
      Reviews The Fire and the Sun as Murdoch's reflec-
tions on Plato's attack on the artist. Declares that
the book is not accessible to a general reader and
that scholars would criticize the lack of clear
references to previous scholarship. Denigrates as too
simple the account of Plato's ideas about the Forms.

Commends mainly the discussion of religious imagery
in art and of the dangers of irony to morality.

1978

1   ABELMAN, PAUL. "The State of the Fiction."
    Spectator 241 (25 November):18.
        Reviews The Sea, The Sea, praising the interweav-
    ing of the three themes and the crisp prose. Criti-
    cizes the "mythological metaphysics" and the treat-
    ment of Hartley, declaring that the book begins to go
    wrong in the second section and collapses in the third.

2   ALLEN, DIOGENES. Review of The Fire and the Sun.
    Theology Today 35 (July):225-26.
        Calls Plato a serious censor and summarizes
    Murdoch's defense of art as leading the person from
    egotistical fantasy to an appreciation of reality's
    incompleteness, moving through the consolation of
    form to the inexplicable in life.

3   "Anger and After." Economist 269 (18 November):153
        Regards The Sea, The Sea as deservedly a best-
    seller, inventive and openended. Finds Murdoch's
    themes to be freedom and reality, with ethics and art
    going hand in hand.

4   ARNAN, GABRIELE. "Murdoch Magic." Listener 100
    (August 24):250.
        Review of The Sea, the Sea that pronouces it a
    philosophical factual thriller, not a tragic novel
    but a comedy. Notes allusions to The Tempest con-
    cerning the renunciation of power and magic.

5   ATWELL, JOHN E. Review of The Fire and the Sun.
    Journal of Aesthetics and Art Criticism 36 (Summer):
    490-93.
        Considers the book to be stimulating and inform-
    ative, well worth reading. Regrets the lack of an
    index and of divisions, finding it difficult to read.
    Declares problematical the difference between Plato's
    understanding of the function of poetry and Murdoch's
    understanding of the function of literature today.

6   BANNON, BARBARA. "PW Forecasts." Publishers Weekly
    214 (9 October):62.
        Brief review of The Sea, The Sea, describing the
    climax as poignant and judging the novel to be a
    major work. Calls it haunting and mystical.

7   BEAMS, DAVID W. "Form in the Novels of Iris Murdoch."
    Ph.D. dissertation, Columbia University, 605 pp.
    Abstract in DAI 39:2282A.

Maintains that the meaning of Murdoch's fiction
resides in her essay "The Idea of Perfection": each
novel is an allegory, embodying a metaphysical concept.

8 BILES, JACK I. "An Interview with Iris Murdoch."
   Studies in the Literary Imagination 11:115-25.
   Topics of discussion include Murdoch as a philosophical novelist, her use of first-person male
narrators, her use of symbolism, and her relation to
contemporary writers versus nineteenth-century writers.

9 BRADBURY, MALCOLM. "Semi-Isle." New Statesman 96
   (25 August):246-47.
   Reviews The Sea, The Sea, perceiving in it a new
complexity of form and increased maturity. Declares
Charles one of Murdoch's most resonant first-person
narrators, acting out patterns of freedom and possession. Asserts that the novel acquires its form slowly,
achieves its mystery and magic, and then dissolves
again into ordinariness.

10 BRUNI, VALERIO. "La doppia funzione dell' 'ingranag-
    gio' in The Italian Girl di Iris Murdoch."
    Spicilegio moderno: Saggie richerche di letterature
    stranier 9:121-35.
    Examines The Italian Girl dialectically through
such themes as light and darkness, innocence and sin,
childishness and maturity, and the openness of the
natural versus the closed world. The characters are
judged existentially as they play against the dialectical themes. The concept of machinery is important
to the story. On the one hand, it represents a
sterile egocentricity that is enclosed in its own
neurotic circle. On the other hand, it assumes a
positive potential, identifying itself with chaotic
flux and the contradictions of existence. For the
characters to overcome being trapped in the machine,
they must accept both the positive and negative elements of life.

11 BURLING, VALERIE. "A Fairly Honourable Defeat:
    Jeux formels." In Recontres avec Iris Murdoch.
    Caen: Centre de recherches de litt. et ling. des
    pays de lang. angl. de l'université de Caen, pp.
    37-42.
    All of the games organized by Julius King are
designed to put to the test theoretical issues about
love. Of special importance in the novel are the
characters' dialogues about love. The many references
to Shakespeare remind the reader that King is setting
the stage for the drama, but as soon as he tries to
become an actor, he loses control of his game. The
first chapter provides a model for reading the novel.

The novel's difference from a play is that the point
of view is not neutral but reflects the characters'
points of view.

12 BYATT, A.S. "The Murdoch Theatre." <u>Books and Book-</u>
    <u>men</u> 24 (October):9-10.
        Review of <u>The Sea, The Sea</u>, characterizing it as
    a combination of magical fable and realistic novel.
    Asserts a major theme to be self-delusion and the
    impossibility of seeing truth. Credits Murdoch with
    successfully treating people undescribed and things
    unsaid, but criticizes Hartley for not quite coming
    to life.

13 CARPI SERTORI, DANIELA. "Per un'interpretazione
    psicanalitica di <u>A Severed Head</u> di Iris Murdoch."
    <u>Lettore di provincia</u> (Ravenna) 33:60-70.
        Psychoanalytic interpretation to explain links
    between the characters in <u>A Severed Head</u>. It refutes
    the existential perspective of Peter Wolfe. The
    study discusses the Oedipus complex, the phenomenon
    of identification, and the concept of taboo, all from
    a Freudian viewpoint. Martin is related to Antonia
    through the Oedipus complex, and Honor Klein enacts
    the notion of taboo.

14 CLARK, JUDITH ANNE. "A Complexity of Mirrors:
    The Novels of Iris Murdoch." Ph.D. dissertation,
    University of Wisconsin-Milwaukee, 413 pp. Abstract
    in <u>DAI</u> 39:3571A.
        Analysis of Murdoch's progress toward her objectives,
    considering character development and the depiction
    of agents in contingent reality in the eighteen novels
    published between 1954 and 1976.

15 CLEMONS, WALTER. "Lesser Murdoch." <u>Newsweek</u> 92
    (27 November):104-6.
        Reviews <u>The Sea, The Sea</u> as not Murdoch's best
    but still clever, witty, and entertaining. Declares
    the theme to be illusion and obession with Charles
    lacking common sense and moral sense.

16 COOGAN, DANIEL. "The Sea, The Sea." <u>America</u> 139
    (December):502.
        Praises the novel's narrative technique, saying
    that Murdoch tries to make the absurd plausible.
    Rates the book as good reading despite the resolution's
    coming one hundred pages before the end.

17 CRITTENDEN, BRIAN. <u>Bearings in Moral Education: A</u>
    <u>Critical Review of Recent Work</u>. Australian Educa-
    tion Review, 12. Hawthorn: Australian Council for
    Educational Research, pp. 11-20.

Explains Murdoch's moral theory as a corrective to the moral philosophies of linguistic analysis and existentialism, asserting that she reintroduced important fundamental themes like an inner self with personal knowledge, rather than an existence with isolated acts of will. Discusses "The Sovereignty of Good" and Murdoch's strong Platonic influence in the primacy of the Good in her moral theory and in her emphasis on metaphors of vision, instead of metaphors of movement.

18 CUNNEEN, SALLY SIMPSON. "The Self and the Sovereign Good: The Moral Vision of Iris Murdoch." Ph.D. dissertation, Columbia University, 193 pp. Abstract in DAI 39:2123A.

Murdoch's chief concern is to illuminate the moral condition of the individual person in the contemporary world. She sees the individual as unclear about his own identity and purpose but as desiring to live more justly. In her best late novels, she reveals her characters' dilemmas and the possibility of transcending them through a loving encounter with reality. Her moral vision is developed from two seemingly incompatible tenets: that the person is unique, valuable, and mysterious, and that the Good is sovereign. By coming to see accurately the reality of the other and of his own life, the ordinary person progresses in understanding appearance and reality. The major obstacle to this vision is the person's egotistic drives and fantasies.

Before 1970, Murdoch was criticizing concepts of the person held by the British empiricists and Sartre. In The Sovereignty of Good, she began to sketch out her positive Platonic alternative. Bruno's Dream, A Fairly Honourable Defeat, and The Black Prince contain the richest expressions of Murdoch's own metaphysical, epistemological, and ethical beliefs.

19 DIPPLE, ELIZABETH. "Iris Murdoch and Vladimir Nabokov: An Essay in Literary Realism and Experimentalism." In The Practical Vision: Essays in English Literature in Honour of Flora Roy. Edited by Jane Campbell and James Doyle. Waterloo, Ontario: Wilfred Laurier University Press, pp. 103-18.

Uses Lolita and The Black Prince as examples of experimentalism and realism in contemporary literature. Claims that the two share a theme, that a work of art confers immortality on the subject, the loved one. The experimental Lolita illustrates human transcendence in Humbert's learning to love Lolita and in Lolita's surviving in the immortality of art. The Black Prince, which is realistic except for the qualification of the forewords and postscripts and for the figure of Loxias, shows art needing the human mortality of the artist

and Bradley learning the necessity of the contingent
and of relatedness. Bradley's manuscript is not cool
and crafted but full of pain in Bradley's momentary
transfiguration in his love for Julian.

20 DRABBLE, MARGARET. "Books of the Year." Observer,
    17 December, p. 33.
        One of Drabble's three choices, The Sea, The Sea,
    she calls glittering with strange happiness, Murdoch
    at her radiant best.

21 DUNBAR, SCOTT. "On Art, Morals, and Religion: Some
    Reflections on the Work of Iris Murdoch." Religious
    Studies 14 (December):515-24.
        Examines Murdoch's essay "God and Good," criti-
    cizing her contemporary philosophy for failing to provide
    a realistic account of human nature. Murdoch's descrip-
    tion of fallen men with the psyche as an egocentric
    system of energy is realistic. She sees moral choices
    and actions emerging from a complex jumble of desires,
    determined by what went on between the acts. Combining
    a Freudian with a Platonic view, she believes that the
    moral pilgrim needs an object of attention outside him,
    the object being God, the transcendent ground of all
    being. Pure attention in contemplating art and nature
    defeats the ego. Art reminds us that the world is
    independent of our wills and that persons are distinct
    and independent of our consciousnesses. To overcome
    egotism is to become moral. Art does show the
    truth.

22 HENZ, ALINE. "Le symbolisme dans les romans d'Iris
    Murdoch." In Recontres avec Iris Murdoch. Caen:
    Centre de recherches de litt. et ling. des pays de
    lang. angle. de l'université de Caen, pp. 44-51.
        In Murdoch's symbol-filled novels, even the
    titles are significant. The names of the characters
    are symbolic. Murdoch reintroduces the same character
    types: the enchanter, the neutral observer, the
    childish woman, the foreigner. She uses typical images
    like water and dark holes. A preoccupation of Murdoch's
    is psychoanalytical symbols and philosophical symbols.
    She even uses artistic symbols, making significant
    the relations between paintings and her characters.
    Symbolism is part of the game between Murdoch and
    the reader who must be cultured to keep up with her.

23 "Holiday Reading." Observer, 23 July, p. 21.
        Brief review of A Word Child, pronouncing it
    timely in its criticism of the educational meritocracy,
    deeply amusing, and full of Murdochian surprises.

24 HUBBART, MARILYN STALL. "Fairy Tale Stereotypes as
    Unique Individuals: A Study of Iris Murdoch and

Anne Sexton." <u>Publications of the Arkansas Philog-
ical Association</u> 4:33-40.
    Compares the use of "fairy tale stereotypes" by
Murdoch and by Anne Sexton. Discusses Sexton poems
and <u>Under the Net</u>, <u>The Flight from the Enchanter</u>,
<u>A Severed Head</u>, and <u>The Unicorn</u> (the Sleeping Beauty
figure). Equates "faily tale stereotypes" with roles
imposed on people by solipsistic and manipulative
others.

25 IRWIN, MICHAEL. "Making Waves." <u>Times Literary
    Supplement</u>, 25 August, p. 945.
    Reviews <u>The Sea, the Sea</u>, commending its life and
its intellectual and imaginative energy but criticizing its flat dialogue and wooden narrative. Accuses
Murdoch of distorting human relationships through
exaggerating them. Values the variety of her talents
and her willingness to attempt so much.

26 JENNINGS, PAUL. "The New Murdoch." <u>Punch</u> 275
    (13 September):415-16.
    States that <u>The Sea, The Sea</u> plays with Sartre's
distinction between <u>etre-en-soi</u>, a person's sense of
himself, and <u>etre-pour-autre</u>, who other people think
he is. Praises Murdoch's admitting her involvement
in the act of writing.

27 KING, FRANCIS. "Love's Spell and Black Magic."
    <u>Spectator</u> 241 (26 August):16.
    Censures the melodramatic dialogue and clumsy
plotting of <u>The Sea, The Sea</u>, saying that it has the
untidiness of autobiography. Identifies guilt as a
major theme. Affirms Murdoch's rich imagination and
grand intellect.

28 KOGER, GROVE. Review of <u>The Sea, the Sea</u>. <u>Library
    Journal</u> 103 (1 September):1962.
    Review of <u>The Sea, The Sea</u> that regards it as a
fascinating and disturbing analysis of love's illusions, one of Murdoch's best since <u>The Black Prince</u>.

29 KUHNER, ARLENE ELIZABETH. "The Alien God in the
    Novels of Iris Murdoch." Ph.D. dissertation,
    University of Washington, 195 pp. Abstract in <u>DAI</u>
    39:2955A.
    A central character in several Murdoch novels,
the alien god is the focus of attention of the other
characters. He is perceived as having power and
focuses the fantasies and enchantment of the other
characters. The alien god is presented with a wealth
of allusive imagery. The figure allows Murdoch to
explore concepts of freedom, love, and fantasy. Five
novels depict the alien god as central: <u>The Flight
from the Enchanter</u>, <u>A Severed Head</u>, <u>An Unofficial</u>

Rose, The Unicorn, and A Fairly Honourable Defeat.
After the latter novel, Murdoch seems to abandon the
alien-god figure because of the artistic temptation
toward power, perceived negatively. The novels that
depict the alien-god figure are, however, strong
artistic statements about the paradox of the human
condition.

30 LAMARQUE, PETER. "Truth and Art in Iris Murdoch's
    The Black Prince." Philosophy and Literature 2
    (Fall):209-22.
         Interpretation of The Black Prince, partly at
    least in the light of The Sovereignty of Good. Asserts
    that Bradley has a double concern with truth--the high-
    minded concern of the artist and the pragmatic concern
    of the falsely convicted man. Discusses the problem
    of Bradley's credibility in relation to the different
    views of him in the postscripts. Says that Murdoch
    here has two concerns with truth: with the truth
    internal to the novel (the truth of Bradley's nar-
    ration) and with the truth revealed through fiction
    about the real world. According to Murdoch, art can
    provide a clearer view of the human situation than
    can the distractions of ordinary life. Bradley
    reflects on the difficulty of achieving objectivity
    and of giving a clear picture of the self and others.
    In trying to sift the evidence about Bradley's cred-
    ibility, the reader gets practice in directing his
    attention to other people, an act of love. Art can
    express truth in its objectivity (as opposed to self-
    serving fantasy) and in its particularity.

31 LE GROS, BERNARD. "Roman et philosophie chez Iris
    Murdoch." In Rencontres avec Iris Murdoch. Caen:
    Centre de recherches de litt. et ling. des pays de
    lang. angl. de l'Université de Caen, pp. 63-72.
         Murdoch is a writer concerned with the absurdity
    of human behavior, a comic, satiric writer. Her
    novels are allegories, comparable to Fellini's films.
    Each of her novels seems to be a message and a novel
    of existential metaphysics, which the reader must
    puzzle out. Murdoch's study Sartre: Romantic
    Rationalist throws light on her thought through an
    examination of their differences. Murdoch goes back
    to Plato's parable of the cave with man a prisoner of
    his ego but with a rudimentary idea of the Good and
    with a capacity to change. Art and love are privileg-
    ed means to attain the Good, but the highest virtue
    is an awareness of others.

32 McCLENDON, JAMES WILLIAM, Jr. "Three Strands of
    Christian Ethics." Journal of Religion and Ethics
    6 (Spring):54-80.

Analyses Christian morality in terms of three
interdependent strands: the splanchnic, the somatic,
and the anastatic. Applies the three strands to the
works of three contemporary moralists: Iris Murdoch,
Stanley Hauerwas, and John Cobb. Murdoch's moral
philosophy relates to the splanchnic strand in which
morality is grounded upon the response of organisms to
their environments.

The two poles of her morality are a real, historical, introspective self, which is the proper subject
of morality, and a real, transcendent, ideal form (the
Good or God), which is the proper object, with the
real world as the indispensable arena in which our
selves apprehend their true object. She takes up and
relates to each other all the characteristic splanchnic
themes: eros, the grounding of the self in the natural world, sin as distorted vision, and salvation as
the true perception of the other as other and of God
as God.

33 MacPHAIL, FIONA, and JEAN-LOUIS CHEVALIER. "A Word
    Child ou l'heauton-timoroumenos." In Recontres
    avec Iris Murdoch. Caen: Centre de recherches de
    litt. et ling. des pays de lang. angl. de l'Uni-
    versité de Caen, pp. 19-36.

In Murdoch's novel, Hilary is the word child,
caught in a circle around a nonexistent center, a concept opposed to Bergson's creative evolution. For
Hilary, language is not a matter of communication but
of control. His knowledge of words and languages is
only a technical satisfaction, not an aesthetic
pleasure. He uses words to protect himself. He
speaks but is afraid to raise emotions that may affect
his life. Hilary is his own prisoner.

At Kitty's death, Hilary realizes that his guilt
is not an exceptional thing, and this knowledge helps
him forget the idea of being the center of an inner
circle. He recovers his freedom after Kitty's death.
Hilary is at peace with the world, accepting his lot
to live alone without any false humility.

34 MAGEE, BRYAN. "Iris Murdoch on Natural Novelists
    and Unnatural Philosophers." Listener, 27 April,
    pp. 533-35.

Interview with Murdoch, edited from the BBC 2
series "Men of Ideas: Creators of Modern Philosophy."
Talk about the difference in Murdoch's language in
philosophy, about the possibility of writing good
philosophical novels. Murdoch asserts that art
involves a moral challenge with the artist really
looking at something other than herself.

35 MASTERS, ANTHONY. "Philosopher Kings." Times
    Educational Supplement, 1 December, p. 23.

Review of The Fire and the Sun, saying that
although it is short, it almost seems like a preface
to Plato's complete works. Compliments Murdoch's
explanation of the theory of Forms and of the theology
of the Timaeus. Regards her defense of art as powerful and moving.

36 MORIN, MICHELE. "Passion et salut dans l'oeuvre
    de Iris Murdoch." In Rencontres avec Iris Murdoch.
    Caen: Centre de recherches de litt. et ling. des
    pays de lang. angle. de l'Universite de Caen, pp.
    52-62.
    Analysis of passion and salvation in Murdoch's
works that sees her ideas as similar to Plato's with
most of her novels enacting Plato's allegory of the
cave. For Murdoch, passion is the psychological force
that moves people to salvation. The article examines
the efficacy of the passions of love, religion, art,
and morality as Murdoch has depicted them.

37 OATES, JOYCE CAROL. "The Novelists." New Republic
    179 (18 November):27-31.
    Reviews The Sea, The Sea, giving an overview of
Murdoch's work so far, saying Murdoch honors life's
random details in eerie, disturbing novels. Finds
some inferior works, some endings too tidy and some
endings provocative and unresolved. Calls Murdoch's
philosophical position classical, stern, and pessimis-
tic. Judges The Time of the Angels implausible but
illuminating in its Death-of-God concerns. Characterizes The Sea, The Sea as intermittently brilliant
with gnomic remarks. Complains that the novel is too
static and many characters too sketchy. Considers
Murdoch's novels to be intelligent and rewarding but
worries that they are becoming perfunctory.

38 "Paperback Choice." Observer, 10 September, p. 33.
    Brief review of Henry and Cato, estimating it as
a satisfying study of the British view of possessions,
praising the descriptions and Murdoch's reflections
on spiritual poverty.

39 "Paperback Choice." Observer, 12 February, p. 27.
    Reviews A Word Child as one of Murdoch's best,
deeply amusing with a surprising plot.

40 Rencontres avec Iris Murdoch. Caen: Centre de
    recherches de litt. et ling. des pays de lang. angl.
    de l'Université de Caen, 95 pp.
    Papers from a conference held at Caen, together
with an opening address by Murdoch, translated into
French, and closing remarks by her in English.

41 Review of <u>The Fire and the Sun</u>. <u>Choice</u> 15 (March):
    54.
        Regards the book as valuable in its organizing
    the relevant texts and in its reconciling in Platonic
    thought a case for beauty as well as truth, establish-
    ing a Platonic aesthetic in spite of Plato's reluctance.

42 Review of <u>The Sea, The Sea</u>. <u>Booklist</u> 75 (1 October):
    276.
        Characterizes the novel as a comedy of manners:
    elegant, psychological, and at the edge of tragedy.

4. Review of <u>The Sea, The Sea</u>. <u>Kirkus Review</u> 46
    (1 October):1087.
        Calls Charles an egotist who gives exquisite
    attention to life's small pleasures and somewhat of
    a stinker. He is now a recluse in a curious old house
    by the sea. A sea monster and other spectral matters
    hint of demons abroad. Although the metaphysical
    games can snarl a bit, this bright play with the
    demons is sly and tantalizing entertainment.

44 Review of <u>The Sea, The Sea</u>. <u>Time</u> 112 (30 October):
    128-29.
        Critique of the book as a familiar Murdoch pot-
    pourri with suspense, philosophy, and supernatural,
    and romantic drama. Declares Charles's story too
    detached and gauges Murdoch better at surfaces than at
    depths.

45 SAGE, LORNA. "Dragons from the Deep." <u>Observer</u>,
    27 August, p. 22.
        Affirms <u>The Sea, The Sea</u> as gossipy, inventive,
    and fantastic. Recognizes the feel of the theater
    world where people are addicted to illusion. The
    reviewer perceives a changed tone with the kidnapping
    of Hartley and with Charles facing ordinariness. She
    sees the novel to be a mirror of contemporary con-
    fusion.

46 SMITHSON, ISAIAH. "Iris Murdoch's <u>A Severed Head</u>:
    The Evolution of Human Consciousness. <u>Southern
    Review</u> (Adelaide) 11:133-53.
        Uses Erich Neumann's <u>The Origins and History of
    Consciousness</u> and <u>The Great Mother</u> to interpret <u>A
    Severed Head</u> as a dramatization of the struggle of the
    ego to emerge from the unconscious into consciousness.
    Perceives Martin as the ego figure and Antonia, Georgie,
    Rosemary, Alexander, and Palmer as Great Mother fig-
    ures who block Martin's growth and self-realization.
    Asserts that Honor Klein is presented in two lights:
    as a Terrible Mother figure that Martin must first
    battle and as the Princess and treasure that Martin
    must rescue and make his own. Relates the incest

motif to the process of the emergence of consciousness.
Tries to reconcile his interpretation to those of
critics like James Gindin who see the novel's main
theme as the overcivilized, overintellectualized man's
estrangement from his emotions.

47 STEWART, JACK F. "Art and Love in Murdoch's The
    Black Prince." Research Studies (Pullman, Wash.)
    46 (June):69-78.
        Examines the art-love theme, especially in the
    Hamlet tutorial, the postscript by Bradley, and the
    editor's postscript. Applies ideas from Murdoch's
    philosophical essays to the novel. Maintains that
    through Hamlet Bradley reaches a synthesis of subject
    and object, self and medium. Finds Bradley's book to
    be self-reflexive. Asserts that by sacrificing to
    art and love, he refines himself virtually out of
    existence and becomes Lover and Artist.

48 TODD, RICHARD. "The Plausibility of The Black
    Prince." Dutch Quarterly Review of Anglo-American
    Letters 8:82-93.
        Declares that Bradley's boot-, sock-, and foot-
    fetishes cast doubt on his "true love" and on the
    reliability of his narrative. Refers to Murdoch's
    critique in "On God and Good" of Freud's picture of
    man. Says that Julian attracts Bradley not because
    he is a repressed homosexual but because in her
    androgynous aspect, she represents the attraction of
    the other, dimly perceived. Declares that Bradley is
    unaware of his self-deception (his sexual obession).
    Maintains that Bradley's narrative unreliability is
    supported by the postscripts and the editorial ap-
    paratus.

49 "Tyger and Kestrel." Philosophy 53:433-35.
        Editorial on the attention given by recent
    philosophers to the relation of animals to humans.
    Alludes to Murdoch's remarks in The Sovereignty of
    Good to the effect that people can forget themselves
    and their self-absorbed moods by observing nature,
    here a hovering kestrel. Murdoch sees the kestrel as
    restoring balance in the person ensnared by subjec-
    tivity. The release is effected because of the
    animal's independent existence.

50 VOLKER, WOLFRAM. The Rhetoric of Love: Das
    Menschenbild und die Form des Romans bei Iris
    Murdoch. Amsterdam: Gruner, 168 pp.
        First surveys trends in criticism of Murdoch as
    a moral philosopher and as a novelist who deals with
    moral and philosophical questions. The goal of the
    study is to show that the form of Murdoch's novels is
    fitted for the implicit reader, used as an internal

communication structure. It also is to show how the
image of man forms the basis of Murdoch's relationship
to reality. The study relates the dialectical identity of the narrative method and the activity of reading to the understood form of her novels. It examines
her image of man from the perspective of her theoretical writings, which seek to correct the failings of
empiricism and existentialism.

Volker analyzes the dimensions of the intended
audience in The Time of The Angels, Bruno's Dream,
and The Black Prince. Murdoch wants the reader to
be active in the work, a consideration more important
than perfection of structure.

51 WILLIAMS, DAVID. "Pick of the Month." Punch 275
    (20 September):472.
      Reviews The Red and the Green, calling it a flop,
muddled and disarrayed. Complains that the historical
events are outside Murdoch's personal experience.

52 WOLFE, PETER. "'Malformed Treatise' and Prizewinner:
    Iris Murdoch's The Black Prince." Studies in the
    Literary Imagination 11:97-113.
      Interpretation of The Black Prince that discusses
Bradley's character, saying he runs away from truth,
wisdom, love, and beauty. Characterizes him as a
repressed Puritan, not admitting his desire for Julian
or his envy of her father. Explores Bradley's self-
defeating behavior, allowing himself to be convicted
of murder. Asserts that he uses his guilt to give
himself an external wholeness, playing saint and
martyr, making his life imitate art, shutting out
contingency. Finds in each postscript new data or a
new slant. Remarks on the tension between Bradley's
pompous style and the unpredictable things that be-
fall him.

1979

1 ADAMS, P.L. "P.L.A." Atlantic 243 (January):98.
     Review of The Sea, The Sea that calls Charles
irresponsible and interfering, although in inventive
ways. Finds the theme to be the tendency of white
magic to linger and become black magic.

2   AIKEN, GAIL ELIZABETH. "This Accidental World: The
    Philosophy and Fiction of Iris Murdoch."   Ph.D.
    dissertation, University of Tennessee, 364 pp.
    Abstract in DAI 40:5047A.
        Structured around four topics discussed in The
    Sovereignty of Good: language, love, art, and death.
    Each chapter places the topic in Murdoch's philosophi-
    cal system, surveys its use as a theme in Murdoch's
    novels, and interprets one novel as an appropriate use
    of the theme.   Analyses A Word Child on language, The
    Sacred and Profane Love Machine on love, The Black
    Prince on art, and Henry and Cato on death.   Concludes
    that Murdoch's philosophical system is developed in
    her philosophical essays and contradicted in her
    novels.

3   CAMPBELL, PAUL NEWELL.   Review of The Fire and the
    Sun.   Quarterly Journal of Speech 65 (February):
    115-16.
        Declares that the book treats the religious
    nature of Plato's hostility to art.   Complains that
    in the first three-fourths Murdoch seems sympathetic
    to Plato's position and that the last fourth is con-
    fusing.   Describes it as provocative but frustrating.

4   CHETTLE, JUDITH. "Playing the Game."   National
    Review 31 (3 August):980.
        Reviews The Sea, The Sea, associating it with
    Lewis Carroll's Alice.   Judges Murdoch to be the
    best English woman novelist today, comparing her
    favorably to John Fowles.   Applauds the sparkling per-
    formance but hungers for more feeling.

5   CUNNEEN, SALLY. "Ingmar Bergman Crossed with Charlie
    Chaplin? What Iris Murdoch Doesn't Know."
    Commonweal 106 (9 November):623-26.
        Review of The Sea, The Sea as a pseudomemoir, a
    fusion of literary form and moral vision.   Asserts
    that from The Nice and the Good on, Murdoch attained
    mastery of her medium, creating believable cross-
    sections of society.   Maintains that A Fairly Honour-
    able Defeat and The Black Prince are her greatest
    achievements, mixing good and evil, comedy and tragedy.
    Praises Murdoch's comic vision.

6 DINNAGE, ROSEMARY. "The Corruption of Love." <u>New</u>
   <u>York Review of Books</u> 26 (8 February):20-21.
      Characterizes <u>The Sea, The Sea</u> as a passionately
   moral story, whose central metaphor is the stage. Perceives Murdoch's theme to be "the corruption of art
   and love by will and self-deception." Murdoch resists
   the temptation to let her philosophical pattern be
   overwhelmed by stagey fictional tricks. Senses in the
   novel real feeling, equal to the contrivances.

7 DRABBLE, MARGARET. "Of Treacle Tarts and Eternal
   Love." <u>Saturday Review</u> 6 (6 January):52.
      Reviews <u>The Sea, The Sea</u>, calling it triumphant
   in holding the reader captive by its tangled relationships and mysterious denouements. Notes numerous
   references to the <u>Iliad</u> and the <u>Odyssey</u>. Calls Murdoch's novels glittering, exhilarating, and magical,
   especially this new one.

8 FLETCHER, JOHN. "Cheating the Dark Gods: Iris
   Murdoch and Racine." <u>International Fiction Review</u>
   6 (Winter):75-76.
      Brief article comparing Murdoch in <u>A Severed</u>
   <u>Head</u> with Racine, both achieving the effect of uncertainty along with that of predetermination. Martin's
   realizing that he loves Honor Klein is like Racine's
   heroes realizing that they are trapped in the tragic
   net. Each is chosen by an inexorable fate.

9 FLETCHER, JOHN. Review of <u>The Sea, The Sea</u>.
   <u>American Book Review</u> 2 (Summer):4-5.
      Evaluates the novel as a major achievement, maybe
   with <u>The Black Prince</u> Murdoch's best. Finds four main
   oppositions: art versus reality, self-deception
   versus self-understanding, the magical versus the mundane,
   and reconciliation and love versus hatred and enmity.

10 FOLEY, BETTY MITCHELL. "Iris Murdoch's Use of Works
   of Art as Analogies of Moral Themes." Ph.D. dissertation, Wayne State University, 203 pp. Abstract
   in <u>DAI</u> 40:2072A.
      This study is an interdisciplinary analysis of
   nineteen Murdoch novels. In eleven she employs specific works of art to give an allegorical dimension to
   the plots. The other eight novels use art as imagery.
   Chapter 1 discusses Murdoch's principles and ideas from
   <u>The Fire and the Sun</u> and <u>The Sovereignty of Good</u>.
   Chapters 2 to 12 discuss eleven novels that include
   a work of art whose subject matter parallels the fiction's theme. Chapter 13 is an overview of the other
   novels in which art defines personality. The characters' ability to attend to a work of art (forgetting
   self) measures the characters' potential for perceiv-

ing reality beneath appearances and their ability to
approach truth.

11 GRIBBLE, JENNIFER. "The Art of Iris Murdoch."
    Quadrant (Sydney) 142 (May):36-39.
        Reviews The Sea, The Sea as Murdoch's best since
    Under the Net. Asserts that this novel develops from
    A Word Child and Henry and Cato. Considers Murdoch's
    strong point to be compassion, transcending irony.

12 HAGUE, ANGELA. "Iris Murdoch's Comic Vision."
    Ph.D. dissertation, Florida State University, 240
    pp. Abstract in DAI 40:5048A-49A.
        Declares that the comic dimensions and ironic
    tone of Murdoch's novels are as important as her use
    of philosophical ideas and mythic patterns. This
    study discusses the relation of comedy to fiction,
    sketching the main characteristics of the contempor-
    ary British comic novel. Explores Murdoch's use of
    comic techniques. Analyzes the comic structure and
    tone of An Accidental Man, The Black Prince, and
    The Sea, The Sea.

13 HOWARD, MAUREEN. "Eight Recent Novels." Yale
    Review 68 (Spring):434-36.
        Review of The Sea, The Sea that sees Charles's
    love for Hartley to be Humbert's love for Lolita,
    turned upside-down. Sees the continuation of Murdoch's
    themes since The Flight from the Enchanter: the
    presence of the accidental and the casual and the dif-
    ficulty of pursuing goodness.

14 JOHNSON, ALEXANDRA. "Iris Murdoch's Seaside Parody."
    Christian Science Monitor 71 (8 January):B2.
        Judges The Sea, The Sea to be less than Murdoch's
    best, repeating too much. Maintains that the real
    Gothic element here is the characters' insistence on
    acting against their true instincts. Commends Murdoch's
    situational irony and sardonic observations about
    human motivation.

15 MAGEE, BRYAN. "Entrevista a Iris Murdoch."
    Dialogos: Artes/Letras/Ciencias (Mexico) 87:17-21.
        Translation into Spanish of the BBC 2 interview
    of Iris Murdoch by Bryan Magee in the series "Men of
    Ideas: The Creators of Modern Philosophy." Murdoch
    discussed the relationship between philosophy and
    literature in general and in her own work.

16 MAGEE, BRYAN. Men of Ideas. New York: Viking
    Press, pp. 262-85.
        Series of interviews with contemporary British
    philosophers, including Murdoch who speaks on the
    connections between philosophy and literature. Murdoch

says that philosophy tries to clarify some very difficult, highly technical problems, while literature
is full of tricks, magic, and deliberate mystification.
It does many things while philosophy does one thing.
Besides the distinction in their aims, their styles
are different, too. An ideal philosophical style has
an unambiguous hardness or plainness. It involves
suppressing the personal voice. Literature involves
controlling and transforming the personal voice.
    Philosophy does not aim at formal perfection for
its own sake. Literature, however, deals with complex
problems of aesthetic form. The philosopher must
have a relentless ability to stay with a problem,
while the artist desires novelty. Literature is
closer to play. A deep motive for literature is the
wish to defeat the formlessness of the world.
    Murdoch sees no general role of philosophy in
literature, although, of course, artists think.
Except for exceptions like Sartre, she resists the
idea that novels make use of philosophical ideas in a
structural way.

17 "Mystical Themes." Christian Century 95 (13 Decem-
    ber):1219-21.
    Review of The Sea, The Sea, saying that Murdoch
mixes the inexplicable, the miraculous, and the farcical. Asserts that she uses bitter social comedy to
meditate on the theme of obsession.

18 "Notes on Current Books." Virginia Quarterly Review
    55 (Spring):58.
    Finds in The Sea, The Sea all of Murdoch's
talents and none of her weaknesses. Praises the
descriptions of the sea, the use of the sea as a
symbol for embroiled thinking, and the rhythm of the
book as ceaseless ebb and flow.

19 O'DONNELL, PATRICK JAMES. "The Fragile Web: Inter-
    pretation as a Subject in Contemporary Fiction."
    Ph.D. dissertation, University of California at
    Davis, 260 pp. Abstract in DAI 40:5050A.
    Analysis of how the process of interpretation as
defined by such thinkers as Sartre, Merleau-Ponty,
Heidegger, Ricoeur, Binswanger, and Derrida is perceived to be important in many contemporary novels.
In some novels the interpretation of reality is a
projection by the hero that demands that the reader
become involved in evaluating the nature of the
interpretive process. Discusses two modes of interpretation (open and obsessed) in novels by Murdoch,
Golding, Cary, Nabokov, O'Connor, Barth, Pynchon,
and Hawkes. In the open mode, the hero is open to

the multiplicity of the universe, accepting its ambiguity. The obsessed hero, however, imposes on the
world a singular pattern of being, reflecting his own
ego.

20 PAULING, TOM. "Books and Writers." Encounter 52
    (January):53-54.
        Criticizes The Sea, The Sea as too academic and
    self-conscious and the style as affected and prepost-
    erous. Censures the novel as an ambitious failure and
    a pointless fantasy.

21 "Pick of the Paperback." Christian Science Monitor
    71 (8 January):B5.
        Brief review of The Nice and the Good, declaring
    that Murdoch here comes close to creating a unified
    whole from her many talents.

22 PIPER, WILLIAM BOWMAN. "The Accommodation of the
    Present in Novels by Murdoch and Powell." Studies
    in the Novel 11:178-93.
        Critical article that asserts that in her first-
    person narratives, Murdoch "exalts the present" making
    each event compelling, while Powell in Dance to the
    Music of Time makes reading "a historical meditation."

23 RADCLIFFE, ELSA J. Gothic Novels of the Twentieth
    Century: An Annotated Bibliography. Metuchen, N.J.:
    Scarecrow Press, p. 156.
        Lists several of Murdoch's novels that reviewers
    call Gothic but finds the designation to be misapplied.
    Judges The Black Prince to be tiresome with no Gothic
    elements and The Unicorn to be a pretentious tale
    about the machinations of an alcoholic.

24 Review of The Sea, The Sea. Choice 16 (April):224.
        Evaluates the novel as one of Murdoch's most
    suspenseful and provocative, lauding her storytelling
    power. Declares that Charles is relieved to retreat
    from human attachments.

25 Review of The Sea, The Sea. Manchester Guardian
    Weekly 120 (January):15.
        Mentions the novel as that year's winner of the
    Booker prize, fresh in people's minds.

26 Review of The Sea, The Sea. West Coast Review of
    Books 5 (January):31.
        Criticizes the lack of subject matter in the
    novel, the overwritten style, the failure to provide a
    tidy ending, and Charles's tiresome assault on Hartley.

27 SCHOLES, ROBERT. "Iris Murdoch's Unicorn." In
    Fabulation and Metafiction. Urbana: University of
    Illinois Press, pp. 56-63.
        Reprinting of the chapter in Fabulation (1967),
    discussing The Unicorn as modern allegory taking as
    its model not God's order but the rage for order in
    the mind of man. In the novel, Murdoch gradually
    redirects the reader from who-done-it to a more philo-
    sophical level of attention. The gradual shift from
    fictional to ideational elements climaxes in the final
    structure of ideas.

28 TODD, RICHARD. Iris Murdoch: The Shakespearian
    Interest. New York: Barnes & Noble, 134 pp.
        Murdoch's novels since 1968 demonstrate a partic-
    ular interest in Shakespeare in his success in reconcil-
    ing the demands of form or plot with the contingent phenom-
    ena of reality. There are numerous allusions to Shake-
    speare from A Severed Head on, although interests predom-
    inate from The Unicorn to The Time of the Angels. The
    Shakespearian interest reappears from The Nice and the
    Good to The Black Prince.
        The seemingly arbitrary pairings of Murdoch's charac-
    ters indicate her belief that characters should be free
    to act surprisingly. Her formalized endings show that
    their style is not cramped by authorial intrusion. A
    group of her novels after A Severed Head contemplate
    Shakespeare's comic sense. They also try to reconcile
    the opposition of a limited cast with a large spread-out
    cast. Northrup Frye's scheme of the three phases in the
    integration of society, used to illuminate Shakespeare's
    comedy, can be applied to Murdoch's comedy.
        A Fairly Honourable Defeat shows indebtedness to A Mid-
    summer Night's Dream, Twelfth Night, and All's Well That
    Ends Well. The concluding chapter of The Nice and the
    Good echoes the last scene of The Merchant of Venice.
    Shakespearian elements, especially the influence of A Mid-
    summer Night's Dream and Measure for Measure, can be seen
    in the novels featuring power figures. Murdoch sees the
    coexistence of form and contingency in the work of Shake-
    speare, a hallmark of good art. Such good art is worthy
    of respect because the contemplation of good art can arouse
    virtue.

29 WALTERS, RAY. "Paperback Talk." New York Times
    Book Review, 15 April, p. 29.
        Briefly reviews A Fairly Honourable Defeat,
    asserting that it explores the problem of evil with
    Julius trying to break up the relationships of two
    loving couples.

30 WEINSTEIN, BERNARD. Review of The Sea, The Sea.
    Best Sellers 38 (March):379-80.

Compliments the novel despite its length and repetitions for its revealing the unexpected in character and situation. Calls it fascinating.

31 WILLIAMS, DAVID. "Dear Diaries." Punch 276 (9 May):826.
    Brief review of The Sandcastle, describing it as full of violent, Gothic happenings. Says it is nostalgic and lovely.

32 WILLIAMS, DAVID. "Dear Diaries." Punch 276 (9 May):826.
    Brief review of Under the Net that characterizes it as a tale of two cities: Paris and London. Finds it fragmentary and kaleidoscopic.

33 WINSOR, DOROTHY ANN. "The Continuity of the Gothic: The Gothic Novels of Charlotte Bronte, Emily Bronte, and Iris Murdoch." Ph.D. dissertation, Wayne State University, 214 pp. Abstract in DAI 40:5882A.
    Examines the Gothic conventions in the novels of the three writers to make clear the unstated assumptions and the world view implied. Studies Murdoch's The Bell, The Unicorn, and The Time of the Angels. All three writers balance realistic and Gothic elements. Murdoch employs the Gothic feminine posture to symbolize a masochistic means of dealing with passion.

1980

1 ABELMAN, PAUL. "Geometric." Spectator, 6 September, p. 20.
    Review of Nuns and Soldiers as better than The Sea, The Sea but as still not working as a whole. Finds the interactions of the characters not convincing. Praises the narrative drive and the independent life of some of the characters in themselves. Concludes that the landscape, psychology, theology, and symbolism are forced together.

2 AMIS, MARTIN. "Let's Fall in Love." Observer, 7 September, p. 29.
    Reviews Nuns and Soldiers as a minor entertainment, not one of the major Murdochs. Remarks that the characters live in an eroticized world, not worrying about health and money. Calls Murdoch addictive, with the reader not wanting the story to end.

3 BIRDSALL, MICHAEL EDWARD. "Art, Beauty, and Morality in the Novels of Iris Murdoch." Ph.D. dissertation, University of Minnesota, 145 pp. Abstract in DAI 41:2114A.
    Examines Murdoch's concept of morality, how that concept is related to quality in art, and how she

uses art-related images and metaphors. Interprets
Murdoch as exploring the difficulty of combining the
randomness of reality with the precision of art.
Follows the analogy between creating good art and
living a good life. The appreciation of art leads to
an understanding of reality and to a good life.

4 BYATT, A.S. "All That Is." New Statesman 100
   (5 September):21.
      Reviews Nuns and Soldiers positively, affirming
the amazing sense of underlying order and the swarm-
ing randomness together. Declares Murdoch is almost
always at her best in the novel. Sees in Tim's and
Gertrude's falling in love a depiction of the total
awareness and hunger of people for each other. Extols
Murdoch's mastery of narrative pace.

5   . "People in Paper Houses: Attitudes to
   'Realism' and 'Experiment' in English Postwar
   Fiction." In The Contemporary English Novel. New
   York: Holmes & Meier, pp. 19-41.
      The reaction against experiment in the British
novel in the fifties was concerned with rejecting the
modernist model of Joyce and Woolf. Later the avant
garde of the sixties and seventies have rejected this
rejection. Critics speaking for realism--John Bayley
in The Characters of Love, Murdoch in "Against Dryness," Bernard Bergonzi, and David Lodge--are anxious
about the future of realism. Critics have accused
Murdoch's novels of failures in density. They have
not grasped that Under the Net is a fable about the
need for concepts and a language of a new realism.
Her later novels are a moral and formal attempt to
achieve the realism she and John Bayley respect.
      Murdoch claims that we can no longer take lan-
guage for granted. This self-consciousness raises
problems. Her truth telling involves abandoning
solipsism and recognizing that reality is other than
ourselves. Art is a technique for discovering the
truth. Byatt examines three novels that embody problems with realism: Murdoch's The Black Prince,
Wilson's As If by Magic, and Lessing's The Golden
Notebook.

6 CHARPENTIER, COLETTE. "The Critical Reception of
   Iris Murdoch's Irish Novels (1963-1976) I: The
   Unicorn." Etudes irlandaises 5:91-103.
      Examines criticism of The Unicorn, using a
synthetic approach, noting what struck most critics
and what elements seem missing. The main bibliographic source was Tominga's and Schneidermeyer's bibliography and a few national bibliographies. All commentators say that love is the main theme with other
suggestions being guilt, innocence, and freedom. Most

critics discuss one or two characters, usually Hannah,
Marian, Effingham, Max or Dennis. Jamesie, Alice,
and Pip are hardly ever examined. Commentators who do
discuss the unicorn usually say that it is Hannah with
Marian as the virgin, but some see that the unicorn
is not necessarily one character. Ten studies discuss
the novel as Gothic. The descriptions of the landscape are praised, but few critics name the location
as Ireland.

7 _____. "Irland ou pas?" Etudes irlandaises 5:
   283-84.
      Review of Iris Murdoch by Donna Gerstenberger.
   Explains the structure of the study: three chapters,--
   on Murdoch's accomplishment, on The Red and the Green,
   and on the Irish connection--with a bibliography alpha-
   betical instead of chronological. Notes Gerstenberger's
   difficulty presenting Murdoch in a series about Irish
   authors but praises her knowledge of Yeats.

8 CHURCH, MARGARET. "Social Consciousness in the
   Works of Elizabeth Bowen, Iris Murdoch, and Mary
   Lavin." College Literature 7:158-63.
      Asserts that the three writers represent a new
   revival of Irish women. Each writer has her own means
   of expressing social consciousness. Murdoch is more
   concerned with the dislocations caused by the social
   injustices of capitalism. The article discusses ideas
   from The Sovereignty of Good and The Fire and the Sun,
   with the first work stressing the role of love and
   the second identifying art as a mainstay of the social
   structure. In "A House of Theory," Murdoch cites
   socialism as the political structure best suited to
   establishing the sovereignty of the good. Church
   perceives political dimensions in The Flight from the
   Enchanter, seeing in it the theme of personal freedom
   with the idea that no one should submit to the will
   of another.

9 COOKE, JUDY. "Bull's Eye." New Statesman 100
   (10 October):22.
      Reviews The Sea, The Sea as a good yarn, winning
   the 1978 Booker Prize. Calls the analysis of love
   tender and truthful. Assures the reader of being
   swept away by the narrative. Says that Murdoch writes
   superbly with an oriental splendor, praising her
   intelligence and her celebration of art.

10 DINNAGE, ROSEMARY. "Inside, Outside." Times
   Literary Supplement. 5 September, p. 951.
      Review of Nuns and Soldiers, criticizing it as
   not one of Murdoch's best. Declares it enjoyable
   reading but complains that the unity between ideas
   and narrative is fragile with a lack of fit between

formality and naturalism. Recognizing familiar Murdoch elements, perceives an underlying structure of
moral debate and characters with more or less realistic life.

11 "Fiction Reprints." Publishers Weekly 217 (16 May):
    210.
         Provides a brief plot summary of The Sea, The
    Sea and quotes an earlier review that called it a
    major work.

12 FOGARTY, MARGARET ELIABETH. "The Search for an
    Aesthetic in the Fiction of Iris Murdoch, with
    Special Reference to The Black Prince." M.A.
    thesis, University of South Africa. Abstract in
    Masters Abstracts 19:325.
         In Murdoch's aesthetic, art and morality are
    inseparable. The Black Prince reveals how Murdoch's
    novels are a fusion of concept and image. A major
    novelist, she comments incisively on the nature of
    art and its function.

13 FURUKI, YOSHIKO. "From the Vicarious to the Im-
    mediate--The Emerging Theme of Iris Murdoch's
    Henry and Cato." Tsuda Review 25:1-16.
         Murdoch's adult bildungsromans describe the
    delayed maturing of men who have long since reached
    manhood. Compared to The Black Prince, Henry and Cato
    is more organically fit, and it conveys a clearer
    message about the theme. The truth that Henry dis-
    covers is that to live is to be engaged in immediate
    experience, rather than vicarious experience.
         Henry has been living in America with the Fishers.
    After a brief affair with Bella, Henry enjoys his
    vicarious position: he has Russell and Bella live the
    married life for him. Henry wants Cato to be his
    agent for doing good and for having faith. Henry also
    identifies himself with Max as a possible artist. So
    Henry has a family, home, religion, and occupation all
    by proxy. His brother's death brings him home to face
    real life.
         One person who helps to awaken Henry is Beautiful
    Joe. Joe kidnaps Cato and tries to rape his sister,
    demanding a large ransom from Henry. Because of his
    fear, Henry comes to see the courage in Colette. He
    is now finally ready for a real relationship. At the
    end of the novel, Henry has seen through the fiction
    of vicarious experience. He has matured to live
    a more common but real life.

14 GAFFNEY, JAMES. "The Fire and the Sun: Why Plato
    Banished the Artists." America 143 (15 November):314.
         Reviews the book as summing up Platonic thought
    so well that it could serve as an introduction or a

source of new insight. Identifies Plato's distrust
of art as religious, concerned with truth.

15 GLENDINNING, VICTORIA. "Vice Is Natural and Virtue
    Is Not." Listener 104 (4 September):308-9.
        Maintains that Nuns and Soldiers is almost a
universal mythology, dramatized and overlaid with the
Christian myth. Regards the elevation of human emotions to the mythological as giving life shape and
significance. Notes the cheerful middle-class realistic details in the embodiment.

16 HIRSCH, PENNEY LOZOFF. "'A Dangerous Delight': The
    Artist as Mage and the Persistence of Theurgic
    Aesthetics from Shakespeare to Singer." Ph.D.
    dissertation, Northwestern University, 381 pp.
    Abstract in DAI 41:2612A.
        This study examines the changing relationship of
theurgy (magic and spiritual preparation for prophetic
experience) to its manifestations in literature. It
looks at works by Spencer, Shakespeare, Coleridge,
Melville, Singer, and Murdoch. The final chapter
discusses the importance of theurgic aesthetics for
Iris Murdoch, Isaac Bashevis Singer, Toni Morrison,
and Maxine Hong Kingston. These writers all explore
questions about art and magic.

17 KELLMAN, STEVEN G. The Self-Begetting Novel. New
    York: Columbia University Press, pp. 87-93.
        Reworks and extends his earlier article (1976)
characterizing Under the Net as a self-begetting novel.
Murdoch's book on Sartre provides a link with the
French reflexive tradition. The self-begetting
novel makes frequent allusions to other literary works.
Each narrator is intent on incorporating and surpass-
ing his predecessors. Murdoch evokes Sartre. This
type of novel recounts the creation of a work very
much like itself; it is also a portrait of a fictive
artist being born. The self-begetting hero typically
occupies center stage throughout the novel.
        Murdoch's reading of Sartre suggests a view of
French fiction as aseptic. She intends to introduce
the stuff of life into the "Continental petrie dish."
As evident in the example of Jake, literature can be an
effective means of accommodating the contingent world.
Under the Net is a striking portrait of the central
protagonist's moral progress.

18 KOGER, GROVE. Review of Nuns and Soldiers. Library
    Journal 105 (15 September):2433.
        A brief note praising the narrative pace, the
inventiveness, and the expansive framework of ideas.

19 LENOWITZ, KATHRYN. "The Controversy over Character:
    An Examination of the Novels of Iris Murdoch and
    Nathalie Sarraute." Ph.D. dissertation, University
    of Colorado at Boulder, 236 pp. Abstract in DAI
    (41):3567A.
        Murdoch, committed to the primacy of character,
    is not really an opposite pole to Sarraute, who
    demands a subtraction of character. Both study not
    isolated individuals but interpersonal human relation-
    ships. Both investigate the role of knowledge in per-
    sonal interactions. Both reject any conceptual model
    that diminishes the psyche.

20 MORITZ, CHARLES, ed. "Iris Murdoch." In Current
    Biography Yearbook. New York: H.W. Wilson, pp.
    268-72.
        Brief assessment of Murdoch's importance in con-
    temporary literature, followed by information on her
    birth, education, childhood writings, war work, begin-
    nings in philosophy, postgraduate education, career
    as a philosophy teacher, and first published work on
    Sartre. Chronological survey of the novels and their
    critical receptions, information on honors and prizes
    she has recieved, mention of her adaptations and
    original plays. Calls Murdoch an outspoken commenta-
    tor on contemporary literature and philosophy.

21 "Paperback Choice." Observer, 5 October, p. 28.
        Brief review of The Sea, The Sea, naming it the
    Booker Prize winner and calling Charles a conscious
    Prospero using wit, emotional greed, and fierce op-
    portunism to survive.

22 Review of Nuns and Soldiers. Kirkus Review, 1 Novem-
    ber, p. 1417.
        Sees the book as expanding a minor romantic
    tangle into a knotty web of intellect and emotion
    with a generous number of Murdoch's characteristic
    themes and devices. Experiences the tension between
    the irony and the highly serious theme of love.

23 Review of Nuns and Soldiers. Observer, 7 December,
    p. 27.
        Brief review. Peter Conrad picks the novel as
    one of the two books he most enjoyed that year.
    Characterizes it as a comedy of erotic enchantment,
    wise, funny, and forgiving.

24 Review of Nuns and Soldiers. Publishers Weekly 218
    (14 November):46.
        Brief review that censures the novel for being
    talky, for lacking real drama, for including improbable
    events and melodrama, and for making the principal

characters too insignificant for the weighty themes
of love and betrayal.

25 SAGE, LORNA. "Female Fictions: The Women Novelists."
    In The Contemporary Novel. New York: Holmes &
    Meier, pp. 67-87.
        Postwar women novelists are at the sensitive
    center of British fiction, mapping the limitations of
    the tradition they are working in. The greatest
    example of countinuity is Murdoch, who resembles
    nineteenth-century serial writers. She differentiates
    the written word from the wider reality, making novels
    out of the approximations and clashes of language with
    reality. She has adopted the various new devices of
    style and structure without accepting their demoral-
    izing contemporary implications. The Black Prince
    sets the hero's narrative in a context of contradic-
    tory accounts without questioning the status of the
    author.
        Murdoch's novels present themselves as objects for
    consumption. They combine contempt for language with
    fluency and gusto. The organizing images and myths
    are localized and not allowed to form any grand pat-
    tern. After discussing The Red and the Green and
    The Black Prince, Sage analyzes the work on Margaret
    Drabble, Muriel Spark, Doris Lessing, Angela Carter,
    and Beryl Bainbridge.

26 _____. "Invasion of Outsiders." Granta 3:131-36.
        States that the English novel is problematical
    today because the language is so much larger than the
    culture and the literature is somewhere in between
    them. The sphere of influence seems always to be
    shrinking. Murdoch remains the grandest and most
    teasing exemplar of the continuity of the past. She
    uses the prestigious techniques of alienation with a
    fine carelessness. The inventiveness of her fiction
    and its deliberate impurity are held up by her con-
    viction that art is second-best. She is an allegor-
    izer aware of the bad faith involved in seeing your-
    self at the center of things. Yet her characters
    sustain a more or less theatrical sense of their own
    importance. That contradiction communicates a sense
    of pervasive, familiar unreality. Murdoch and Angus
    Wilson demonstrate the English novel's capacity for
    de-naturing itself without breaking with the past.

27 SANDERS, HANS JOCHEN. "Menschliche Natur und
    Individualitat in Fielding's Tom Jones und im
    spatburgerlichen englischen Roman." Zeitschrift
    für Anglistik und Amerikanistik (Leipzig) 28:
    237-43.
        Noted in the 1981 MLA Bibliography as exploring
    Fielding's influence on Iris Murdoch and William Golding.

28 SCANLAN, MARGARET.   "Fiction and the Fictions of
    History in Iris Murdoch's The Red and the Green."
    Clio 9:365-78.
         States that Murdoch's novel is not a typical his-
    torical novel and identifies the central theme as the
    confrontation between literature and history. Both
    artists and revolutionaries seek to shape reality. In
    the Irish independence movement, what the artist
    imagined of it was translated into action, a reversal
    of the usual process of the artist portraying history.
    In the novel each character is given a political role
    and a set of political opinions. Scanlan finds al-
    lusions to Joyce and Yeats with Barney like Leopold
    Bloom and Pat like Stephen. The novel suggests a less
    glamorous reality behind Yeats's famous interpretation
    of Easter Week. The epilogue, however, seems to shift
    the tone and to affirm the terrible beauty of commit-
    ment and violent death.

29 SCOTT-KILVERT, IAN.   Review of Nuns and Soldiers.
    British Book News, November-December, p. 760.
         A mixed review, praising the virtuosity of her
    Shakespearian symbolism, her powers of description
    and verismilitude, and her insight into emotional
    experience, but assessing the actions, characters, and
    relationships here implausible, and the character
    Gertrude hard to reconcile with the moral law.

30 SLAYMAKER, WILLIAM E.   "The Labyrinth of Love: The
    Problem of Love and Freedom in the Novels of Iris
    Murdoch." Bluegrass Literary Review 1:39-44.
         All Murdoch's twenty novels and most of her
    philosophical essays concern the idea of freedom. In
    the 1950s and 1960s she attacked the romantic, promoth-
    ean freedom in Sartre's philosophy and Stuart Hamp-
    shire's careful rational analysis of freedom. By the
    1970s she believed in the severe limitations of human
    freedom. Her mataphors of mechanism, especially of
    the machinery of the human ego, imply the difficulty
    of attaining freedom. She says, however, that freedom
    is possible for those who can love and accept the
    other. In the novels of the 1970s the characters'
    freedom is severely limited by the dark force of sex-
    uality, by complications of human motivation, and
    by the murkiness of human psychology. The Black Prince
    uses Greek myth to depict the lack of freedom of
    Bradley Pearson, and the novels after it are similarly
    pessimistic about attaining freedom.

31 STEWART, IAN.   "Recent Fiction." Illustrated
    London News 268 (November):102.
         Reviews Nuns and Soldiers, asserting that Murdoch
    celebrates sexual love and the development of relation-
    ships with determined subtlety. Defines the nuns as

those who find their meaning in something other than
sexual satisfaction and the soldiers as those who
cling to an honorable, self-sacrificing role. Judges
the narrative treatment full but not always convincing.

32 STEWART, JACK F. "Dialectics in Murdoch's The Bell."
    Research Studies 48 (December):210-17.
        The dialectics here are objectivism, embodied in
    James Tayper Pace, and subjectivism, embodied in
    Michael Meade, seen especially in their different ser-
    mons. Relates the sermons to th objective-subjective
    dialectic with its poles of convention and neurosis,
    ordinary language man and totalitarian man, formal
    and contingent--terms from Murdoch's The Sublime and
    the Good. Declares that she has moved from subjectiv-
    ism to objectivism, from Hegel and Sartre through Kant
    back to Plato, and from the idea of freedom to that
    of love.

33 WALTERS, RAY. "Paperback Talk." New York Times
    Book Review 85 (10 August):31.
        Brief review of The Sea, The Sea, taking pleasure
    in Murdoch's intelligence, portraying Arrobwby's com-
    pulsion to become a good man instead of a liar.

34 WELDHEN, MARGARET. "Morality and Metaphor." New
    Universities Quarterly 2:215-28.
        Exploration of ideas from The Sovereignty of the
    Good and from other philosophical works to support
    the idea that metaphor is the base of morality because
    it is the key to the ordering of experience. Starts
    with Murdoch's position on how to relate moments of
    choice to our inner states of being. Sets up the
    distinction between poeta, the language of metaphor,
    and techne, the language for the manipulation of
    things. Investigates how morality is involved with
    creativity and uses Murdoch's idea of language as con-
    stituting the fabric of human life. Relates morality
    and art to the perception of the real. Murdoch
    associates the development of consciousness with the
    use of metaphors.

35 WILLIAMS, DAVID. "Good Companions." Punch 279
    (15 October):662.
        Brief review of The Sea, The Sea, calling it
    uneven and objecting to the male narrator and to
    Murdoch's liking for the Gothic and the pathetic fal-
    lacy. Considers it less than her best: Under the
    Net and Bruno's Dream.

36 WINSOR, DOROTHY A. "Iris Murdoch and the Uncanny:
    Supernatural Events in The Bell." Literature and
    Psychology 30:147-54.

The eerie, supernatural elements that Murdoch
uses consistently in her novels are closely connected
with hidden aspects of man's inner life. Winsor uses
Freud's analysis of the uncanny to illuminate the
supernatural events in The Bell. Freud links adult
perceptions of seemingly supernatural events to the
loss of the social facade usually covering primitive
needs. Like Freud, Murdoch ties her uncanny elements
to primitive psychic drives and opposes them to forces
like organized religion.

A problem in Murdoch's novels is that if the
characters remain conventional, they are destructive
and unloving toward reality. If they attempt to
recognize primitive elements from their pasts, they
become frightened by these forces. Love seems possible only in the abstract and not in actual relationships between human beings. Murdoch's distrust of
man's maturity haunts the novels in the form of supernatural events.

1981

1 ASHWORTH, ANN M. "Venus, Cupid, Folly, and Time:
   Bronzino's Allegory and Murdoch's Fiction."
   Critique: Studies in Modern Fiction 23:18-24.
       Discusses the use of Bronzino's painting "Allegory
   of Time and Love" in The Nice and the Good. The
   painting and the novel expose the illusory nature of
   erotic love. Paula remembers Richard's interpretation
   of the painting, noting its cool beauty but the dom-
   inance of Truth. The moral dilemma of love unites
   the characters thematically. Murdoch admits the
   standard of goodness of human love, along with the
   higher standard of Indian mysticism. She also values
   the gaze of attention.

2 BELL, PEARL K. "Games Writers Play." Commentary
   71 (February):69-73.
       Review of Nuns and Soldiers that characterizes
   Murdoch as a game-playing novelist whose characters
   are sexual pawns. Maintains that she keeps an ironic
   distance with no hint of commitment to the dance of
   love and death. Her plots are full of intricacy,
   accident, and tempestuous adultery.

3 CHARPENTIER, COLETTE. "The Critical Reception of
   Iris Murdoch's Irish Novels (1963-1976) II: The
   Red and the Green." Etudes irlandaises 6
   (December):87-98.
       Survey of criticism of The Red and the Green.
   The book has mainly been seen as a historical novel,
   but Hicks and Baldanza see it as a comedy of manners.
   Critics discuss the significance of the epilogue and

Murdoch's obsession with family relationships and the
idea of fratricide. Many critics have considered the
setting and characters, praising Murdoch's descriptions
of Ireland. Characters most often discussed include
Barney, Pat, Millie, Frances, Christopher, Andrew,
Hilda, and Cathal. E. Pell says that the novel has
two climaxes, one a parody of sex and one a parody of
war. Some critics of the novel find the bedroom farce
to be fatal to it.

4   COHAN, STEVEN. "From Subtext to Dream Text: The
    Brutal Egoism of Iris Murdoch's Male Narrators."
    In Men By Women. Edited by Janet Todd. New York
    and London: Holmes & Meier, pp. 222-42.
        Out of twenty novels, Murdoch wrote six in the
first-person, each using a male narrator and none
using a female. She employs a male voice to artic-
ulate a sense of lived experience unique to another
self, ironic because her male narrators are convinced
that no one else can understand them. Her many plots
involving sexual comedy bring into relief the ideological function of the male and female characters. The
sexual comedy appears as a metaphor for the tension
between form and contingency. The world of form is
ruled by the male, the world of contingency by the
female. Murdoch's plots question whether the male's
sense of power and control can accommodate the instability of his emotional confrontation with the female.
The female exposes the male's egotism as well as his
inability to control the world beyond the self. The
female embodies the opacity of other persons that
eludes his understanding and manipulation.
        In The Sea, The Sea, Murdoch achieves the objec-
tivity of third-person narration without lessening the
singularity of her narrator's vision. The layered
plots allow her to work the narrative out of the
contingency-form tension so that it does frame the
critical view of men as a commentary on their unconscious brutality in the name of love.

5   CONRADI, PETER. "The Metaphysical Hostess: The
    Cult of Personal Relations in the Modern English
    Novel." ELH 48 (Summer):427-53.
        With the incomplete emancipation of women and in
a time of cultural pessimism, the hostess figure
appears in novels. She typifies the cult of personal
relations in an age of substitute religions, an alternative to the cult of business, money, and power. Personal relations, love and friendship, constitute a
separate realm of value. The hostess brings people
together in a relationship transcending other means
of communication. In Forster and Woolf, the metaphysical hostess becomes an organizing principle, suggesting a way in which things in the modern world

might be held together. Symbolizing the author's own
values, the metaphysical hostess stands for the life
force, dissolving differences and achieving accommodation and reconciliation.

   Murdoch's novels make use of the type but present
her mainly in a negative light. By aestheticizing
experience, the hostess may come to view people as
objects to be collected, like Kate Gray in The Nice
and the Good. The woman, like Clara Tisbourne in
An Accidental Man, may be flirtatious, confusing love
and friendship. An important feature of these characters is their stupidity and only partial emancipation.
A Severed Head uses Antonia Lynch-Gibbon, the apotheo-
sis of the type, to dramatize the degeneration of the
cult of personal relations into sexual confusion and
entanglement. Murdoch's intense suspicion of the
hostess is related to her Platonic doubts about the
value of art itself and her hostility to any false
consolation.

6   . "Useful Fictions: Iris Murdoch." Critical
   Quarterly 23 (Autumn):63-69.
   Nuns and Soldiers is a love story against a quasi-
religious background. Murdoch employs an operatic
realism, an intensely visual drama of instant loves,
stolen letters, and physical concealments. She re-
invents the arbitrary nature of the real world. The
plot is a series of ordeals to expose the moral
resources of the characters. The idea of God's ubiqui-
ty is a useful fiction, according to Gertrude. Nuns
and Soldiers also shows the usefulness of fictions.

7 CUNEEN, SALLY. "The Post-Divine Comedy of Iris
   Murdoch." Christian Century 18 (20 May):573-77.
   Defends Nuns and Soldiers against Stade's
caustic review, asserting that the center of the novel
is a powerful sexual realtionship. Contends that
Murdoch's view of love is more Platonic than Christian.
Declares that Stade's problem with the novel is his
inability to accept her ironic vision of human potential. Calls for a retrospective look to help general
readers understand Murdoch's complex strategies.

8 DICK, BERNARD F. Review of Nuns and Soldiers.
   World Literature Today 55 (Summer):472-73.
   Brief discussion that perceives the novel as
disjointed and too long. Objects to her allusions to
the arts, seeing the book polarized between art and
life, between academic and general readers.

9 FLETCHER, JOHN. "Reading Beckett with Iris Murdoch's
   Eyes." Journal of the Australasian Universities
   Language and Literature Association 55 (May):7-14.

Proposes to examine the function of the comic
hero and comic narrative in Under the Net as they are
influenced by Samuel Beckett's Murphy and Raymond
Queneau's Pierrot mon ami. Documents the influence
from a Murdoch interview with Harold Hobson. All
three of the novels are comic in a wry way and have
intricate plots. The tone of the three is similar,
that of a Chaplinesque sadness under the drollery.
Also in all three, language is a comic protagonist in
its own right. All three novels center around a
clearly defined symbol: Under the Net is dominated
by Jake's friendship with Hugo.

10 FORD, SAMUEL DENNIS. "The Intolerable Vocation:
    An Introduction to the Moralist as Critic." Ph.D.
    dissertation, Syracuse University, 246 pp. Abstract
    in DAI 42:2176A.
        Chapters 1 and 2 review the work of Iris Murdoch
and Stanley Hauerwas to point up the inadequacies of
contemporary images of the moralist. The two thinkers
propose that the moralist be seen not through the
concept of decision or choice but through the image of
the storyteller or artist. Chapters 3, 4, and 5
examine the idea of the moralist as critic from the
perspectives of epistemology, theology, and literary
criticism. Chapters 7 and 8 offer examples of
exemplary moral critics like Matthew Arnold and F.R.
Leavis. Chapter 8 looks at criticism concerning
Under Western Eyes by Joseph Conrad. The final chapter
reviews the argument and concludes that understanding
ethics through the imagery of criticism would have a
substantial effect on ethics.

11 FURBANK, P.N. "Between Past and Present." Times
    Literary Supplement, 11 May, p. 563.
        Review of J.G. Farrell's The Hill Station. Fur-
bank charges Murdoch and other writers of "the higher
entertainments" with sacrificing human truth to
pretty effects because readers must be kept pleased.

12 FURUKI, YOSHIKO. "Iris Murdoch Ron." Eigo seinen
    [Rising generation], (Tokyo) 126:602-6.
        Examines how the writer and the philosopher co-
exist in the novels of Murdoch, discussing especially
ideas from "The Sublime and the Beautiful Revisited"
and "Against Dryness." Murdoch is a novelist who
incorporates the ethics of a philosopher and who tries
to achieve the goal of a philosopher by writing novels.
Throughout her work is the backbone of a concern with
moral development. Contrasts her novels with the
elite, hard-to-read novels of the nineteen twenties.

13 GANNER, RAUTH H. "Iris Murdoch and the Bronte
    Heritage." Studies in English Literature (Tokyo)
    58:61-74.
        Discussion of the reworkings of Brontean motifs
    and narrative devices in The Unicorn and The Sacred
    and Profane Love Machine. Disputes Peter Wolfe's view
    of The Unicorn as influenced by Wuthering Heights.
    Sees more influence on The Sacred and Profane Love
    Machine.

14 HALIO, JAY L. "Fiction about Fiction." Southern
    Review 17 (Winter):233.
        Reviews The Sea, The Sea as an example of writers
    writing about their craft. Detects Murdoch's typical
    conflict between reality and illusion and sees her
    use of modern themes portrayed according to nineteenth-
    century models.

15 HOSKINS, ROBERT. "Hamlet and A Severed Head."
    American Notes and Queries 20:18-20.
        A discussion of Hamlet's importance to A
    Severed Head with Martin Lynch-Gibbon as a recogniz-
    able Hamlet figure with an excessive tendency to
    rationalize. The juxtaposition of Martin's dilemma
    with Hamlet's underscores the superficiality of
    Martin's life. Both Martin and Hamlet have a problem
    of inaction and of impulsive, violent action. The
    relationship between Martin and Antonia mirrors that
    between Hamlet and Gertrude, and Georgie, like Ophelia,
    is linked romantically with the hero and becomes a
    victim of the larger dilemma.

16 "Interview with Iris Murdoch." Vogue 171 (March):
    329, 167.
        Brief account of an interview with Murdoch, ask-
    ing first how the novelist and philosopher work togeth-
    er in her fiction. Murdoch says that philosophy may
    affect the way she thinks about morals, but she is a
    traditional novelist. The ideas in her head occur
    through her characters. She is preoccupied with evil,
    the self-assertion of the human ego. The goal of life
    is to become unselfish, despite the difficulty of
    changing. Art is connected with overcoming the ego
    in the artist and in the audience. Murdoch sees hope
    in the simple but powerful desire for happiness, which
    keeps people sane.

18 JEFFERSON, DOUGLAS. "Iris Murdoch: The Novelist
    and the Moralist." In The Uses of Fiction: Essays
    on Modern Novel in Honour of Arnold Kettle. Edited
    by Douglas Jefferson and Graham Martin. Stoney
    Stratford, England: Open University Press, pp.
    261-72.
        Notes the extraordinary variety and abundance of

Murdoch's early work. Under the Net with its picaresque and episodic charm is moral and a small masterpiece. The Flight from the Enchanter indicates that
Murdoch could have done well writing elegant, light
entertainment. A Severed Head is a classic comedy of
manners that makes a reductio ad absurdam: what if
everybody is doing it? In The Bell, perhaps her best
novel, the most important relationship is handled with
insight and a sense of moral truth.

19 LEHMAN-HAUPT, CHRISTOPHER. "Nuns and Soldiers."
    New York Times, 6 January, p. 20.
        Calls the novel an intriguing love story, con-
    vincing and compelling. But accuses Murdoch of symbol-
    mongering, making the book a Christian allegory, an
    examination of different courses of action in a world
    where God is dead.

20 LIVELY, PENELOPE. "Five of the Best: New Fiction."
    Encounter 56 (January):56-58.
        Sees Nuns and Soldiers as an operatic performance
    that make absolute the emotional life. Regards the
    central theme as deception. Criticizes the style but
    feels caught up in the powerful fantasy.

21 MARTINDALE, KATHLEEN MARY. "For Love of the Good:
    Moral Philosophy in the Later Novels of Iris Murdoch."
    Ph.D. dissertation, University of Toronto (Canada).
    Abstract in DAI 42:4459A.
        The study investigates the effect Murdoch's
    philosophy has had on her later fiction from The Time
    of the Angels (1966) to Nuns and Soldiers (1980). Her
    novels and her essays embody the same large philosophi-
    cal concerns. Her earlier characters grew morally by
    attending to the beauty of the world and to other
    people. Her later characters grow by substituting
    contemplation for activity, especially when they love.
    Murdoch's moral dilemmas are usually erotic because
    she treats love as the center of ethical crisis. In
    the later novels, she associates sexuality with death.
    Only self-renunciation resulting from a right under-
    standing of death makes love possible.

22 MAY, DERWENT. "The Murdoch Magic." Saturday Review
    8 (January):62.
        Review of Nuns and Soldiers, declaring it one of
    Murdoch's best. Appreciates her energy and optimism,
    stating modern English fiction to be more sordid with-
    out her. Praises her evocations of London and especial-
    ly her magical descriptions of French landscapes.

23 McEWAN, NEIL. The Survival of the Novel: British
    Fiction in the Later Twentieth Century. Totowa,
    N.J.: Barnes & Noble Imports, pp. 7-8, 13, 19.

Discusses ideas from "Against Dryness," including the contrast between modern characters and the characters in nineteenth-century novels and Murdoch's distinction between journalistic and crystalline novels. Murdoch wants to recover the traditional purposes of the novel and to discover a new moral philosophy. Under the Net is concerned with knowing truth and with preserving a moral sense with honesty.

24 "Notes on Current Books." Virginia Quarterly Review 57 (Autumn):135.
Briefly reviews Nuns and Soldiers, admitting its stylistic flaws but judging Murdoch one of the most morally perceptive writers and one of the more important writing now in English.

25 PHILLIPS, BARBARA. "Murdoch: Journey Dazzling, Destination Uncertain." Christian Science Monitor 73 (9 February):33.
Review of Nuns and Soldiers that calls its solutions to the characters' crises improbable but engrossing. Finds the plot contrived and the ideas more provocative than the characters but enjoys the detailed descriptions and the rich patchwork of dialogue.

26 PHILLIPSON, JOHN S. Review of Nuns and Soldiers. Best Sellers 40 (March):427.
Maintains that the novel is about innocence and experience as well as love and human relationships generally, alleging that in the end the characters find order unexpectedly.

27 "Picks and Pans." People Weekly 15 (1 February): 12-13.
Reviews Nuns and Soldiers as heavy-going, except for an occasional vivid scene, with too many parables and too many symbols except for Murdoch's most devoted fans.

28 "SR Recommends." Saturday Review 8 (February):101.
Very brief review of Nuns and Soldiers, calling it one of Murdoch's best, joyfully endorsing love, duty, and innocence.

29 SEYMOUR SMITH, MARTIN. "The British Novel 1976-1980." British Book News, June, pp. 325-28.
Includes The Sea, The Sea in his list of fifty-three important novels of the time, naming it Murdoch's most substantial achievement in those years. Declares that criticism of her work stems mainly from her overexposure but that she maintains her readers' interest with enormous skill.

30   "Short Reviews." <u>Atlantic Monthly</u> 247 (March):90
     Regards <u>Nuns and Soldiers</u> as a delight, an
exceptionally full book with questionings, symbols,
ideas, and characters caught in the web of life.
Identifies central questions as whether it is possible
to live purely, to love honestly, to act wisely. Considers Murdoch's technique perfected.

31   STADE, GEORGE. "A Romance for Highbrows." <u>New York
     Times Book Review</u> 86 (4 January):1, 14-15.
     Affirms that critics take Murdoch seriously as
one of the most accomplished postwar British novelists.
Attacks her for writing Harlequin romances for highbrows, for being a neo-Christian apologist, and for
mixing romance and religion. Censures her writing as
too bad to be faked. Criticizes <u>Nuns and Soldiers</u> for
its cluttering symbolism and simpering play on the
language of devotion.

32   STRANG, STEVEN MACDONALD. "Iris Murdoch: Novelist
     of Moral Intent." Ph.D. dissertation, Brown Univer-
     sity, 296 pp. Abstract in <u>DAI</u> 43:443A.
     Declares that Murdoch's novels are either novels
of knowledge or novels of awareness. Novels of knowledge are novels of ideas or of manners. In them the
third-person narrator is morally aloof from the actions
and the characters. This category includes <u>A Fairly
Honourable Defeat</u>, <u>An Accidental Man</u>, <u>The Time of the
Angels</u>, and <u>The Nice and the Good</u>.
     Novels of awareness are narrated in the first-
person. Murdoch leads us through the tortured,
twisted consciousness of modern man. Novels of
awareness include <u>A Word Child</u>, <u>The Black Prince</u>, and
<u>A Severed Head</u>.
     Strang closely examines several of Murdoch's
novels: <u>The Time of the Angels</u>, <u>The Black Prince</u>,
<u>A Word Child</u>, and <u>A Fairly Honourable Defeat</u>. A
second major goal is to examine Murdoch's use of form,
including her experiments with form.

33   STUEWE, PAUL. "Snaps for the Tsar and Shark Cuisine."
     <u>Quill and Quire</u> 47 (January):32.
     Brief review of <u>Nuns and Soldiers</u>, finding it
predictable, stylish without substance, and basically
soap opera.

34   TURNER, ALICE K. "Hey, Hey, the White Swan."
     <u>Nation</u> 232 (17 January):58-59.
     Reviews <u>Nuns and Soldiers</u> as an ironic account of
English manners. Compares Murdoch to Agatha Christie
for delivering whimsical mayhem, inspirational coziness,
and a regular output of reliable content. Declares
Murdoch too entertaining, too prolific, and too sen-
sational to be taken seriously as a writer.

35 UPDIKE, JOHN. "Worlds and Worlds." New Yorker 57
    (23 March):148-54.
        Review of Nuns and Soldiers, objecting to the
    bossy, intervening author and to the spoiled, selfish
    characters. Fears that Murdoch with her sly spooki-
    ness has teased the reader about religion. Judges
    the book marvelous in many ways but puzzles over a
    sense of thinness or hollowness.

36 WICKENDEN, DOROTHY. "A Comedy of Instruction."
    New Republic 184 (24 January):39-40.
        Regards Nuns and Soldiers as Murdoch's version
    of the human comedy with romantic love marred by
    possessiveness and other human frailty. Considers
    the relationship between Gertrude and Tim funny and
    compelling but finds the Count and Ann with their meta-
    physical questionings tiresome, an example of Murdoch's
    deflating the quest for spiritual enlightenment. Calls
    the narrative devices well worn and the prose bloated
    with Christian motifs and metaphors of imprisonment
    and sacrifice.

37 WINSOR, DOROTHY A. "Solipsistic Sexuality in Iris
    Murdoch's Gothic Novels." Renascence 34 (Autumn):
    52-63.
        Asserts that Murdoch's experiments with Gothic
    conventions are an exploration of the tension between
    the inner and the outer world and its expression in
    sexuality. The Gothic conventions focus on the inner
    world, with nature merely being a reflection of the
    central characters' feelings. Examines The Bell,
    The Unicorn, and The Time of the Angels as Murdoch's
    portrayals of the dangers of this solipsistic world
    view and as her exploration of the possibilities for
    transforming its primitive sexuality into eros.
    Although Murdoch may use some Gothic elements again,
    she never again tries to use the Gothic version of
    sexuality as an adult basis for love.

                          1982

1 DIPPLE, ELIZABETH. Iris Murdoch: Work for the
   Spirit. Chicago: University of Chicago Press,
   353 pp.
       Book investigating the moral and religious con-
   texts of Murdoch's achievement. Murdoch studies the
   realms of ethics and spirituality, depicting art as
   equally elusive and difficult to attain. Her novels
   peel off layers of bourgeois complacency and prejudice
   existing in the characters' worlds. Murdoch modifies
   realism with a Platonic religious apprehension of
   existence. She is committed to reality, and her ironies, tricks, and games demonstrate her reluctant

acceptance of the artifice of form. For her, the real
function of art is truthtelling.
        The idea that underlies all of Murdoch's novels
is that of human aspiration to the Platonic Good. The
route to it involves self-denial and the knowledge
that there is no reward and no end to the process.
Becoming an artist involves the same discipline and
self-denial. Although Murdoch is against egocentricity, she allows her characters autonomy to be
egocentric. Her use of circular structures expresses
our entrapment in selfhood. The study examines
Murdoch's novels through Nuns and Soldiers (1980).

2   Interview with Iris Murdoch. In The Radical Imagin-
    ation and the Liberal Tradition: Interviews with
    English and American Novelists. Edited by Heide
    Ziegler and Christopher Bigsby. London: Junction
    Books, pp. 209-30.
        Interview in London on 5 December 1979, discuss-
ing first influences on Murdoch's philosophy and then
her practice as a novelist. Discusses her relation to
existentialism, Wittgenstein, Buddhism and Christianity, Plato, and Kant. She asserts that art has got
to have form and authority, a strong internal structure. Rejects any connection between characters as
coercive plotters and the author as a coercive plotter,
writing fiction. Relates free characters to ones
not bound by the writer's prejudices with D.H.
Lawrence as a negative example. Equates moral sense
with common sense, recognizing duty and working to
transform oneself. Discusses The Sea, The Sea;
The Black Prince; and A Fairly Honourable Defeat.

3   JEFFREYS, SUSAN, and MARY ANNE BONNEY. "Paperback
    Shortlist." Punch 282 (17 February):285.
        Brief review of Nuns and Soldiers, finding fam-
iliar elements like the threat of drowning, religious
and cosmic experiences, and various love relationships.
Praises the excellent writing and the superb expertise.

4   KOGER, GROVE. Review of Elizabeth Dipple's Iris
    Murdoch: Work for the Spirit. Library Journal
    107 (1 April):730.
        Brief notice that marks it as the only comprehen-
sive study since Frank Baldanza's in 1974. Says
that Dipple sees Murdoch exploring the connection
between Platonic reality and traditional literary
realism. Calls Dipple's readings commonsense but
sometimes defensive.

5   LLOYD, GENEVIEVE. "Iris Murdoch on the Ethical
    Significance of the Truth." Philosophy and Litera-
    ture 6:62-75.
        Begins with Plato's criticism of literature as

confined to the production of appearances whereas
philosophy has access to the real.   Contemporary
thinkers can bypass Plato's objection by saying that
art is not concerned with truth but with creating
beautiful objects.   Murdoch challenges the separation
of art from truth, wanting to defend literature from
Plato's attack and still take seriously his preoccupation with truth.   Lloyd's purpose is to attempt
to clarify Murdoch's defense of the ethical significance of truth, truth seen as a correspondence between
mental representations and the real.   Discusses Murdoch's defense of the importance of the inner life
of thought and perception, including the case of M and
D in The Sovereignty of Good.

6   McDOWELL, EDWIN.   "One's Name in Print."   New York
     Times Book Review 87 (14 February):34.
        Brief anecdote involving Morris Philipson's ded-
     icating a novel to Murdoch and her simple enjoyment
     of it.

7   "Paperback Choice."   Observer, 14 February, p. 32.
        Brief review of Nuns and Soldiers, calling it one
     of Murdoch's lighter and slighter novels, written
     however with passion and engagement.

8   "Paperbacks New and Noteworthy."   New York Times
     Book Review 87 (7 March):35.
        Reviews Nuns and Soldiers briefly as rich and
     complex according to many critics but as a Harlequin
     romance according to Stade.

9   SLAYMAKER, WILLIAM.   "Myths, Mystery and the
     Mechanisms of Determinism: The Aesthetics of Free-
     dom in Iris Murdoch's Fiction."   Papers on Language
     and Literature (Southern Illinois University) 18:
     166-80.
        Discusses Murdoch's idea of freedom in her philo-
     sophical essays, concluding that they show the theo-
     retical possibility of freedom through love of the
     true, the beautiful, and the good, but Murdoch's
     recent novels show the failure of that scheme.   The
     forces of the selfish ego and the mechanical physical
     and psychological drives make freedom an unrealized
     dream.
        In The Black Prince, Pearson does not measure up
     to Murdoch's definition of freedom.   Instead, he is
     determined by uncontrollable urges.   The postscripts
     show that his book may be based on a complete delusion.
     Art may be possible for Pearson, but the love affair
     between him and Julian is doomed.   The novel uses
     Greek myth to show the confusion and lack of freedom
     Pearson experiences.   It demonstrates Murdoch's
     growing skepticism about the possibility of freedom.

10 WIDMER, KINGSLEY. "The Wages of Intellectual-
    ity . . . and the Fictional Wagers of Iris Murdoch."
    In Twentieth Century Women Novelists. Edited by
    Thomas F. Staley. Totowa, N.J.: Barnes & Noble,
    pp. 16-38.
        Declares that Murdoch partly modernizes trad-
itional English fiction with sophisticated disillusion-
ments and existential awareness. Focuses on the protagonists as self-destructive and deluded intellectual
males with the sexual and moral perplexities of
middle age. Says that the protagonists are put into
unwinnable games, into comic-horrific muddles. Asserts
that love opens up onto an endlessly complicating
labyrinth.
        Concludes that most of the Murdoch novels in the
1970s explore variations of aging male intellectual
egoism. Discusses The Sandcastle, The Unicorn, The
Italian Girl, The Flight from the Enchanter, The Bell,
The Times of the Angels, A Severed Head (a fuller discussion than the others), An Unofficial Rose, The
Nice and the Good, Henry and Cato, Bruno's Dream,
A Fairly Honourable Defeat, The Sea, The Sea (dis-
missed as least interesting), An Accidental Man,
The Sacred and Profane Love Machine, A Word Child, and
The Black Prince.

                            1983

1 ADAMS, PHOEBE. "Short Reviews." Atlantic 252
    (August):100.
        Brief review of The Philosopher's Pupil, calling
the lengthy novel a lamentable bore and George a minor
public nuisance. Finds the characters garrulous and
ill-tempered.

2 AMIS, MARTIN. "To the Nth Degree." Observer,
    1 May, p. 28.
        Reviews The Philosopher's Pupil, complaining of
faults of style and of raggedness to the novel. Her
characters as usual inhabit an eroticised world,
untouched by cares concerning work, health, or money.
Her narrator sometimes enjoys full authorial omniscience
and sometimes functions as an ordinary member of the
cast. The reader can, however, perceive Murdoch's
fierce belief in and love for her characters.

3 ARNOLD, DAVID SCOTT. "Liminal Tellings: Interpre-
    tations of Otherness in Readings of Moby-Dick,
    Ulysses, and A Severed Head." Ph.D. dissertation
    Emory University, 250 pp. Abstract in DAI 44:3681A
        An inquiry into the experience of reading fic-
tional narrative, focusing on the process by which
the reader ur erstands three particular novels.

Chapter 1 investigates three critical approaches, those of Coleridge, of Northrop Frye, and of Wolfgang Iser. The next three chapters interpret the three novels in order. A Severed Head is interpreted, focusing on the dialectic of character and reader in the light of Murdoch's announced critical program.

4 BANNON, BARBARA. "P.W. Forecasts." Publishers Weekly 223 (20 May):223.
   Reviews The Philosopher's Pupil as influenced by Dostoevski from Professor Rozanov's Russian name to the theme of the hunger for salavation. Censures the first two-thirds of the novel as bloodless and lacking in power. Criticizes the characters as too many, sketchily drawn and unconvincing and the narrator as having no compelling function. Says that in the final third, Murdoch's wit and storytelling ability reassert themselves but complains that the characters just chatter about ideas.

5 "Best and Worst Books of the Year." Spectator 251 (17 December):54.
   Mark Amory names The Philosopher's Pupil as not the most inept book of the year but as a disappointing novel by a clever, admired writer.

6 "Books." Antioch Review 41 (Fall):509.
   Brief review of The Philosopher's Pupil that calls it Murdoch's most entertaining novel. Finds the antics of the characters outrageous and their illusions absurd in view of their intelligence.

7 BRADY, PATRICIA. Review of The Philosopher's Pupil. Boston Review 8 (October):37-38.
   Sees the novel as a critique of modern scientific philosophy, which suggests that everything can be explained and fixed. Contends that George refutes that view, George driven and demonic. Asserts that our rational, psychological prose cannot fully express the real mystical experiences in life. Praises Murdoch's flawed but noble efforts to express them.

8 COALE, SAMUEL. Review of The Philosopher's Pupil. America 149 (10 December):378.
   Calls the book a fat dazzling novel that illustrates the penetration of morality into ordinary life. Notes the webbed and intricate plot, shimmering as a comedy of coincidence. Sees Murdoch interested in mysterious connections between her characters.

9 DAVIES, ALISTAIR, and PETER SAUNDERS. "Literature, Politics, and Society." In Society and Literature, 1945-1970. Edited by Alan Sinfield. New York: Holmes and Meier, pp. 13-50.

Discusses Murdoch with the group of writers who
began their careers in the 1950s, a group with philosophical explicitness and a commitment to liberal values. Compares her to Angus Wilson, both questioning
the efficacy of the liberal tradition in British
politics and culture. Analyses The Flight from the
Enchanter. The subsequent fiction of the two reversed
their early pessimism. In The Sandcastle Murdoch
challenged the ethics and aesthetics of Bloomsbury.
Discusses her views on mass technology, small-scale
technology, small-scale socialism, and Britain's
entry into the Common Market.

10 DAVIES, ROBERTSON. "Iris Murdoch's Crowded Canvas."
    Book World, The Washington Post, 26 June, pp. 1-2.
        Review of The Philosopher's Pupil that mentions
    the rambling, discursive plot, the leisurely pace,
    and the pleasure in describing natural surroundings.
    Considers Rozanov a silly man who, having lived most
    of his life in his mind, doesn't know how to deal with
    emotion. Calls Murdoch a real storyteller who con-
    vinces us of the truth of what she tells.

11 DAVIS, HOPE HALE. "Half a Mystery." New Leader 66
    (8 August):17-18.
        Review of The Philosopher's Pupil that perceives
    the central conflict of Rozanov struggling against
    George's violent dependence to be augmented by depic-
    tions of family relationships and marriages, love
    variously received, and vivid beach and spa scenes.
    Criticizes Murdoch generally for using a thriller
    framework, for appealing to the head not the emotions,
    and for frustrating the anticipations she creates.

12 DESALVO, LOUISE A. "This Should Not Be: Iris
    Murdoch's Critique of English Policy towards
    Ireland in The Red and the Green." Colby Library
    Quarterly 19:1113-24.
        Interprets the novel as an attack on English
    policy toward Ireland and on English imperialism,
    seeing a parallel between morality in politics and
    good loving. Names Frances, with Marxist and feminist
    leanings, the fiercest revolutionary besides the
    Dumay brothers. Asserts that the way that Andrew
    holds Frances at arm's length is the way the English
    treat the Irish. States that the novel is also an
    attack on U.S. intervention in Vietnam, citing Murdoch's
    article "Political Morality" in 1967, denouncing
    American imperialist policies in Vietnam.

13 Deveson, Richard. "Of Course." New Statesman 105
    (29 April):28.
        Review of The Philosopher's Pupil that calls it
    soap opera, mentioning the flying saucers, megalithic

ring, foxes, and gypsies. Says that one doesn't read
Murdoch for naturalistic plausibility but for the
knot of characteristic ideas, one of which is morality
permeating all life. Sees Rozanov and George in a
parallel state of intellectual crisis but declares
that the people and events are finally preposterous.

14 DICK, KAY. "A Feast." Spectator 250 (30 April):26.
        Praises unreservedly The Philosopher's Pupil
for the intellectual pleasure it provides, characterizing it as a novel for adults. Mentions the large
cast of striking characters and the exuberant passion
in Murdoch's creation. Finds it hugely funny and
luxurious in its range of motives, personalities, and
counterpoint.

15 DOLLIMORE, JONATHAN. "The Challenge of Sexuality."
        In Society and Literature, 1945-1970. Edited by
        Alan Sinfield. New York: Holmes & Meier, pp.
        75-76.
        States that English novels of the early postwar
period treat homosexuality with extreme caution and
then discusses the relationship of the homosexual
lovers Simon and Axel in A Fairly Honourable Defeat.
Murdoch portrays their sex and gender as irrelevant
to their love. The inadequacy of marriage as a pre-
scribed form is a recurring theme, especially in
The Bell, An Unofficial Rose, and The Black Prince.

16 DRABELLE, DENNIS. "Murdoch's Latest Isn't Trendy,
        Just Fascinating." U.S.A. Today, 15 July, p. 30.
        Compares Murdoch to Graham Greene as producing
so much first-rate fiction, in reviewing The Philosopher's Pupil. Attributes to Rozanov an international
reputation and local star quality. Perceives the
theme to be the ethics of charm, love, and friendship.

17 ELDER, RICHARD. "The Conjuring Magic of Murdoch."
        Los Angeles Times Book Review, 3 July, pp. 2,8.
        Review of The Philosopher's Pupil that agrees
with other critics that the book is too long with too
many characters described too completely. Declares
that Murdoch writes about the corners of hell subtly
and with a surprising gaiety. Explains that she
blends the realistic novel and the magical tale.

18 EMERSON, SALLY. "Recent Fiction." Illustrated
        London News 271 (May):76.
        Criticizes The Philosopher's Pupil as not a smooth
read. Compares the characters to figures from a nightmare in perverse or anguished relationships. The
philosopher mirrors the God-like power of the novelist,
controlling the destinies of the characters.

19 FAULKS, SEBASTIAN. Review of The Philosopher's
    Pupil. Books and Bookmen, May, p. 35.
        Calls it a great fat beast of a book with impres-
    sive inventiveness but with a structure that fails to
    do it justice. Praises the engrossing nature of the
    naturalistic surface, the steady human sympathy of
    Murdoch's morality, and the high quality of the
    entertainment. Says that her last properly shaped
    novel was The Black Prince.

20 FEENEY, JOSEPH J. Review of The Philosopher's Pupil.
    Best Sellers 43 (September):206.
        Judges the novel one of Murdoch's best: mysteri-
    ous, rational, magical, and superb. Praises her wit,
    her clever plotting, and her compassion as well as
    her clear mind, which recognizes forces that cannot
    be fully analyzed: passion, hate, and love. Calls
    the scene in the midnight garden mythic and Hawthorn-
    esque.

21 FLETCHER, JOHN. "Iris Murdoch." In Dictionary of
    Literary Biography: British Novelists since 1960.
    Vol. 14, no. 2. Detroit: Gale Research, pp. 546-61.
        Article includes some biographical information,
    some general comments on Murdoch's work, and brief
    explications of several of her novels. Murdoch is
    one of the dominant figures of postwar British litera-
    ture, prolific like Dickens, Thackeray, and Wilkie
    Collins. Perhaps the most intelligent novelist since
    George Eliot, she extends the English tradition in
    important ways. Her books are fictional engines like
    those of Vladimir Nabokov, and her mentors are Elias
    Canetti, Samuel Beckett, and Raymond Queneau. Her
    chief themes are self-deception versus self-knowledge,
    art versus reality, reconciliation and love versus
    enmity and hatred, and the mysterious versus the
    mundane. Under the Net is for many readers her
    finest and most characteristic work, demonstrating
    maturity, elegance, and stylishness with familiarity
    with other contemporary comic masterpieces and with
    the authority of its moral concern. Her later novels
    fall into two categories: ironic tragedies and bitter-
    sweet comedies. Her subject matter is usually love,
    but her true concern is with art.

22 GRAY, PAUL. "Figures in a Moral Pattern." Time 121
    (27 June):72.
        Review of The Philosopher's Pupil that sees a
    metaphysical design submerged in the profusion of
    details, naming Murdoch's method allegory, a tool for
    testing beliefs. Describes Rozanov, who is supposed
    to have all the answers, without the will or the
    power to save George, in despair, saying that at the

bottom it is all jumble. The narrative voice natters
away as if the nineteenth-century novel were alive and
well.

23 HAFFENDEN, JOHN. "In Conversation with Iris Murdoch."
    Literary Review (London) 58:31-34.
         Interview in which Murdoch discusses questions
    about The Philosopher's Pupil, saying that it has less
    to do with philosophy than with the pupil-teacher
    relationship. John Robert is a figure who can't help
    exercising power. The teacher is a powerful and
    potentially destructive person, and an absolutist in
    something like philosophy could transfer that absolut-
    ism into real life. George wants the emotional drama
    to make a bond between him and John Robert, even if
    that bond is one of rage.
         Not wanting to be dominated by her own mythology,
    Murdoch made this novel very scattered with numerous
    characters that she hopes exist in their own right.
    But if the novel is to be any good, it must contain
    within it also the fire of a personal unconscious
    mind.
         Murdoch says that she has gotten all sorts of
    interesting ideas from Freud--the idea of the super-
    ego and the id, the idea of anamnesis, of the
    unconscious mind, and the idea of eros as fundamental
    energy that includes sex--all ideas that Freud got
    from Plato. What Murdoch is afraid of is finding out
    that it doesn't matter how you behave, that morality
    is just superficial. She thinks that a novelist
    should be truthful and not project personal daydreams
    like dreams of power or of being terribly sexually
    attractive. A novel should depict what it is like for
    someone to be good or bad and the contingency of life.
    She feels that she has to prevent the form of a novel
    from determining the emotion of the book by creating
    surprises in the opposite direction. A novel is a
    mode of explanation, examining the characters and
    their motives. The novelist reveals his own morality
    in judging the characters.

24 HARPER, MICHAEL. "Nominees, 1983 Fiction Prize."
    Los Angeles Times Book Review, 13 November, p. 6.
         Review The Philosopher's Pupil as providing many
    of the joys of old-fashioned realism with believable
    characters in a richly detailed social setting.
    Apprehends Murdoch's ultimate concern, however, to be
    the spiritual, with her looking at the everyday world
    through the lens of theology. Regards the novel as
    her most ambitious so far.

25 HEUSEL, BARBARA STEVENS. "Patterned Aimlessness in
    the Mature Novels of Iris Murdoch." Ph.D. disserta-

tion, University of South Carolina, 229 pp. Abstract
in DAI 44:1092A.
Asserts that four of Murdoch's novels--The Black
Prince, A Word Child, The Sea, The Sea, and Nuns and
Soldiers--reveal the mystery of human nature through
dramatizations of modern life. These novels employ
the Wittgensteinian analyses of language, routine,
love, death, and art, as Murdoch explained them in
The Sovereignty of Good. This study explores Ludwig
Wittgenstein's deep influence on Murdoch's ideas and
methods. The four novels depict man's preference for
illusion over reality and his escapist strategies.
They display Murdoch's portrayal of the contingent
world and her use of formal patterns.

26   JACKSON, MARNI. "Cheerful in the Absence of Reason."
     Maclean's 96 (2 May):58.
        Discerns a tireless intelligence in The Philos-
opher's Pupil but considers it repetitious, needing
to be edited. With Rozanov's obsession with his grand-
daughter, the illusion of a rational universe collapses.
Characterizes the novel as playful, ambitious, and
strangely cheerful.

27   KOGER, GROVE. Review of A Philosopher's Pupil.
     Library Journal 108 (1 June):1158.
        Briefly discusses the novel as a profound study
of human frailty presented as interesting melodrama.
Calls the town and the hot springs solidly realized.

28   LEHMAN, DAVID. "Water Torture." Newsweek 101
     (20 June):75.
        Reviews The Philosopher's Pupil as a ghastly
attempt to combine religious allegory, the didactic
novel of ideas, and British comedy of manners. Con-
demns the novel as having all of Dostoevski's hysteria
without his genius, pronouncing the McCaffrey
brothers poor stand-ins for the Karamazovs. Criticizes
the style as prolix with too many adjectives.

29   LEHMANN-HAUPT, CHRISTOPHER. "Books of the Times."
     New York Times 132 (29 June):C25.
        Calls The Philosopher's Pupil Murdoch in an antic
mood. Interprets the frantic, repetitive activity of
the characters as her striving for a mechanical
quality like slapstick. Perceives a wonderful con-
catenation of misunderstandings, alternately funny
and appalling. Maintains that besides the Oedipal
clashes, the book is about the inadequacy of philosophy in the face of human passion. Commends the vivid
characters and the furious comic energy.

30   McLOUGHLIN, JANE. "Dubliners." Punch 284 (27
     April):78

Calls The Philosopher's Pupil a rattling good
yarn about the nature of the responsibility between
teacher and pupil with Rozanov abusing power by feeling no responsibility to others. Finds humor in Murdoch's setting up a tenet of Protestantism and knock-
ing it down with cold reality.

31 MALLON, THOMAS. "Books in Brief." National Review
    35 (14 October):1297.
        Review of The Philosopher's Pupil that finds it
a disappointment, complaining that none of the characters are likeable with Rozanov and George acting like
"psychological Kryptonite." Criticizes the repetitive
philosophical discussions and the hundreds of adjectives.

32 MASON, DEBORAH. "Manners, Morals, and Murdoch."
    Vogue, July, p. 47.
        Describes The Philosopher's Pupil as bracing and
incorrigibly civilized with the characters imbued with
moral ardor. Appreciates that the characters suffer,
love, inflict pain, but always learn. Views the novel
as a magnificent passion play in which love is crush-
ed and healed, gods are toppled, and salvation is
granted.

33 MINER, VALERIE. "Catalyst at Large." Progressive
    47 (December):42-44.
        Review of The Philosopher's Pupil as compelling
and rich with dramatic action. Asserts that the spa
is a metaphor with characters seeking forgiveness
and a new life and also a realistic scene of business
transactions, political debate, courtship, and death.
Extols Rozanov as fascinating, presenting a distorted
mirror for characters like the McCaffreys. Calls for
Murdoch's intellectual complexity to be balanced by
an increased emotional texture.

34 MITCHELL, LARRY. "Iris Murdoch: Fifth Columnist
    for the Good." M.A. thesis, California State
    University, Chico, 241 pp.
        The purpose is to explain that Murdoch's power
as a novelist comes from the force of the Good and
from her double role as novelist and philosopher.
Discusses how she uses the novel to concretize her
philosophy and how she manipulated false goods to
snare the reader and to goad him on in the quest for
the true Good. Two-fifths of the thesis deals with
The Red and the Green. Provides some reflections on
Bruno's Dream and a sustained reading of Henry and
Cato.

35 MOSLEY, NICHOLAS. "The Philosopher Fails--The
    Artist Succeeds." Listener 109 (28 April):19-20.

Compares The Philosopher's Pupil unfavorably with
The Black Prince and A Word Child, concentrated, gripping narratives. Sees Rozanov as a philosopher who
wants the world to be logical and without contradictions. Considers as fascinating enough the different
stories of passion and the attempts to manipulate
others.

36 OATES, JOYCE CAROL. "Love and Other Illusions."
    New York Times Book Review 88 (17 July):1, 20-21.
        Describes Murdoch's general formula before dis-
cussing The Philosopher's Pupil as characters chasing
about after the fantasies they have of each other.
From appearing sympathetic at the beginning, Rozanov,
one of Murdoch's enchanters, develops into a monster.
Complains of a certain thinness to the novel and wants
to know more about N., part puppet and part puppet-
master.

37 PRITCHARD, WILLIAM. "Some August Fiction."
    Hudson Review 36 (Winter):748-49.
        States that there is much in The Philosopher's
Pupil that is entertaining, like the descriptions of
places, but says that it lacks depth and the human
aspect, calling the novel automatic and self-propelled.

38 Review of The Philosopher's Pupil. Kirkus Review
    51 (15 April):480.
        Regards the novel as rich and freshly challenging,
an enchanted journey into metaphysics, told in dense
Murdoch prose. Names as familiar symbols the dog,
water, and a flash of antlers.

39 REYNOLDS, GRAHAM. Review of A Year of Birds.
    Apollo 117 (February):145-46.
        Says that Murdoch's first volume of verse adds to
the tradition concerning the orderly succession of
the seasons. Maintains that she defines the relationship between the month and the chosen bird with
haikulike concentration. Praises the epigrammatic
quality of Reynolds S. Stone's images.

40 SCOTT-KILVERT, IAN. Review of The Philosopher's
    Pupil. British Book News, July, p. 453.
        Alleges that the novel combines realistic detail
and conduct with strange states of mind. The author
has widened her focus from the haute bourgeoisie to
take on an entire town with its history, architecture,
sociology, and genealogy. Perceives at the end a
controlling design but criticizes the solutions as
contrived.

41 STEPHEN, KATHY FIELD. "World Class Writers."
    Christian Science Monitor 75 (6 July):9.

Review of The Philosopher's Pupil that calls it
unrealistic and exhausting with exaggerated characters
and a jarring plot. The discussions of philosophy and
religion are only a little self-consciously woven into
the narrative. Deplores the unappealing minor characters and the perverse and negative relationships.

42 STRAWSON, GALEN. "Compounding Error with Excess."
    Times Literary Supplement, 29 April, p. 421.
        Finds The Philosopher's Pupil to have psychologi-
    cal insight and inspired realistic detail but to lack
    narrative momentum. Sees the book as an illustration
    of "The Sovereignty of Good" with the psyche desiring
    consolation and continually asserting the self. Cen-
    sures the triplets of adjectives, the lists of com-
    pound feelings, and the gushing intensifiers, and
    stresses that the novel should be cut.

43 TAUBMAN, ROBERT. "Double Life." London Review of
    Books 5 (19 May):23.
        Reviews The Philosopher's Pupil, noting Murdoch's
    juggling with reality and illusion, sometimes mock-
    ing her puppet characters. Distinguishes familiar
    elements: The Peter Pan motif, women in love, and
    the supernatural. Observes two styles, the narrator's
    cool style and a hot style for moments of emotional
    stress and devastation.

44 UPDIKE, JOHN. "Books." New Yorker 59 (14 November):
    197-25.
        Judges The Philosopher's Pupil as one of Murdoch's
    biggest and best. Percieves in the opening scene her
    symbol-prone intelligence behind the actuality, say-
    ing that she provides "delightfully individual toads
    in botanically specific gardens." Calls Enniston a
    solid stage for the drama, with its friendly indus-
    trial grit. Regards as realistic her depiction of
    attempts to rescue religion from them. Compares the
    novel to The Flight from the Enchanter, missing the
    feminine sharpness of the early novel but evaluating
    the later one as large as life.

45 WADE, ROSALIND. "Quarterly Fiction Review." Con-
    temporary Review 243 (July):45-46.
        Review of The Philosopher's Pupil that considers
    impressive the portrayal of the complicated mosaic of
    family interactions. Appreciates the range of
    philosophical debate, despite the unreal sounding
    dialogue. Considers it Murdoch's most satisfying
    recent novel.

46 W., C. "Random Notes." National Review 35 (8 July):
    828.

Brief announcement of The Philosopher's Pupil,
comparing it unfavorably to Dostoevski's novels.

47 WEEKS, BRIGITTE. "Steam Bath." New Republic 189
    (18 July):36-37.
    Pronounces A Philosopher's Pupil a rambling rag-
bag, too long with a ceaseless battering of patterns
and symbols. Sees the novel's center to be the baths,
the steamy inferno that draws the characters together,
and Rozanov, not lovable or profound, with more
evidence needed to believe his international importance
and his sinister influence.

48 WIDMER, KINGSLEY. "Iris Murdoch." In Thinkers of
    The Twentieth Century: A Biographical, Biblio-
    graphical and Critical Dictionary. Edited by Eliza-
    beth Devine, Michael Held, James Vinson, and George
    Walsh. Detroit: Gale Research, pp. 408-10.
    Critical entry with bibliography, stating that
Murdoch became a professional moral philosopher and
then a prolific, witty novelist. In essays she
staked out a qualified modern Platonism. Her philosophical essays are not exceptionally rigorous or
persuasive, but her novels are. She injects into
traditional forms an ironic modern consciousness and
self-conscious fictional gaming. Her novels include
much realistic description of London, eccentric
characters, and sharp wit.
    Murdoch's usual subject is the moral muddle of
the English upper-middle-class intellectual male in
a sexual and moral bind. The story usually proposes
a transcendent Good, which is undercut and dissolved
into a conventional love-ethic. Sometimes it falls
back on affirming the ordinary decencies. Her gothic
melodramas present some of her philosophical arguments
like egotism versus goodness and Luciferian solipsism
versus compassion for others. A Severed Head is the
best of her early fictions. The later family sagas
display moral sentimentality, although often with
perception and metaphoric flair. Perhaps the best
of them is The Sacred and Profane Love Machine.
Murdoch is an intellectual ironist who creates witty
catharses to affirm conventional decencies while
yearning for some more significant Good.

Index